JUST URBAN DESIGN

Urban and Industrial Environments

Series editor: Robert Gottlieb, Henry R. Luce Professor of Urban and Environmental Policy, Occidental College

For a complete list of books published in this series, please see the back of the book.

JUST URBAN DESIGN

THE STRUGGLE FOR A PUBLIC CITY

EDITED BY KIAN GOH, ANASTASIA LOUKAITOU-SIDERIS,
AND VINIT MUKHIJA

FOREWORD BY LAWRENCE J. VALE

THE MIT PRESS   CAMBRIDGE, MASSACHUSETTS   LONDON, ENGLAND

The MIT Press would like to thank the anonymous peer reviewers who provided comments on drafts of this book. The generous work of academic experts is essential for establishing the authority and quality of our publications. We acknowledge with gratitude the contributions of these otherwise uncredited readers.

This book was set in Stone Serif by Westchester Publishing Services. Printed and bound in the United States of America.

Library of Congress Cataloging-in-Publication Data

Names: Goh, Kian, editor. | Loukaitou-Sideris, Anastasia, 1958– editor. | Mukhija, Vinit, 1967– editor. | Vale, Lawrence J., 1959– writer of foreword.
Title: Just urban design : the struggle for a public city / edited by Kian Goh, Anastasia Loukaitou-Sideris, and Vinit Mukhija ; foreword by Lawrence J. Vale.
Description: Cambridge, Massachusetts : The MIT Press, [2022] | Series: Urban and industrial environments | Includes bibliographical references and index.
Identifiers: LCCN 2021060539 (print) | LCCN 2021060540 (ebook) | ISBN 9780262544276 (paperback) | ISBN 9780262371070 (epub) | ISBN 9780262371087 (pdf)
Subjects: LCSH: City planning—Social aspects. | Communication in city planning. | Social policy.
Classification: LCC HT166 .J87 2022 (print) | LCC HT166 (ebook) | DDC 307.1/216—dc23/eng/20220106
LC record available at https://lccn.loc.gov/2021060539
LC ebook record available at https://lccn.loc.gov/2021060540

10 9 8 7 6 5 4 3 2 1

publication supported by a grant from
The Community Foundation for Greater New Haven
as part of the **Urban Haven Project**

To our students

CONTENTS

FOREWORD

Lawrence J. Vale

The quest to merge urban design and justice into "just urban design" is welcome, noble, and necessary. As a counterpoint to rampant nationalism and lingering segregation, this is also very difficult to do.

In taking on this difficult quest, this book ambitiously resets the theory and practice of urban design in a fully fleshed-out spatial justice framework. The editors and contributors do so with a commendable blend of epistemological sophistication and grounded examination of particular instances of projects, practices, and processes.

First, and perhaps most fundamentally, *Just Urban Design* brings the agenda for urban design more fully into conversation with the rest of planning and urban development. Too often, urban design is treated as a "big architecture" extension of aesthetics, devoid of linkage to political processes and power dynamics. This book explodes that myth of autonomous design once and for all. Second, and related, the book dramatically and appropriately widens the targeted audience for urban design because its focus on justice forces consideration of the impact of the built environment on marginalized individuals and groups—while also opening possibilities for how input from those margins can enhance both the relevance and influence of urban design practice. Third, by setting up a framework for explaining how justice—in its many guises—is linked to the goal of a "public city," the volume succeeds in illuminating not only what urban design is—and can be—but it also helps ground the more abstract notions of *justice* and *public* in more tangible and visceral lived realities. Finally, by combining the work of senior scholars with a variety of rising stars, the set of contributors—working around the globe—itself conveys the vitality of the field.

Urban design is the right scale for interrogating spatial justice since urban designers see themselves as having a core responsibility for shaping the public realm of the lived city. One problem, though, is that urban designers don't actually have much control over their own professional domain—any more than planners and architects do. In seeking to make urban design more just, we need to confront this disconnect between a privileged expertise that lacks a corresponding privileged position for exercising it. One part of coping with that limitation paradoxically entails *sharing* that privilege of expertise—by welcoming and insisting upon co-creation of design solutions with affected communities. Even so, part of the challenge is more structural: Who decides whether to accord these designer-community teams resources and centrality of decision making?

What happens when professional urban designers have to balance the needs of a particular community with that of a larger city? This is not merely a conundrum for theorists concerned about justice; it is a quotidian aspect of practice. Consider, for example, the case of installing bike lanes in a community that wants more buses. How does one serve people in the community while also serving those who want to bike quickly *through* or *past* that community to get to some other destination? Or, even more pointedly, how should urban designers act when some stakeholders view street space in those communities as a pathway for leisure rather than a usable streetscape supporting local commerce? The shaping of the public realm offers both constraints (and "othering") as well as opportunities for fuller urban citizenship. A more just form of urban design entails sensitive engagement with multiple positionalities.

Neil Adger and colleagues (2005) laid out four criteria for successful climate adaptation,[1] and I think these apply equally well to our collective quest for just urban design. The first two—*effectiveness* and *efficiency*—are, broadly speaking, more technical kinds of tasks. Effectiveness challenges us to ask whether an adaptive intervention can effectively reduce vulnerability, while the second criterion asks whether it does so efficiently in terms of time, space, and financial resources. Proposals for "resilient cities" or resilient settlements have, thus far, tended to remain focused on these two issues—even as a concern for quality urban design has also foregrounded concern for improving the attractiveness, as well as the protectiveness, of public space.

Adger and colleagues (2005) argue, convincingly to me, that there need to be two additional criteria beyond effectiveness and efficiency. Adding in these two other considerations can get us much closer to the transformative aspiration of just urban design. To get us to this next stage, we will need to devote more attention to the underlying politics of urban design and take seriously two other key elements of implementation: *equity* and *legitimacy*.

Taken together, these two terms ask basic questions: Who benefits? And who decides? In the context of just urban design, equity has two main dimensions. First, environmental vulnerability is distributed highly unevenly, with the most socioeconomically disadvantaged residents of cities often facing the greatest endangerment, whether this is daily exposure in the public realm or susceptibility to acute hazards. There is also a second dimension to measuring equity through just urban design. Urban design projects, whether taking the form of infrastructure or some other large intervention, often disproportionately harm the poor, either directly (through displacing poor communities or shifting risk onto those people who can least afford to address it) or indirectly (through displacement by "green gentrification" following the creation of new amenity landscapes).

But the politics of just urban design is about more than just trying to tally who gains and who loses. If the goal is increased equity, legitimacy is a necessary precondition. Legitimacy entails judgment about the *inclusiveness of a process*—its input and its throughput—whereas equity may fully be judged only in terms of outcome—its output. Legitimacy, especially in the context of urban design, depends on the engagement of those most directly affected. If it is nothing else, just urban design ought to be in service of enhancing human dignity. Only then can we be sure that outcomes are equitable.

Just urban design can help us identify exemplary projects but also—if legitimacy and equity are central aspects—will cause us to question exactly what it means to cocreate better public space. Imported practitioners must learn from local "tactitioners." Just urban design, as a framework, asks a double question: Who controls decisions about the public realm? Who gets to challenge that, and on what basis?

Ultimately, the pursuit of just urban design entails operating across time as well as space. Urban designers have a triple responsibility. They need to begin with an awareness of past site-based injustices, give sustained attention to processes playing out in the present, and invigorate respectful dialogue based on visions of imagined alternative shared futures. This book shows us how to do that.

NOTE

1. For an application of this to urban design, see Lamb (2020).

REFERENCES

Adger, W. N., Arnell, N. W., and Tompkins, E. L. (2005). "Successful Adaptation to Climate Change across Scales." *Global Environmental Change* 15 (2): 77–86.

Lamb, Z. (2020). "Connecting the Dots: The Origins, Evolutions, and Implications of the Map that Changed Post-Katrina Recovery Planning in New Orleans." In Laska, S. (ed.). *Louisiana's Response to Extreme Weather: A Coastal State's Adaptation Challenges and Successes*, 65–91. New York: Springer.

ACKNOWLEDGMENTS

We gratefully acknowledge our contributors. Their intellectual generosity and collaboration underpin this book. We thank them for their participation in this endeavor, which included a speaker series hosted by the UCLA Department of Urban Planning during the 2019 academic year. We are indebted to the faculty, staff, and students at the UCLA Luskin School of Public Affairs for their collegiality, camaraderie, and engagement. We thank Tammy Borrero and Robin McCallum, who provided valuable support for the organization of the speaker series. We are appreciative of the UCLA Department of Urban Planning, which provided financial support for the speaker series through funds from the Harvey S. Perloff Endowment, as well as the UCLA Lewis Center for Regional Policy Studies, which also supported the series. We would also like to acknowledge the team at the MIT Press, especially Robert Gottlieb, Beth Clevenger, and Anthony Zannino, for their support and guidance, as well as the anonymous reviewers for their insight. We would like to thank Larry Vale for providing an eloquent foreword for this book, and also for serving as a discussant during a session at the Association of Collegiate Schools of Planning conference in 2020, during which some of the book's contributors presented their preliminary findings. We also thank our graduate research assistant Claire Nelischer for putting together the book's index. Lastly, but importantly, we thank our students. Our interactions with them have allowed us to explore and deepen the ideas presented in this book.

INTRODUCTION

Kian Goh, Anastasia Loukaitou-Sideris, and Vinit Mukhija

The ideal of the city as a commons and space for all persists in any notion of the "good city." Cities are held up as progressive beacons, spaces of diversity and inclusion, even sanctuaries, which protect against reactionary politics and promote access to safety and resources for all. In contrast, market-driven, neoliberal urban policies often hold residents in cities, especially those already marginalized and oppressed, captive to development pressures. Following the whims of finance capital, the goal in the design of urban form in such cities is often to achieve economic advantage rather than justice or inclusivity. Unjust cities and physical interventions favoring certain groups of urban residents over others certainly existed prior to the initiation of neoliberal urban policies. Nevertheless, the market-driven urbanism of the last decades has exacerbated injustice through privatization, gentrification, displacement, and exclusion. At stake is the notion of the city as a public sphere, in which all city residents can make political and spatial claims of citizenship and have a right to city life and livelihoods. In this book, we and our collaborators explore the roles of urban design and urban designers in strengthening the potential of cities and city regions to foster inclusive urban public life.

More specifically, we are interested in examining the possibility of envisioning and delivering social, spatial, and environmental justice in cities through urban design and the material reality of built environment interventions. Too often, the opposite is true. As cities relax regulations aimed at the public interest to accommodate the preferences of powerful corporate and real estate interests, they frequently use urban design interventions as tools for the creation of what some call the "private city": downtowns revitalized with public investments for largely corporate uses and users, elite parks supposedly open to the public but controlled by nongovernmental organizations and funded by private foundations and corporations, gated communities and new forms of privatized urban enclaves, and gentrified neighborhoods, which attract corporate ventures, tourist dollars, and wealthy consumers but exclude marginalized groups. These design interventions do not promote an urban commons but rather perpetuate social inequalities and deepening divisions between wealthy and poor residents, private and public interests, and formal and informal spaces.[1]

Justice in cities is intrinsically linked to their spatial, physical environments. But by and large, the concept of justice rarely appears as an explicit concern in urban design discourse and design practice. In contrast, in this book, we aim to bring to the fore the notion of justice and the public city, its struggles and challenges, and the role of urban design in achieving it. We see the city as a public good, which should provide its benefits and opportunities to all members of society. This public city should be open to all and characterized by institutional processes and outcomes that are inclusive and equitable. In particular, we interrogate the role of urban design and spatial interventions in delineating conflicts over what constitutes public(s) in cities and pose ideals or alternatives. Thus, the chapters that follow use case studies to discuss the following questions: What makes a public city? Who is it for? How is it made? What is the role of urban design? And what is "just urban design"?

JUSTICE AND THE CITY

Cities are sites of inclusion and exclusion. From the early 1900s, formative urban sociologists including Georg Simmel (1950) characterized modern cities as places demanding new attitudes of detachment and providing new forms of liberty. Chicago School sociologist Louis Wirth (1938) described cities as large, dense, and heterogeneous places that can offer freedom through anonymity and chosen and constructed communities. Indeed, cities have long been places of refuge for immigrants, ethnic and racial minorities, and people of different and diverse sexualities. On the other hand, cities are also economic centers—the command-and-control posts of the global market and its often exploitative mechanisms (Sassen 1991)—and where inequalities are magnified.

Because of the contrasting possibilities of liberation and coercion, urban researchers have long investigated the question of justice in the city. They have conceptualized justice from multiple perspectives, including the point of view of philosophical thinking. Iris Marion Young (1990), for example, questions philosophical concepts of justice that focus on distribution and instead points to concepts of domination and oppression as ways to shine a light on the importance of group difference and social movements. Young offers a concept of justice more in line with the ideals of urban life, where different people live in proximity. Susan Fainstein (2010) synthesizes key philosophical concepts to argue for a "just city" characterized by three guiding principles of urban justice: equity, diversity, and democracy; she goes on to advocate for the value of justice as an urban policy norm.

Other scholars have posed ideas about justice and the city through the point of view of Marxist political economy. Thus, for David Harvey (2009), the city is a spatial, physical manifestation of processes of unequal and unjust capitalist accumulation—the more just corrective of which involves the democratic control of the means and processes of economic production. Similarly, Edward Soja (2010) emphasizes the spatiality of issues of justice in the city, viewing space as a critical factor that influences and, in turn, is influenced by social relations.

Others have pointed to the ways systems of oppression underlie unjust processes and outcomes in cities. Laura Pulido (2000) and Ryan Holifield (2001) assert the ways disparate environmental conditions in cities go beyond specific cases of intentional discrimination, revealing systemic patterns of discrimination and racism. Echoing Young, Holifield contests the distributive frameworks of justice that characterize some environmental justice research in favor of aspects of justice that are more in tune with ideals of progressive social movements. This point is increasingly pertinent as cities confront and respond to the increasingly urgent problem of climate change in ways that can exacerbate existing inequalities (see, e.g., Anguelovski et al. 2019; Goh 2021).

Building on but distinct from such philosophic and political-economic bases, urban planning scholars have argued for a normative basis for justice in the city. John Friedmann (1987; 2000) has advocated for planning theory to provide "images of the good city," claiming the need to search for the "common good," which a city should serve. Other planning scholars, including Leonie Sandercock (2004) and Faranak Miraftab (2009), have continued to call for transformative visions for the city in response to systemic urban inequalities and oppressions.

JUST URBAN DESIGN

But while such ruminations about justice and the city have formed core lineages of urban research, few of the primary debates account for the possibility of spatial interventions to change and create more just processes or outcomes. Indeed, Friedmann's (2000) call for "guiding, normative images" of the city acknowledges the lack of such thinking, pointing readers to Allan Jacobs and Donald Appleyard's (1987) "urban design manifesto." As we discuss in the first chapter, considerations of the interrelationship between design (or physical transformations of the city) and justice are often missing from the classic texts on the just city.

The conventional disregard for justice in urban design is problematic. Urban design is often seen as a practice of beautification quite apart from fundamental concerns of wellbeing, equity, and justice. But formative ideas about urban design emerged from observations of injustice. Overcrowded European and American cities of the late nineteenth century prompted early explorations of the relationship between spatial form and social good. Visions such as Ebenezer Howard's garden city (1898) and Tony Garnier's cité industrielle (1899–1917) imagined utopian spaces with calibrated and separated zones for living, working, and playing. The architects of the Congrès Internationaux d'Architecture Moderne (CIAM), or International Congresses of Modern Architecture, believed that good city design accounts for the organization of ideal social and spatial relationships. The Athens Charter (1933), in fact, prioritized the human scale and the interests of the community over the individual. CIAM architects called for better housing and recreational spaces for workers in the city and came up with ideas and proposals for minimum standards for space, light, and air. However, modernist urban design projects envisioned wholesale redevelopment of congested neighborhoods without enough attention to how the lives and livelihoods of workers and residents were dismantled and disrupted on the road to progress.

Such visions are now often criticized as universalist, rational, hierarchical, and authoritarian (Boyer 1983). In the era after the rejection of modernist planning, epitomized by Jane Jacobs (1961) in her classic book *The Death and Life of Great American Cities* and reflected in the demolition of the Pruitt-Igoe public housing complex in St. Louis in 1972, utopian visions for cities have generally receded in the minds of spatial planners and urban designers. So have more ambitious considerations of justice in urban design.

In recent years, some exceptions have explicitly focused on the possibilities and challenges of design interventions contributing to justice. For example, Toni Griffin and her colleagues (2015) share their personal reflections on "what a just city would look like." David De La Peña and his colleagues (2017, 1), in the edited book *Design as Democracy,* examine the process and techniques of participatory design and challenge designers to "seek meaningful, ethical, and effective ways to design with communities." Jeffrey Hou (2010) and his collaborators in the edited book *Insurgent Public Space: Guerilla Urbanism and the Remaking of Contemporary Cities* and Gordon Douglas (2018) in the more recent book *The Help-Yourself City: Legitimacy and Inequality in DIY Urbanism* critically examine bottom-up design interventions in cities as forms of community and civic engagement and as ways of achieving a more just urban form. While not focusing specifically on the urban design and architecture of cities, Sasha Costanza-Chock's (2020) recent book *Design Justice* also calls for inclusivity in design.

This book is in the same spirit as these recent interventions and attempts to center justice as the object of research in design scholarship. It specifically asks: How might urban planning and urban design researchers and practitioners reconsider concepts of urban design as central to considerations of justice in cities?

BOOK ORGANIZATION

The book is organized into four parts. Part I, following this introductory chapter, asks: *What Is Urban Design for Justice?* Part II extends the discussion and focuses on asking *What Is the Public City and Inclusive Urbanism?* Part III elaborates on *Participation and Organizing for Just Design.* Lastly, Part IV, *Design for Difference*, examines design within the context of a diverse public city that prioritizes the most marginalized communities. Below, we discuss in more detail the context of each of the four parts of the book and preview the chapters included in them.

PART I: WHAT IS URBAN DESIGN FOR JUSTICE?

Traditionally, urban design has been seen either as art preoccupied with aesthetic issues of form and appearance or as technical expertise, untangling technical problems related to the construction of urban form (Loukaitou-Sideris 1996). But as early as 1933, the first seeds of a social conscience in the profession emerged in CIAM's Charter of Athens, detailing modern movement's concerns away from buildings for the elite and toward the creation of well-lit, well-aired housing and workspaces for a larger public. It was not until 1981, however, that Kevin Lynch, in his *A Theory of Good City Form*, explicitly named "justice" as a "meta-criterion" toward achieving a good city form. Ten years prior to this publication, political philosopher John Rawls (1971) had issued his *Theory of Justice*, and Lynch drew from this classic treatise to discuss the distributive inequality of what he considered as five essential performance characteristics of city form: vitality, sense, fit, access, and control. Lynch's conception of justice focused on "distributive justice"—how the five attributes of good city form were inequitably distributed in urban and metropolitan landscapes. This discussion remained mostly normative, with no explicit suggestions of how an urban design for justice could be achieved. In more recent decades, Setha Low and her collaborators (2005) introduced two additional concepts of justice: "procedural justice"—concerned with how just and inclusive the processes of design and decision making are in the construction of urban form—and "interactive justice"—concerned with how different subgroups of users interact but may be treated differently and unequally in designed spaces. Subsequently, Setha Low and Kurt

Iveson (2016) added the concept of "recognitional (or representational) justice," which is concerned with how design recognizes and responds to the needs and values of marginalized groups.

Various scholars within the urban design field react and respond to these four conceptions of justice. Tending to distributional justice, John Chase, Margaret Crawford, and John Kaliski (1999) in *Everyday Urbanism* want to take the attention of urban design from elite, primary spaces in the city to the spaces of everyday life. Tending to procedural justice, efforts around participatory design and coproduction of space focus on democratizing the urban design process (De La Peña et al. 2017), while design movements such as guerilla urbanism (Hou 2010) and DYI urbanism (Douglas 2018) seek to take the agency of space production from the "designer-expert" to a larger collective of citizens and neighborhood groups. Tending to interactional justice, various recent discussions and treatises on the "architecture of cooperation" (Sennett 2012), "inclusive design," and "design for difference" examine how urban design and designed spaces can not only simultaneously accommodate the needs but also promote the interaction of a diverse public, also giving emphasis on vulnerable or marginalized groups (women, ethnic and sexual minorities, immigrants, older adults, people with disabilities, etc.). Lastly, tending to "recognitional justice," Vinit Mukhija and Anastasia Loukaitou-Sideris (2014) in the *Informal American City* ask for a broadening of the scope of the field of urban design to encompass and recognize the spaces and activities of informal workers and informality in cities.

In addition to chapter 1, which offers a critical review of foundational urban design literature, the other two chapters in this section further interrogate what urban design for justice is. Chapter 1 seeks to trace how urban design scholarship treats or most often ignores the value of justice. In this chapter, with Christopher Giamarino, we examine the key theoretical developments in urban design scholarship to assess how urban design thinkers consider equity and justice in their ideas and proposals. We are interested in understanding and analyzing urban design both as the subject and the object of research and practice. We closely read thirty-one key urban design texts to examine if they consider the concept of justice in distributive, procedural, interactional, or recognitional ways. We find that the vast majority of these texts, which are primarily written by white, male writers of the Global North, pay only cursory if any, attention to concepts of justice.

In chapter 2, Setha Low expands her original discussion on justice and public spaces (Low, Taplin, and Scheld 2005) by proposing six dimensions for social justice in urban design—distributive, procedural, interactional, informational, representational, and ethic of care. She applies this framework within the context of reduced access to public spaces experienced by older adults during the COVID-19 pandemic to demonstrate how the satisfaction of these six dimensions can help cities create more just public spaces for them. The six dimensions she proposes draw from her thirty years of ethnographic research on public spaces. Thus, she offers a theoretical and practice framework for the evaluation of public space from a just design perspective.

In chapter 3, Michael Rios argues that urban design as a field has been slow to realize and respond to the multiple "intersectional" injustices in the city. He draws from Iris Marion Young's (2013) "responsibility for justice" dictum, her "social connection model," and other scholarship on race and space to interrogate how an ethical urban design praxis can advance justice by agitating and reacting to these injustices. He believes that a just urban design requires different ways of imagining, knowing, and doing that produce counterimaginaries, make visible previously marginalized forms of social life, and multiple and differentiated visions of the "good city."

PART II: WHAT IS THE PUBLIC CITY AND INCLUSIVE URBANISM?

Following Edward Soja's (2010) call for spatial consciousness in the quest for justice and Susan Fainstein's (2010) emphasis on cities and urban centers, the chapters in this section adopt an explicitly spatial lens at the urban scale to understand social justice and the publicness of cities. The publicness of a city (or "publicity," as Diane Davis calls it) is defined by its inclusivity and ability to integrate all residents and their diverse and disparate histories, demands and needs, and access to resources. Inclusive urbanism does not solely respond to the needs and values of dominant, powerful, or well-represented groups. It also tends to those who theorist Nancy Fraser (1990) calls "subaltern counter-publics," acting to foster, preserve, and expand settings where nondominant or marginalized social groups, such as gender, religious, and racial/ethnic minorities, would feel safe.

Urban design scholarship is largely devoid of detailed inquiries on how to recognize and meet diverse needs through design, often tending instead to universalizing concepts of human needs. Similarly, the design praxis is frequently aiming at satisfying the "average user," often patterned after white, male, cisgender individuals (Loukaitou-Sideris 1995). Certainly, bright exceptions exist, such as earlier feminist critiques of sexist city design and its reimagining, including Dolores Hayden's (1980) treatise *"What Would a Non-Sexist City Be Like?"*; Daphne Spain's (1992) *Gendered Spaces*; Leslie Kanes Weisman's (1992) *Discrimination by Design*; and, more recently, work by Yasminah Beebeejaun (2017) on *Gender, Urban Space and the Right to Everyday Life* and Leslie Kern's (2020) *Feminist City*. We have also recently witnessed some much-needed scholarly attention to design and placemaking in communities of color, including *Diálogos* by Michael Rios and Leonardo Vazquez (2012), *Black in Place* by Brandi Thompson Summers (2019), and *Black Landscapes Matter* by Walter Hood and Grace Mitchell Tada (2020).

The authors of Part II also focus on inclusivity and are interested in just design outcomes, including the procedural and interactional dimensions of justice, as these are present or absent in urban design process and practice. They suggest that whereas urban citizenship confers equal rights to all residents, it also requires collective responsibilities. While Martha Nussbaum (2011) focuses on governments and public policy and their roles in advancing justice, these chapters focus more directly on the built environment and urban designers. They do, nonetheless, have an expansive and ambitious conception of what constitutes urban design and its material domains and the corresponding responsibility of urban designers. The lessons and principles the authors identify draw their inspiration from cosmopolitanism (Appiah 2007), aspiring to foster progressive cosmopolitanism as an outcome that extends beyond narrow and confining municipal boundaries.

In chapter 4, Diane E. Davis uses the lens of sovereignty to posit a just and inclusive city where residents have shared rights and equal citizenship. She provocatively makes a case for sovereignty at the city scale rather than at the national level as a political approach for developing a shared urban community. Highlighting her arguments with examples from two conflict cities—Jerusalem and Belfast—she privileges the case for progressive urban politics and local decision making with implications beyond urban boundaries. She argues for cosmopolitan cities in the US and elsewhere as a bulwark against parochial nationalism. Thus, she presents urbanism as a political aspiration juxtaposed against nationalism and places urban designers and planners at the forefront of progressive political discourse and action.

In chapter 5, Vinit Mukhija examines inclusive urbanism through access to housing and its material configurations. He argues that an open and inclusive housing market with flexible housing forms and patterns—or the private realm of housing—defines the public city and its cosmopolitan character. Housing forms, particularly single-family housing, need to change to accommodate the more diverse needs in cities. But making housing characteristics fit the diverse needs of various social groups requires inclusive deliberation of all stakeholders—not just the privileged groups. Mukhija uses the case of Vancouver's informal and locally driven neighborhood changes to show how participatory processes helped establish the basis for city-level interventions for opening single-family neighborhoods to four units per lot.

In chapter 6, Alison B. Hirsch approaches inclusive urbanism by making inequities and conflict in the city visible and argues for urban designers to confront, recognize, and address injustices in the built environment. She focuses on Los Angeles in the wake of the 1992 urban unrest (following the Rodney King verdict) as the city's turning point. She considers the challenge of making conflicts visible, including the inherent difficulties involved in fairly selecting and identifying significant struggles and discords. Nonetheless, she makes a case for awareness of conflict and inequities to provoke mitigating responses and interventions that counter spatial injustices and lead to inclusive urbanism.

In the final chapter of Part II, Rebecca Choi explains how a modern bureaucracy of urban design governance emerged during the late 1960s and early 1970s in New York City. Choi shows how its driving forces were political, procedural, and oriented toward market-based efficiency and expediency rather than justice. While elite institutions, including the

Museum of Modern Art (MoMA), Columbia University, and the Chase Manhattan Bank, were crucial in establishing the city's new political economy of urban design, its Black and Puerto Rican residents were systematically disenfranchised and left out of the urban design process.

PART III: PARTICIPATION AND ORGANIZING FOR JUST DESIGN

Increasingly, researchers have looked to social movements and group difference as the foundations for thinking about concepts for justice and the city (Young 1990). They have also emphasized the importance of urban governance and policy (Friedmann 2000; Fainstein 2010). These invocations of social movements and urban governance require analytical attention beyond ideas about distribution or individual equity. They require analyses of how different groups gain power, rights, and access in cities and how individuals, agencies, and other policymaking facets of city governments respond to claims for rights and access.

Some planning scholars have looked to ideas about communication and participation as the modes of planning through which more equitable processes and outcomes might be sought (Innes 1995; Forester 1999). Many of these planning ideas appeared in direct response to the perceived inequality of top-down processes of modernist planning. Planning scholars have also contested simplistic notions of participation and have instead called for more reflexive planning attuned to the different ways that planners interact with diverse groups (De Souza Briggs 1998) as well as more radical notions of participatory agency beyond inclusion (Miraftab 2009).

Planning ideas about urban design have often underemphasized or neglected participation and organizing. This happens in two ways. Some have noted how standard urban design practices have often sidelined participation and more generally have paid insufficient attention to the lived experiences of those affected by the design proposals (Peattie 1987). Others have ignored the ways and possibilities that urban design tools, strategies, and processes might actually enable new forms of participation and organizing.

Emerging scholarship on urban design takes a more concerted look at aspects of participation and organizing. The contributions in this section take on the institutions, scales, and practices of urban design in contested spaces and contexts. In chapter 8, Jeffrey Hou explores the ways in which long-term institutional relationships offer the platform for urban design to empower community-building in Seattle's rapidly changing Chinatown-International District. He uses the case study of a two-decades-long process of community-engaged urban design to show how sustained community-university partnerships and participatory design methods can help shape a just city. He emphasizes how a focus on capacity-building can guide the way for knowledgeable and capable community engagement in built environment interventions. He also reminds readers that capacity-building and community engagement in urban design can lead to socially transformative outcomes that transcend the projects seeking genuine community engagement.

In chapter 9, Chelina Odbert explains how innovative design thinking with and for communities in marginalized places can open opportunities for creating public spaces as pathways to just urban design. She offers examples of the work of Kounkuey Design Initiative (a community development and design nonprofit organization) in Mendoza, Argentina, and in the Coachella Valley and Los Angeles, California, to illustrate her claims. She shows how urban designers can use their technical expertise to read clues in the built environment to understand the needs and wants of marginalized communities and collaborate with residents who have local knowledge to design new public spaces.

In chapter 10, Rachel Berney emphasizes the role of disadvantaged communities in making urban design decisions about their neighborhoods and built environments. She focuses on Seattle to explain how a coalition of historically Black churches and their leaders—the Nehemiah Initiative—working with progressive city agencies and academic units attempts to change the oppressive historical patterns of urban development in the city and enable more just claims on space. She details the coalition's concerns about affordable housing, gentrification, and displacement, and its role in training future urban design professionals. She describes the initiative's work as a just design movement focused on expanding both the *invitation* to use the city to traditionally disadvantaged community groups, as well as the *imaginary* of who urban designers should design for.

In the last chapter of Part III, Kian Goh examines the ways that new organizations of resilient urban design have impacted struggles for recognition and justice in New York City after Hurricane Sandy in 2012. She focuses on the case of Rebuild by Design, a design competition for resilient solutions for storms and sea-level rise, which has become a model initiative for urban interventions around climate change. She examines and assesses how underlying design concepts and concerns of design have affected ongoing struggles for social, spatial, and environmental justice in the city—particularly the events and politics around the Lower East Side in Manhattan. Thus, her focus is on examining how the politics of design, including participation and organizing, contribute to just resilience.

PART IV: DESIGN FOR DIFFERENCE

Who is urban design for? For too long and too often, urban design has favored the wealthy and the powerful and has concentrated its efforts in the prime spaces of the city. As a result of highway development, suburbanization, and more recent neoliberal urban policies, many inner-city neighborhoods remain neglected in both physical and economic terms. Certain design and infrastructural projects have produced negative instead of positive impacts on poor communities or marginalized urban groups, such as when the building of a prison further stigmatized a poor community; the intrusion of a highway effectively cut it off from the rest of the city; and walls and fences were built to "protect" gated communities from the fear of "other" groups. In recent decades, neoliberalist urban design has given its attention to creating city brands, wooing the corporate world and "creative professionals" in revitalized downtowns, and attracting tourists and conventioneers to the "buzz" and often privatized spaces of high culture (Judd and Fainstein 1999). Even in cases when such injustices and inequities by design have not taken place, urban design often consciously or unconsciously follows the tastes, needs, or preferences of more white, more male, and more affluent groups (Loukaitou-Sideris 1995).

Henri Lefebvre (1996, 158) described the right to the city as a "transformed and renewed *right to urban life.*" If this is the case, then just urban design should enable not only access to city amenities but also the ability to claim and reconfigure spaces of opportunity for even the most marginalized communities. The chapters in this section take on this challenge exploring how urban design can enhance the right to the city for marginalized or vulnerable groups and communities. Thus, drawing from their research and design practice, Teddy Cruz and Fonna Forman in chapter 12 take us to planning and design interventions in neighborhoods in Medellín and Bogotá, Colombia, and at the San Diego/Tijuana border to discuss how design is exercised by and for immigrant groups there in ways that enhance their right to the city. Urban rights, they argue, are grounded in the agency of marginalized groups and their entitlement to coproduce a just and equitable city. In particular, Cruz and Forman are motivated by and focus on immigrants and their informal spaces and practices as building blocks of an urban design of justice.

In chapter 13, Francesca Piazzoni and Anastasia Loukaitou-Sideris detail the spatial tactics of Bangladeshi street vendors who operate and often live in one of the most exclusive spaces in the world, the historic center of Rome. They discuss how just urban design can support these tactics through physical design interventions, which they call "empowering placemaking strategies." They suggest that urban designers can support vendors by enhancing their opportunities for commerce in prime spaces; by ensuring that they have accessible amenities for satisfying their needs; and by providing spaces to claim and appropriate for their unique practices and histories. These placemaking strategies, they argue, can ensure a more just design of prime city spaces that welcome rather than exclude vulnerable groups.

Arguing that Black urbanism has been almost completely neglected from urban design narratives, Matthew Jordan-Miller Kenyatta, in chapter 14, uses Leimert Park, a historically Black neighborhood in Los Angeles, as an example of how Black-owned businesses and artists have developed a spatial Pan-Africanist imaginary that enhances their belongingness to place. He draws a connection between Black economic geographies with arts and culture and their power as culturally based, place-making platforms of inclusion. Miller reframes Black urbanism as an asset-oriented approach and Blackness as a dynamic community resource for urban designers interested in spatial justice to draw on, as well as actively support.

In the last chapter of this section, Anastasia Loukaitou-Sideris elaborates on the significant role of physical mobility in creating opportunities for socioeconomic development and healthy living and highlights the role of sidewalks in mobility. She details a study based on walking in an inner-city Los Angeles neighborhood with older adults, mostly immigrants and minorities. Through their descriptions of their walks, it becomes clear that their right to the city is severely compromised by dangerous and age-unfriendly sidewalks and public spaces. The chapter discusses these elders' everyday concerns for safety, the necessity of a just urban design for inclusive sidewalks, and how such sidewalks can be achieved through just urban design.

Thus, in the book's four parts, we and our collaborators contextualize the state of knowledge about urban design for justice; present the idea of the inclusive "public city" as the key to considerations of justice in the city; affirm the ideas about community participation and organizing as cornerstones in more equitable processes; and assert that just urban design is design that tends to the needs of publics, counter-publics, and, indeed, centers and privileges the most marginalized individuals and communities in our cities.

The primary premise of this book is that urban design can and must play an important and constructive role in the development of cities as a public good. We suggest that urban design scholars have paid inadequate attention to the larger questions of justice and the more focused inquiry on the role of spatial interventions in enabling social justice and making cities accessible and open to all. Urban designers have the agency to transform cities—for better or worse. To be more just and inclusive, practices of city design need to be transformed by an ethic of privileging the most vulnerable and disadvantaged groups. In the following chapters, we and our colleagues show pathways of progress in urban design scholarship and practice. We present both broader theoretical perspectives on justice in cities and urban design and also more specific considerations of sites, strategies, and groups involved in the making of the public city.

NOTE

1. For discussions about the "urban commons" see, for example, Gidwani and Baviskar (2011), Chatterton (2016), and Dellenbaugh et al. (2015).

REFERENCES

Anguelovski, I., Connolly, J. J., Pearsall, H., Shokry, G., Checker, M., Maantay, J., Gould, K., Lewis, T., Maroko, A., and Roberts, J. T. (2019). "Opinion: Why Green

'Climate Gentrification' Threatens Poor and Vulnerable Populations." *Proceedings of the National Academy of Sciences* 116 (52): 26139–26143.

Appiah, K. A. (2007). *Cosmopolitanism: Ethics in a World of Strangers*. New York: Norton.

Beebeejaun, Y. (2017). "Gender, Urban Space, and the Right to Everyday Life." *Journal of Urban Affairs* 39 (3): 323–334.

Boyer, M. C. (1983). *Dreaming the Rational City: The Myth of American City Planning*. Cambridge, MA: MIT Press.

Chase, J., Crawford, M., and Kaliski, J. (1999). *Everyday Urbanism*. New York: Monacelli Press.

Chatterton, P. (2016). "Building Transitions to Post-Capitalist Urban Commons." *Transactions of the Institute of British Geographers* 41 (4): 403–415.

Costanza-Chock, S. (2020). *Design Justice: Community-Led Practices to Build the Worlds We Need*. Cambridge, MA: MIT Press.

De La Peña, D., Jones Allen, D., Hester, Jr., R., Hou, J., Lawson, L. L., and McNally, M. J. (eds.). (2017). *Design as Democracy*. Washington, DC: Island Press.

Dellenbaugh, M., Kip, M., Bieniok, M., Müller, A., and Schwegmann, M. (2015). *Urban Commons: Moving beyond State and Market*. Basel: Birkhäuser.

De Souza Briggs, X. (1998). "Doing Democracy Up-Close: Culture, Power, and Communication in Community Building." *Journal of Planning Education and Research* 18 (1): 1–13.

Douglas, G. C. C. (2018). *The Help-Yourself City: Legitimacy and Inequality in DIY Urbanism*. New York: Oxford University Press.

Fainstein, S. (2010). *The Just City*. Ithaca: Cornell University Press.

Forester, J. (1999). *The Deliberative Practitioner*. Cambridge, MA: MIT Press.

Fraser, N. (1990). *Rethinking the Public Sphere: A Contribution to the Critique of Actually Existing Democracy*. Durham, NC: Duke University Press.

Friedmann, J. (1987). *Planning in the Public Domain: From Knowledge to Action*. Princeton, NJ: Princeton University Press.

Friedmann, J. (2000). "The Good City: In Defense of Utopian Thinking." *International Journal of Urban and Regional Research* 24 (2): 460–472.

Gidwani, V., and Baviskar, A. (2011). "Urban Commons." *Economic and Political Weekly* 46 (50): 42–43.

Goh, K. (2021). *Form and Flow: The Spatial Politics of Urban Resilience and Climate Justice*. Cambridge, MA: MIT Press.

Griffin, T., Cohen, A., and Maddox D. (eds.). (2015). *The Just City Essays: 26 Visions for Urban Equity, Inclusion and Opportunity. Vol. 1*. New York: J. Max Bond Center on

Design for the Just City at the Spitzer School of Architecture, City College of New York, Next City and The Nature of Cities.

Harvey, D. (2009). *Social Justice and the City*. Rev. ed. Athens: Georgia University Press.

Hayden, D. (1980). "What Would a Non-Sexist City Be Like? Speculations on Housing, Urban Design, and Human Work." *Signs* 5 (3), Supplement. Women and the American City, S170–S187.

Holifield, R. (2001). "Defining Environmental Justice and Environmental Racism." *Urban Geography* 22 (1): 78–90.

Hood, W., and Tada, G. M. (eds.). (2020). *Black Landscapes Matter*. Charlotte: University of Virginia Press.

Hou, J. (ed.). (2010). *Insurgent Public Space: Guerilla Urbanism and the Remaking of Contemporary Cities*. New York: Routledge.

Innes, J. (1995). "Planning Theory's Emerging Paradigm: Communicative Action and Interactive Practice." *Journal of Planning Education and Research* 14 (3): 183–189.

Jacobs, A., and Appleyard, D. (1987). "Towards an Urban Design Manifesto." *Journal of the American Planning Association* 53 (1): 112–120.

Jacobs, J. (1961). *The Death and Life of Great American Cities*. New York: Random House.

Judd, D., and Fainstein, S. (eds.). (1999). *The Tourist City*. New Haven, CT: Yale University Press.

Kern, L. (2020). *Feminist City: Claiming Space in a Man-Made World*. London: Verso.

Lefebvre, H. (1996). *Writings on Cities*. Oxford: Blackwell.

Loukaitou-Sideris, A. (1995). "Urban Form and Social Context: Cultural Differentiation in the Meaning and Uses of Neighborhood Parks." *Journal of Planning Education and Research* 14 (2): 101–114.

Loukaitou-Sideris, A. (1996). "Cracks in the City: Addressing the Constraints and Potentials of Urban Design." *Journal of Urban Design* 1 (1): 91–103.

Low, S., and Iveson, K. (2016). "Propositions for More Just Urban Public Spaces." *City* 20 (1): 10–31.

Low, S., Taplin, D., and Scheld, C. (2005). *Rethinking Urban Parks: Public Space and Cultural Diversity*. Austin: University of Texas Press.

Lynch, K. (1981). *A Theory of Good City Form*. Cambridge, MA: MIT Press.

Miraftab, F. (2009). "Insurgent Planning: Situating Radical Planning in the Global South." *Planning Theory* 8 (1): 32–50.

Mukhija, V., and Loukaitou-Sideris, A. (eds.). (2014). *The Informal American City: Beyond Taco Trucks and Day Labor*. Cambridge, MA: MIT Press.

Nussbaum, M. (2011). *Creating Capabilities: The Human Development Approach*. Cambridge, MA: Harvard University Press.

Peattie, L. (1987). *Planning: Rethinking Ciudad Guyana*. Ann Arbor: University of Michigan Press.

Pulido, L. (2000). "Rethinking Environmental Racism: White Privilege and Urban Development in Southern California." *Annals of the Association of American Geographers* 90 (1): 12–40.

Rawls, J. (1971). *A Theory of Justice*. Cambridge, MA: Harvard University Press.

Rios, M., and Vasquez, L. (eds.). (2012). *Diálogos: Placemaking in Latino Communities*. London: Routledge.

Sandercock, L. (2004). "Towards a Planning Imagination for the 21st Century." *Journal of the American Planning Association* 70 (2): 133–141.

Sassen, S. (1991). *The Global City: New York, London, Tokyo*. Princeton, NJ: Princeton University Press.

Sennett, R. (2012). "The Architecture of Cooperation." Public lecture, Harvard Graduate School of Design, February 28, 2012.

Simmel, G. (1950). "The Metropolis and Mental Life." In Wolff, K. H. (ed. and trans.). *The Sociology of Georg Simmel*. New York: Free Press.

Soja, E. (2010). *Seeking Spatial Justice*. Minneapolis: University of Minnesota Press.

Spain, D. (1992). *Gendered Spaces*. Chapel Hill: University of North Carolina Press.

Summers Thompson, B. (2019). *Black in Place: The Spatial Aesthetics of Race in a Post Chocolate City*. Chapel Hill: University of North Carolina Press.

Weisman Kanes, L. (1992). *Discrimination by Design: A Feminist Critique of the Man-Made Environment*. Urbana: University of Illinois Press.

Wirth, L. (1938). "Urbanism as a Way of Life." *American Journal of Sociology* 44 (1): 1–24.

Young, I. M. (1990). *Justice and the Politics of Difference*. Princeton, NJ: Princeton University Press.

I

WHAT IS URBAN DESIGN FOR JUSTICE?

1

JUST URBAN DESIGN SCHOLARSHIP?
EXAMINING URBAN DESIGN THEORIES THROUGH A JUSTICE LENS

Christopher Giamarino, Kian Goh, Anastasia Loukaitou-Sideris, and Vinit Mukhija

Urban design is concerned with designing and making urban places. It is influenced and constrained by aesthetic, economic, environmental, political, and social demands, with their attendant implications for justice. Ideas about justice in urban space have developed in critical ways in recent years (Soja 2010; Fainstein 2011; Low and Iverson 2016). Just and unjust practices are contested through urban politics, materialized through spatial practices, including urban design, and become visibly and physically inscribed in space. Our late colleague Edward Soja (2010) argued that justice and space are inextricably linked. Socially produced spaces create structures of unevenly distributed geographical advantages and disadvantages. Because of design's role in envisioning and making these spaces, particular forms of injustice are intertwined and perpetuated or conversely mitigated by urban design.

But to what extent are urban design theories centrally concerned with justice in the city? In this chapter, we examine the key theoretical developments in urban design scholarship over the last 120 years to understand this. We identify thirty-one classic books that have influenced and continue to influence built environment processes and outcomes and urban design pedagogy worldwide. We ask: Did the foremost urban design thinkers concern their theories and visions with equity and justice issues? If so, how did they incorporate notions of justice into urban design? Was justice envisioned through top-down or bottom-up design? Was it outcome- or process-oriented, or something else?

Our objective in this chapter is to search for and identify ideas of justice present in scholarly works that encompass urban design's primary shared body of knowledge. Scholars have constructed frameworks to explore justice at multiple spatial scales and illustrate how spatial structures combined with group characteristics (gender, race, age, class) can impair certain groups' right to the city (Israel and Frenkel 2018). Most often, these writings come from disciplines outside urban design. We critically assess and build on conceptual frameworks inquiring about urban design as the subject and object of research, juxtaposed against broader theories of social justice and the city, to formulate an analytical framework of justice in urban design. Drawing from these texts, we first operationalize and discuss an analytical framework of justice composed of four domains: distributive, procedural, interactional, and recognitional. Next, we turn to the urban design literature and closely read and analyze essential urban design texts to explore whether justice is a central consideration in the proffered visions.

We find that theories of urban design rarely focus on justice and that the attention given to justice in urban design scholarship is often cursory. Only two out of the thirty-one reviewed books explicitly focus on multiple justice domains. Four other texts focus on at least one domain of justice explicitly. To be fair, several urban design texts consider an area of justice implicitly, particularly interactional justice. However, the texts are significantly deficient in discussing recognitional aspects of justice explicitly or implicitly. Ten books do not discuss any domain of justice at all. Collectively, these texts suggest that justice is not particularly important to urban designers.

In this chapter, we first develop our framework for analyzing justice in urban design scholarship. Next, we identify important urban design texts for analysis and explain how we selected them. In the subsequent section, we share our research and findings. We conclude with a reiteration of the chapter's main arguments. By identifying notions of justice present (or absent) in the prevailing theories of urban design, we argue for a broadening of the urban design discourse to become more diverse, inclusive, and sharply focused on justice in the city.

CONCEPTUALIZING DOMAINS OF JUSTICE AS AN ANALYTICAL FRAMEWORK

JUSTICE AS A FUZZY CONCEPT FOR URBAN DESIGN

Justice is a "fuzzy concept" that has historically been difficult to operationalize for empirical study (Markusen 2003). This is partly because the concept of justice has traditionally been compartmentalized into segregated epistemologies, which reside in different academic disciplines. Literature from political philosophy (Rawls 1971, 2001; Young 1990, 2011; Sen 2009; Nussbaum 2011), neo-Marxist critical urban geography (Harvey [1973] 2009; Soja 2010), urban planning theory (Marcuse et al. 2009; Fainstein 2011), and urban design (Lynch 1981; Lowery and Schweitzer 2019) diverge in their conceptualization of justice. Scholars associate justice with universal fairness to equal rights and distribution of socioeconomic goods from an "original position" (Rawls 1971); the capability for people to choose freedoms and rights so essential that without them, their basic human dignity would be nonexistent (Sen 2009; Nussbaum 2011); the establishment of baseline outcomes to achieve democracy, diversity, and equity in planning and policy outcomes (Fainstein 2011); and the assurance that different social groups can claim their right to the city through recognition and the ability to shape processes and outcomes in the production of space (Lefebvre 1968; Fraser 1995; Lowery and Schweitzer 2019).

Justice is a normative goal in key urban design literature (Jacobs and Appleyard 1987; Loukaitou-Sideris 1996; Lowery and Schweitzer 2019). However, scholars have rarely operationalized the concept of justice for urban design in a comprehensive way. Operationalizing justice in urban design requires a typology of analytically distinct yet ontologically interconnected domains of justice. Drawing on prior literature by theorists who have developed such a typology (Low and Iveson 2016; Moroni 2019), we compose a four-part operational framework for justice in urban design (table 1.1) and discuss it below.

DISTRIBUTIVE JUSTICE

Scholars often equate justice with fairness in the distribution of socioeconomic goods provided by political, social, and economic institutions

Table 1.1 An operational framework for justice in urban design

Justice concept	Operational definition
Distributive	Design outcomes that *redistribute public investments and opportunities in cities and regions* to produce a more equitable distribution of social amenities, infrastructure, and resources in the built environment.
Procedural	Design processes that *ensure that underprivileged groups are well represented and have a voice in creating urban form* by actively promoting participation and collaborative decision making.
Interactional	Design processes and outcomes that *treat all individuals with dignity and make underrepresented groups feel welcome in the production and consumption of built form* by encouraging multiple users and activities to interact and share the public realm.
Recognitional	Design processes and outcomes that *prioritize the cultural claims of marginalized social groups* by recognizing diverse users and activities in the public realm.

in society. However, there have been disagreements about how this just distribution is conceived. Debates have ranged from liberal, individualist concepts of societal distribution to neo-Marxist formulations that seek to address class-based inequities by transforming capitalist modes of production.

Political philosopher John Rawls's (1971, 2001) liberal utilitarian construction intended to maximize the redistribution of benefits for the less well-off in society without harming others. This concept has been extended by Amartya Sen (2009) and Martha Nussbaum (2011) in their "capabilities" approaches. These liberal conceptualizations of justice have been critiqued for ignoring, underplaying, or obfuscating the systemic or structural power relationships underlying differences among diverse social groups. In contrast, neo-Marxist urban geographers, including David Harvey ([1973] 2009) and Edward Soja (2010), conceived of injustice in the city as the uneven social and spatial outcomes caused by the exploitation of the working class through capitalist modes of production. They envisioned more just societal distribution through a revolutionary—and materially redistributive—transformation of the processes of capitalist urbanization.

Recognizing urban design's role in the social and spatial processes of urbanization, we define and operationalize distributive justice as design outcomes that spatially redistribute public investments and opportunities in cities and regions to produce a more equitable distribution of social amenities, infrastructure, and resources in the built environment. To explicitly focus on distributive justice, scholars must discuss redistribution to disadvantaged groups.

PROCEDURAL JUSTICE

Procedural justice focuses on the processes of decision making, asking who is involved, who is represented, and who counts. Moving away from top-down, technocratic processes, advocacy planning in the 1960s popularized the notion of including a plurality of voices in processes leading to planning and design outcomes (Davidoff 1965). Later known as collaborative planning (Healey 1997, 2003), this shift to a focus on relational interactions between laypeople and experts seeks to understand how social, economic, and environmental dynamics lead to different types of outcomes. Grounded in Jürgen Habermas' "ideal speech situation" (1984), the communicative turn in planning articulated that collaborative processes could create more just practices and place-based outcomes.

Supporters of this process-based emphasis on justice argue that design processes must be open and inclusive to ensure just outcomes (Lake 2017). However, some scholars have also criticized the neglect of power relationships, social group differences, and political and economic contexts that often shape participatory processes (Fainstein 2000; Innes and Booher 2004; Campbell 2006). Notwithstanding these debates, encouraging procedural justice in urban design can help ensure that marginalized groups possess the capability to participate in decision-making processes that affect them and impact the public realm's design according to their needs.

We define and operationalize procedural justice as design processes that ensure that underprivileged groups are well represented and have a voice in creating urban forms by actively promoting participation and collaborative decision making. To explicitly focus on procedural justice, scholars must discuss participation by marginalized and underrepresented groups.

INTERACTIONAL JUSTICE

The concept of interactional justice involves the quality of interpersonal interactions and comes from the literature on organizational justice (Cropanzano, Prehar, and Chen 2002). Interactional justice is achieved when individuals are treated with dignity and respect. Those impacted by outcomes are transparently notified and are given clear explanations as to why processes were used in a particular way and how outcomes were subsequently distributed (Muzumdar 2012).

Examining this concept in the context of design, interactional justice is achieved when design actions by those in power—architects, designers, and planners—involve outreach and engagement strategies so that different members of the public are well informed and have the opportunity to express their views regarding the actions. Interactional justice is encountered in urban design scholarship in works that discuss how to increase the quality of encounters among different urban residents (Low and Iveson 2016), encourage inclusive interactions in design processes (Loukaitou-Sideris 2012), or foster a sense of conviviality among multiple users who are all given the right to occupy space and be treated with respect (Chiu and Giamarino 2019).

We define and operationalize interactional justice as design processes and outcomes that treat all individuals with dignity and make underrepresented groups feel welcome in the production and consumption of built form by encouraging multiple users and activities to interact and share the public realm. To explicitly focus on interactional justice, scholars must discuss the interactions of marginalized and underrepresented groups in the built environment.

RECOGNITIONAL JUSTICE

Recognitional justice promotes the representation and celebration of diverse cultural, social, racial, class, and gender groups in policymaking and design outcomes (Fainstein 2011; Low and Iveson 2016). Iris Marion Young (1990, 2011) stresses that the concept of justice should include acknowledging and addressing the domination and oppression of marginalized social groups. According to Nancy Fraser (1995, 92), justice is multidimensional and requires more than material distribution. It must also prioritize a "deconstructive cultural politics" to eliminate cultural domination and alienation, celebrate other cultures that have been rendered invisible by authoritative interpretations, and abolish cultural stereotypes represented in the media and everyday life.

The recognition of social group differences is a vital domain of social justice because social relations and institutional conditions tend to reinforce the oppression of some groups and the domination of other groups. This leads to uneven decision-making processes that preclude "the development and exercise of individual capacities and collective communication and cooperation" (Young 1990, 39). Young suggests that city life, in its ideal, offers the setting for an empowering and emancipatory politics of recognition. Justice as recognition in urban design produces environments that accommodate differentiated social networks without spatial exclusion, serve a diverse array of cultural activities, and celebrate group differences, the embodied participation and presence of different voices in civic life, and interactions among strangers.

With urban design scholarship in mind, we define and operationalize recognitional justice as design processes and outcomes that prioritize marginalized social groups' cultural claims by recognizing diverse users and activities in the public realm. To explicitly focus on recognitional justice, scholars must address the recognition of marginalized and underprivileged groups.

CLASSIC URBAN DESIGN SCHOLARSHIP

CHOICE OF TEXTS

We selected thirty-one classic writings in urban design to explore if and how urban design discourses have considered the aforementioned four justice domains (table 1.2). To develop our list, we (1) focused on books or monographs, including edited volumes, rather than articles; (2) selected texts written by designers (architects, landscape architects, urban designers, physical planners); and (3) excluded books that mainly focused on the history of urban design or urban form. However, we made an exception to the second criterion to include works by Jane Jacobs (1961) and William H. Whyte (1980), who, while not designers, produced highly influential texts for urban design. Next, we surveyed a variety of "must-read"

Table 1.2 Classic urban design texts

	Title	Date	Author	List
1.	*The Art of Building Cities*	1889	Camillo Sitte	A, P
2.	*Garden Cities of To-Morrow*	1898	Ebenezer Howard	A, L8
3.	*Town Planning in Practice*	1909	Raymond Unwin	A, APA, P
4.	*Towards a New Architecture*	1923	Le Corbusier	APA
5.	*The City of To-Morrow and Its Planning*	1929	Le Corbusier	A
6.	*Toward New Towns for America*	1951	Clarence Stein	APA
7.	*The Living City*	1958	Frank Lloyd Wright	APA
8.	*The Image of the City*	1960	Kevin Lynch	A, AD, APA, P, L8
9.	*The Death and Life of Great American Cities*	1961	Jane Jacobs	A, AD, APA, L8, P
10.	*The Architecture of the City*	1966	Aldo Rossi	A, P
11.	*Design of Cities*	1967	Edmund N. Bacon	APA, L8
12.	*Design with Nature*	1969	Ian McHarg	A, APA, L8, P
13.	*The Concise Townscape*	1971	Gordon Cullen	A, AD, APA, P
14.	*Life between Buildings*	1971	Jan Gehl	A, AD, APA, P
15.	*Learning from Las Vegas*	1972	Robert Venturi, Denise Scott Brown, and Steven Izenour	A, AD, P
16.	*Urban Design as Public Policy*	1974	Jonathan Barnett	APA
17.	*A Pattern Language*	1977	Christopher Alexander, Sara Ishikawa, and Murray Silverstein	A, AD, APA, P
18.	*Delirious New York*	1978	Rem Koolhaas	AD, P
19.	*Collage City*	1978	Colin Rowe and Fred Koetter	A, AD
20.	*Urban Space*	1979	Rob Krier	A, P

Table 1.2 (continued)

	Title	Date	Author	List
21.	*The Social Life of Small Urban Space*	1980	William H. Whyte	A, APA
22.	*Livable Streets*	1981	Donald Appleyard	APA, P
23.	*A Theory of Good City Form*	1981	Kevin Lynch	A, APA, P
24.	*The Granite Garden*	1984	Anne W. Spirn	AD, APA
25.	*Finding Lost Space*	1986	Roger Trancik	A
26.	*A New Theory of Urban Design*	1987	Christopher Alexander et al.	A
27.	*The Next American Metropolis*	1993	Peter Calthorpe	A, APA
28.	*Everyday Urbanism*	1999	John Chase, Margaret Crawford, and John Kaliski (eds.)	A
29.	*Suburban Nation*	2000	Andres Duany, Elizabeth Plater-Zyberk, and Jeff Speck	P
30.	*Design for Ecological Democracy*	2006	Randolph T. Hester	APA
31.	*Landscape as Urbanism*	2016	Charles Waldheim	L8

Legend: A = Araabi (2016); AD = AD (2020); APA = APA (2019); L8 = Land8 (2016); P = Toderian (2013)

book lists on city design put together by the American Planning Association (2019), *Planetizen* (Toderian 2013), Landscape Architects Network (Land8 2016), and the editorial team of *Architecture Digest* (AD Editorial Team 2020). Lastly, we consulted the lists created by Hooman Foroughmand Araabi (2016), who analyzed the frequency of texts in urban design syllabi at Australian, UK, and US universities. While our positionalities as urban design scholars played a role in choosing specific books over others, the texts we selected repeatedly appear in syllabi of urban design courses or must-read lists in popular architecture, design, or planning outlets indicating their prominence and influence in the field of urban design.

TEXT ANALYSIS

First, we grouped each text according to its associated design movement (*i.e.*, modernism, townscape, postmodernism, new urbanism, landscape urbanism, everyday urbanism) to better understand how it was initially formed, contextualized within the urban political economy and landscape, critiqued by other texts, and connected to ideas of justice. Next, we closely read each book with our four-part domains of justice in mind. In particular, we looked for explicit and implicit emphasis on justice in the texts. We took copious notes on each book's main arguments and ideas and extracted quotes from the text related to the four justice domains. Third, we wrote short summaries of each book's main arguments, design ideas, relationship to prior design movements, and how many justice domains were present. The exercise helped us contextualize how each design idea related to or was influenced by other urban design theories and whether justice was considered. Fourth, we deliberated on our analysis as a group and finalized our assessment of each classic text by consensus. Thus, what follows is a collaborative, qualitative, and subjective assessment of justice in exemplary urban design scholarship.

Our content analysis of influential urban design texts is not without its limitations. For one, we examined only urban design literature written in English and focused on texts that are widely taught and covered in the US, UK, and Australia. Even though some of these texts have been translated into other languages, and some may appear in urban design curricula of non-English-speaking countries, we cannot claim a global applicability of our findings. Additionally, our content analysis did not examine the particular historical contexts or circumstances in which the authors worked—possibly flattening the complexity and nuance of how their particular ideas were formed.

ENCOUNTERING CONCEPTS OF JUSTICE IN CLASSIC URBAN DESIGN TEXTS

A first observation, evident even before we reviewed the texts, is that the authors of these thirty-one books were very homogenous: European and American men in institutions of the Global North wrote most of the texts presented in table 1.2. Of the thirty-one books, only six (19 percent) were written or cowritten by women. Additionally, with the exception of Sara Ishikawa, who is one of the coauthors of *Pattern Language*, all other authors and coauthors are white.

A second observation that became evident after we reviewed the texts is that urban design scholarship pays only cursory attention to justice. Table 1.3 summarizes our findings: Of the thirty-one classic texts that we identified for this analysis, only Kevin Lynch (1981) in *A Theory of Good City Form* and Randolph Hester (2006) in *Design for Ecological Democracy* explicitly focus on multiple justice domains. Also, Ebenezer Howard (1898), *Garden Cities of To-Morrow*; Jane Jacobs (1961), *The Death and Life of Great American Cities*; Donald Appleyard (1981), *Livable Streets*; and John Chase, Margaret Crawford, and John Kaliski (1999, eds.), *Everyday Urbanism*, focus explicitly on one domain of justice. While many urban design texts implicitly consider a domain of justice, particularly interactional justice, almost all ignore recognitional aspects of justice. Several books that promote design that implicitly recognizes interactional justice do not explicitly state which underrepresented groups should be treated with more dignity and included in the public realm's consumption and production. For justice as recognition, only two books—*Everyday Urbanism* and *Design for Ecological Democracy*—explicitly focus on prioritizing the cultural claims to the public realm of diverse groups by discussing how to learn from and design for groups like immigrant street vendors and unhoused people of color.

Strikingly, almost a third of the reviewed urban design books do not discuss any of the four justice domains. These texts often develop an innovative or provocative theory concerned with addressing or correcting design issues related to harmonious aesthetics, experiences in, and functions of urban form. For example, Camillo Sitte (1889) is concerned with the "artistic principles" of traditional European plazas, including the study of their irregular streets and enclosed squares. Le Corbusier (1923, 1929) looks to technological advances of the "machine age" to advocate for the reorganization of urban form into functionally separated land uses. Edmund Bacon (1967) supports strong "design ideas" to guide urban development along with systems of movement and circulation. Gordon Cullen's (1971) "serial vision" theory aims to develop urban design guidelines to stimulate artistic experiences in the city and perceptions of dramatic visual sequences. Colin

Table 1.3 Classic urban design texts and explicit/implicit emphasis of justice domains

	Author (date of book publication)	Justice domain			
		D	P	I	R
1.	Sitte ([1889] 1945)				
2.	Howard ([1898]1965)	E		i	
3.	Unwin ([1909] 1911)	i			
4.	Corbusier ([1923] 1974)				
5.	Corbusier ([1929] 1989)				
6.	Stein (1951)	i			
7.	Wright (1958)	i			
8.	Lynch (1960)		i		
9.	Jacobs (1961)			E	
10.	Rossi ([1966] 1982)			i	
11.	Bacon ([1967] 1974)				
12.	McHarg (1969)				i
13.	Cullen (1971)				
14.	Gehl ([1971] 1987)			i	
15.	Venturi, Brown, and Izenour (1972)			i	
16.	Barnett (1974)		i		
17.	Alexander, Ishikawa, and Silverstein (1977)		i		
18.	Koolhaas (1978)			i	
19.	Rowe and Koetter (1978)				
20.	Krier (1979)				
21.	Whyte (1980)		i	i	
22.	Appleyard (1981)		E	i	
23.	Lynch (1981)	E	E	i	
24.	Spirn (1984)				

Table 1.3 (continued)

	Author (date of book publication)	Justice domain			
		D	P	I	R
25.	Trancik (1986)			i	
26.	Alexander et al. (1987)				
27.	Calthorpe (1993)			i	
28.	Chase, Crawford, and Kaliski (1999)		i		E
29.	Duany, Plater-Zyberk, and Speck (2000)			i	
30.	Hester (2006)	i	E	E	E
31.	Waldheim (2016)				

Legend: D = Distributive; P = Procedural; I = Interactional; R = Recognitional
E = Explicit i = Implicit
Works that focus explicitly on at least one justice domain

Rowe and Fred Koetter's (1978) "collage city" concept supports the architect as a bricoleur who layers traditional elements of urban design with utopian notions of future form to create pluralistic urban design practices. Rob Krier's (1979) "urban space" serves as a backward-looking encyclopedia of good design associated with the public realm to ameliorate the negative externalities produced by modernism.

Anne Spirn (1984) advocates for designing with nature in *The Granite Garden* to ensure that every resident has access to health, safety, and welfare. Still, she does not reflect on how to redistribute environmental burdens equitably. Nonetheless, in later work, such as in the article "Restoring Mill Creek" (2005), justice becomes a central consideration for Spirn. Christopher Alexander and coauthors (1987) proffer the concept of "wholeness" to produce an autonomous form of urban design where buildings define how new development proceeds and create local symmetry defined by inviting public spaces. Their emphasis is only on aesthetic and formal wholeness. Charles Waldheim (2016), who has played a pivotal role in developing concepts of landscape urbanism, surveys how different design discourses associated with the landscape solve spatial and social issues. But his main emphasis and contributions are to critique the shallow design theory associated with new urbanism.

Below, we discuss the texts that pay attention to the four domains of justice in more detail. We also highlight in table 1.4 six of these texts, which explicitly refer to at least one justice domain.

URBAN DESIGN AND DISTRIBUTIVE JUSTICE

Concerned by London's overcrowded conditions, the proximity of industrial and residential uses, and proliferation of diseases and social ills, Ebenezer Howard argues in *Garden Cities of Tomorrow* that the

Table 1.4 Summary/explanations for selected design texts that explicitly consider notion(s) of justice

Author (date)	Explicit justice domain	Explanation
Howard ([1898] 1965)	Distributive	Howard explicitly proffers garden cities as a democratic socialist, anticity alternative to overcrowded, industrial cities. Employing economic and architectural analyses, the book explains how redistributions of property ownership, land uses, and populations can create affordable rents, collectively stewarded agricultural lands, and wealth redistribution.
Jacobs (1961)	Interactional	Jacobs notes the benefits that a dense, mixed-use sidewalks can have for everyday life in the city. The mixture of old and new buildings and "sidewalk ballet" encourage the inclusion of diverse populations, increase security based on informal social networks, and produce both a society and public spaces that are more tolerant to different types of users and activities.
Appleyard (1981)	Procedural	Appleyard's case studies show the conflicts associated with wealthier residents who push back against bike lanes, wider sidewalks, and other traffic calming techniques. He argues that inclusive participatory planning processes can reduce conflicts and ensure that overlooked groups, such as lower income communities and older adults, have a say in planning and urban design projects.

Table 1.4 (continued)

Author (date)	Explicit justice domain	Explanation
Lynch (1981)	Distributive and procedural	Lynch proposes five performance dimensions—vitality, sense, fit, access, and control—for a normative theory of good city form and two metacriteria—efficiency and justice. The performance dimensions should be equitably distributed and must afford people a chance to participate in the control of what settings look like and what activities are allowed in the public realm.
Chase, Crawford, and Kaliski (1999)	Recognitional	Chase, Crawford, and Kaliski encourage urban designers and architects to learn from place-based vernaculars associated with diverse social, spatial, and aesthetic meanings, claims, and uses of public space. Incorporating everyday activities in design can produce social change and blur race and class boundaries. Different social group identities and cultural practices can be recognized and celebrated by focusing on everyday urbanism.
Hester (2006)	Procedural, interactional, and recognitional	Hester prioritizes the integration of different users and activities into urban form and explicitly discusses how ecological democracy can foreground inclusive participatory processes for different social groups. He also advocates for an increase in biological and cultural diversity and articulates that allowing different cultures to express themselves in design concretizes their recognition.

decentralization of urban populations into town-country magnets of thirty thousand residents would produce self-sufficient agricultural and industrial land uses as well as housing with adequate light and access to gardens and would also promote cooperative land ownership where the "distribution of wealth forms so created [would] take place on a far juster and more equitable basis" ([1898] 1965, 130). Howard envisions that these self-sufficient radial cities would be environmentally sustainable, economically self-sufficient, and socially equitable. Rents would be affordable, open space would be plentiful, and different socioeconomic and racial groups would come together to steward cooperatively owned land. Howard's explicit cooperative interest and emphasis on social restructuring are evident from the original title of his book, *To-Morrow: A Peaceful Path to Real Reform*, published in 1898.

English town planner Raymond Unwin, considered the godfather of the modern town planning movement, sought to blend the irregularities of German towns with the top-down order of American street grid systems when considering how to redistribute and integrate them into holistic city and suburban design. He aimed to prevent overcrowded conditions while also providing for beauty and individuality of form and an affordable, inclusive mixed-income housing stock. Unwin was against residential segregation and actively promoted the redistribution of different housing types to reach a just estimate of mixed-income communities. As he states in his book, *Town Planning and Practice* ([1909] 1911, 294): "There is nothing in the prejudices of people to justify the covering of large areas with houses of exactly the same size and type. The growing up of suburbs occupied solely by any individual class is bad, socially, economically, and aesthetically." Like Howard, albeit less explicitly, Unwin's ideas focus on ideals related to material and spatial redistribution to create more just cities. Howard and Unwin inspired Clarence Stein's book *Toward New Towns for America (1951)*. Stein conceptualizes his new towns according to local economics, political realities, and climatological and topographical environmental conditions. The goal of his American garden city suburbs is "the building of balanced communities, cut to the human scale, in balanced, regions, which would be part of an ever widening national, continental, and global whole" (17).

Frank Lloyd Wright combined Jeffersonian antiurban sentiments and ideals of individualized property ownership with Henry George's interest in socializing land value in his proposals for Broadacre City. Every family would receive a one-acre lot. He writes, "Optimistic, nonpolitical, ex-urban, vernal, spacious, free! All this—yes. In practical outline here is the feasible idea of organic social democratic reconstruction of the city belonging to creative society—the living city. Abolish not only the 'tenement' and wage-slavery but create true capitalism. The only possible capitalism if democracy has any future" (1958, 158).

Kevin Lynch, who studied with Wright but disagreed with his individualistic philosophy, explicitly proposes justice as a metacriterion in *A
Theory of Good City Form* (1981). In terms of distributive justice, he writes,
"Distributions of particular goods might then safely remain unequal,
because of individual valuations and the resulting prices and patterns of
spending, while the general ability to choose would be equitable" (225).

URBAN DESIGN AND PROCEDURAL JUSTICE

Traditionally, the designer was perceived as the real expert, not needing
society's input on shaping the urban form. But starting in the 1960s, as
urban designers and city planners began working more closely with local
communities, some urban design scholars started considering participation and procedural justice.

In *A Theory of Good City Form*, Lynch identifies five performance dimensions of "good" urban design—vitality, sense, fit, access, and control. He
also recognizes that the distribution of the dimensions would require an
inclusive, and at times conflictual, process: "All decisions are made by
struggle and compromise; few values are held in common" (1981, 46).
Approximately twenty years earlier, in *The Image of the City* (1960, 117),
Lynch had proposed mental mapping as a participatory planning tool. He
argues, "Citizens could be taken into the street, classes could be held in
the schools and universities, the city could be made an animated museum
of our society and its hopes. Such education might be used, not only to
develop the city image, but to reorient after some disturbing change. An
art of city design will wait upon an informed and critical audience. Education and physical reform are parts of a continuous process." In *A Theory of
Good City Form* (1981, 321), Lynch elaborates on the sweeping potential of
such processes, "Mapping the accessibility of a city to diverse social groups,
or their relative control of its elements, would be a radical analysis."

Similarly, Donald Appleyard's planning and design work in Berkeley,
Oakland, and San Francisco highlights the importance of inclusive processes. A student of Kevin Lynch, Appleyard understood that design interventions in the built environment, such as the development of livable
streets, were political actions. He believed that the public's participation

in implementation, evaluation, and modification processes should be maximized. He argues: "The intent is to expose the attitudes, values, and political forces at work in neighborhood traffic schemes so that neighborhood groups, engineers, and planners can become more sophisticated in how they go about improvement efforts" (1981, 154–155).

For Randy Hester, participation and procedural justice are central elements of urban design and democracy. In *Design for Ecological Democracy* (2006, 95), he argues, "Creating a city that expresses fairness in its procedures and form enables more citizens to participate meaningfully and contribute to a strong ecological democracy. For those most interested in appearances, fairness creates more aesthetically pleasing urban landscapes. . . . No landscape can be more beautiful than it is just." He adds, "To maximize stewardship, the design of every part of the city should provide opportunities for meaningful citizen involvement. There should be a place at the table for everyone to participate. This requires a diversity of table settings" (371).

URBAN DESIGN AND INTERACTIONAL JUSTICE

Jane Jacobs focused on cities as sites of diversity, vibrant street life, social intercourse, and interaction. From personal observations in her Greenwich Village neighborhood, she hypothesized that mixed uses, walkable blocks, a mixture of old and new buildings, and population density were generators of urban diversity. In *The Death and Life of Great American Cities*, Jacobs (1961, 62) criticizes modernist planning and design as alienating residents and segregating human activity. She argues that "it is possible to be on excellent sidewalk terms with people who are very different from oneself and even, as time passes on familiar public terms with them."

Similarly, Hester advocates for designs that enable people to actively comingle and participate in the public realm; create resilient forms that withstand political upheavals, economic shocks, and environmental calamities; and instill a sense of joy and relaxation in residents and designers when appropriating and occupying public space. He argues, "Enabling form helps us to get to know unfamiliar neighbors and facilitates working with them and others to solve difficult problems" (2006, 8). He adds,

"Socially mixed neighborhoods offer one way to overcome repression, discrimination, and prejudice. Mixed neighborhoods also help us expand world views that are artificially simplified by segregation" (190).

The writings and design suggestions of several other urban designers also focus on the importance of public spaces in bringing people from diverse walks of life together in the city. We consider them as aiming at interactional justice, albeit in implicit and limited ways. For example, architect Jan Gehl published *Life between Buildings* in 1971 (later translated into English in 1987), based on his experience of redesigning the center of Copenhagen into a bike- and pedestrian-friendly city. Gehl encourages urban design that provides a physical framework to "affect the possibilities for meeting, seeing, and hearing people—possibilities that both take on a quality of their own and become important as background and starting point for other forms of contact" (15). Similarly, Roger Trancik in *Finding Lost Space* proposes an integrated theory of urban design to fill in the voids or leftover spaces in ways that respond to local cultural needs and particular local contexts. He believes that this "urbanism of addition" would reconnect elements in the built environment, encourage the presence of diverse users and rich function, and make sure "lost exterior spaces become new arenas for social and physical interaction" (1986, 23).

New urbanists like Peter Calthorpe (1993) and Andres Duany, Elizabeth Plater-Zyberk, and Jeff Speck (2000), in their writings, also promote a revitalized public realm. They claim that designing walkable public spaces and transit-oriented developments will reverse the proliferation of racially and economically segregated gated communities, anti-immigrant suburbs, and sprawling placelessness.

URBAN DESIGN AND RECOGNITIONAL JUSTICE

In *The Aesthetics of Equity* (2007), African American architectural theorist Craig Wilkins criticizes the institutional whiteness present in academic design institutions and in design practice. Through an analysis of different sites, he identifies how architecture and urban design have been systemically oppressive, resistant, and exclusive of diverse cultures' contributions to architectural history and practice, particularly from African Americans. He also describes "celebratory heterotopias"—deviant spaces of resistance purposefully chosen, appropriated, and remade by the hip-hop community to promote the recognition of difference and the construction of cultural identities within various spaces of the African American diaspora. This "hip hop spatial paradigm" allows for designers and laypeople to reuse materials from the postindustrial inner-city to communicate the mixture of hip-hop music and African American culture spatially, symbolically, and materially. *The Aesthetics of Equity* epitomizes justice as recognition in urban design.

In the late 1990s, a group of urban designers demonstrated the transformative possibilities for urban design if practitioners actively learned from overlapping socio-spatial and aesthetic meanings, tactical practices, and displays of cultural and political resistance taking place in the mundane spaces of everyday life. In *Everyday Urbanism* (1999), Chase, Crawford, and Kaliski expand the scope of urban design to include interventions for street vendors, garage sale patrons, guerrilla gardeners, and persons experiencing homelessness. They propose that "juxtapositions, combinations, and collisions of people, places, and activities . . . create a new condition of social fluidity that begins to break down the separate, specialized, and hierarchical structures of everyday life" (34). As they argue, "The intersections between an individual or defined group and the rest of the city are everyday space—the site of multiple social and economic transactions, where multiple experiences accumulate in a single location. These places where differences collide or interact are the most potent sites for everyday urbanism" (11).

Walter Hood's chapter "Urban Diaries" in *Everyday Urbanism* serves as a paradigmatic example of transformative sociocultural recognition through urban design for persons experiencing homelessness and for African Americans in West Oakland's Durant Minipark. Like Wilkins, Hood offers provocative design visions with mutable programmatic pieces that serve multiple users and activities, including alcoholics, sex workers, and children. He argues that "no single programmatic piece dominates the space—the ethos of difference and inclusion creates a place with multiple meanings, one that underscores many neighborhood practices at odds with normative societal values and attitudes" (1999, 162). But this ethos of difference and inclusion in the design of public spaces for all walks of life is absent in most classic urban design texts. Without attention to the history, behaviors, and social characteristics of a place, it is impossible to provide spaces for underrepresented groups to feel welcome.

One notable exception is Hester, who explicitly considers recognitional justice in urban design. He argues that "sometimes diversity must be pursued with the same vigor that we need to pursue shared values in decision making. Cities that are diverse are more resilient but only when that diversity is within a framework that is delineated by the particularness of the given regional landscape, social respect, and cooperation" (2006, 171). Hester, however, also realistically recognizes the limitations of justice through urban design. As he notes, "Expressing cultural difference in design makes diversity concrete and therefore more comprehensible. With a modest amount of mutual respect, differences can be appreciated, admired, and enjoyed, but design is no match for extreme ethnocentrism or xenophobia" (187).

CONCLUSION

In 1987, Allan Jacobs and Donald Appleyard published "Toward an Urban Design Manifesto." They criticized urban design theories and practices for failing to attend to the local context and address political, social, economic, and environmental problems in cities. The manifesto foregrounded justice as a critical goal in urban design. Jacobs and Appleyard (1987, 116) argued for a "commitment to a larger whole, to tolerance, justice, law, and democracy." In recognition and advocacy for disadvantaged groups, they added, "in supporting the small against the large . . . more justice for the powerless may be encouraged" (119–120). The field of urban design mostly ignored this advice, but today their ideas are more relevant than ever. Neighborhood inequities exposed by the COVID-19 pandemic, the precipitous rise in homelessness, and the protest movements of Black Lives Matter, sparked by the murders of George Floyd and countless other Black people in the US and around the world, underscore the need for a radical change of the public sphere, the public realm, and urban design. As urban design can help transform the settings of everyday life, the way that urban design scholars and practitioners theorize needs and practice design to address contemporary issues like the current public health crisis, ongoing racism, inequality, and homelessness matters.

In this chapter, we have developed an analytical framework for justice in urban design that has four domains: distributive justice, procedural justice, interactional justice, and recognitional justice. We propose that this justice framework is at the fore of future urban design inquiries, theories, and practice. In so doing, the design of the public realm will always consider economic and spatial redistribution, social group representation and vocalization in design workshops, fair treatment in the production and use of cities, and inclusion of cultural claims and recognition of difference in public spaces for underrepresented groups such as persons experiencing homelessness, indigenous communities, communities of color, and the LGBTQIA+ community, among others.

But in using our framework to analyze how classic urban design texts consider concepts of justice, our findings are disappointing. In part, this is because we focused on books (and excluded publications like Jacobs and Appleyard's manifesto). However, books are still a primary currency for exchanging ideas about urban design. Key books, including the thirty-one texts we analyzed, drive pedagogy in urban design programs and discourse in practice. Our analysis shows that urban design scholars rarely focus on justice. Most often, their attention to justice is only superficial. About a third of the key texts do not discuss any domain of justice. Moreover, they are written only from the dominant Global North perspective by white and primarily male authors. A more inclusive perspective that incorporates diverse voices and underrepresented groups is entirely missing from this design canon. The texts' primary focus is not on justice but on physical transformations and design solutions to respond to social, economic, and environmental processes in cities. There is a problematic lack of attention to ensuring fairness in design processes (procedural justice) and designing to include diverse social, cultural, and ethnic groups in the public realm (justice as recognition).

There is very little attention given to who benefits from urban design and how the benefits can be shared more broadly, particularly with disadvantaged groups. We hope that this chapter, and indeed this book, encourage a further reexamination of the urban design canon. Urban design's shared body of knowledge needs to be more inclusive and attentive to all different justice domains. This will help increase urban design's scope, perspective, and impact toward building a just city.

REFERENCES

AD Editorial Team. (2020). "125 Best Architecture Books." *Archdaily*, April 21, 2020. https://www.archdaily.com/901525/116-best-architecture-books-for-architects-and -students.

Alexander, C., Hajo, N., Anninou, A., and King, I. (1987). *A New Theory of Urban Design*. New York: Oxford University Press.

Alexander, C., Ishikawa, S., and Silverstein, M. (1977). *A Pattern Language: Towns, Building, Construction*. New York: Oxford University Press.

American Planning Association (APA). (2019). "*100 Essential Books of Planning*." https://www.planning.org/library/greatbooks/.

Appleyard, D. (1981). *Livable Streets*. Berkeley: University of California Press.

Araabi, Foroughmand H. (2016). "A Typology of Urban Design Theories and Its Application to the Shared Body of Knowledge." *Urban Design International* 21 (1):11–24.

Bacon, E. N. ([1967] 1974). *Design of Cities*. New York: Viking Press.

Barnett, J. (1974). *Urban Design as Public Policy*. New York: Architectural Record Books.

Calthorpe, P. (1993). *The Next American Metropolis: Ecology, Community, and the American Dream*. New York: Princeton Architectural Press.

Campbell, H. (2006). "Just Planning: The Art of Situated Ethical Judgment." *Journal of Planning Education and Research* 26: 92–106.

Chase, J., Crawford, M., and Kaliski, J. (eds.). (1999). *Everyday Urbanism*. New York: Monacelli Press.

Chiu, C., and Giamarino, C. (2019). "Creativity, Conviviality, and Civil Society in Neo-liberalizing Public Space: Changing Politics and Discourses in Skateboarder Activism from New York City to Los Angeles." *Journal of Sport and Social Issues* 43 (6): 462–492.

Corbusier, L. ([1923] 1974). *Towards a New Architecture*, 7th ed. (Translated by Frederick Etchells). New York: Praeger.

Corbusier, L. ([1929] 1987). *The City of To-Morrow and Its Planning*. (Translated by Frederick Etchells). Mineola, NY: Dover.

Cropanzano, R., Prehar, C., and Chen, P. (2002). "Using Social Exchange Theory to Distinguish Procedural from Interactional Justice." *Group & Organization Management* 27 (3): 324–351.

Cullen, G. (1971). *The Concise Townscape*. Oxford: Architectural Press.

Davidoff, P. (1965). "Advocacy and Pluralism in Planning." *Journal of the American Institute of Planners* 31 (4): 331–338.

Duany, A., Plater-Zyberk, E., and Speck, J. (2000). *Suburban Nation: The Rise of Sprawl and the Decline of the American Dream*. New York: North Point Press.

Fainstein, S. (2000). "New Directions in Planning Theory." *Urban Affairs Review* 35 (4): 451–478.

Fainstein, S. (2011). *The Just City*. Ithaca, NY: Cornell University Press.

Fraser, N. (1995). "From Redistribution to Recognition? Dilemmas of Justice in a 'Post-Socialist' Age." *New Left Review, no.* 212: 68–93.

Gehl, J. ([1971] 1987). *Life between Buildings: Using Public Space*. New York: Van Nostrand Reinhold Company.

Habermas, J. (1984). *The Theory of Communicative Action. Volume 1, Reason and the Rationalization of Society*. Cambridge: Polity Press.

Harvey, D. ([1973] 2009). *Social Justice and the City*. Athens: University of Georgia Press.

Healey, P. (1997). *Collaborative Planning: Shaping Places in Fragmented Societies*. Vancouver: University of British Columbia Press.

Healey, P. (2003). "Collaborative Planning in Perspective." *Planning Theory* 2 (2): 101–123.

Hester, R. T. (2006). *Design for Ecological Democracy*. Cambridge, MA: MIT Press.

Hood, W. (1999). "Urban Diaries: Improvisation in West Oakland, California." In Chase, J., Crawford, M., and Kaliski, J. (eds.). *Everyday Urbanism*, New York: Monacelli Press, 152–173.

Howard, E. ([1898] 1965). *Garden Cities of To-Morrow*. (Edited by F. J. Osborn). Cambridge, MA: MIT Press.

Innes, J. E., and Booher, D. E. (2004). "Reframing Public Participation: Strategies for the 21st Century." *Planning Theory & Practice* 5 (4): 419–436.

Israel, E., and Frenkel, A. (2018). "Social Justice and Spatial Inequality: Toward a Conceptual Framework." *Progress in Human Geography* 42 (5): 647–665.

Jacobs, A. B., and Appleyard, D. (1987). "Toward an Urban Design Manifesto." *Journal of the American Planning Association* 53 (1): 112–120.

Jacobs, J. (1961). *The Death and Life of Great American Cities*. New York: Vintage.

Koolhaas, R. (1978). *Delirious New York: A Retroactive Manifesto for Manhattan*. New York: Oxford University Press.

Krier, R. (1979). *Urban Space*. New York: Rizzoli.

Lake, R. W. (2017). "Justice as Subject and Object of Planning." *International Journal of Urban and Regional Research* 40 (6): 1206–1221.

Land8: Landscape Architects Network. (2016). *"Top 10 Books to Make You a Better Urban Designer."* September 30, 2016. https://land8.com/top-10-books-to-make-you-a-better-urban-designer/.

Lefebvre, H. (1968). *Le Droit à La Ville*. Paris: Anthropos.

Loukaitou-Sideris, A. (1996). "Cracks in the City: Addressing the Constraints and Potentials of Urban Design." *Journal of Urban Design* 1 (1): 91–103.

Loukaitou-Sideris, A. (2012). "Addressing the Challenges of Urban Landscapes: Normative Goals for Urban Design." *Journal of Urban Design* 17 (4): 467–484.

Low, S., and Iveson, K. (2016). "Propositions for More Just Urban Public Spaces." *City* 20 (1): 10–31.

Lowery, B. C., and Schweitzer, L. A. (2019). "Justice and Urban Design." In Banerjee, T., and Loukaitou-Sideris, A. (eds.). *The New Companion to Urban Design*, London: Routledge, 509–518.

Lynch, K. (1960). *The Image of the City*. Cambridge, MA: MIT Press.

Lynch, K. (1981). *A Theory of Good City Form*. Cambridge, MA: MIT Press.

Marcuse, P., Connolly, J., Novy, J., Olivo, I., Potter, C., and Steil, J. (eds.). (2009). *Searching for the Just City: Debates in Urban Theory and Practice*. London: Routledge.

Markusen, A. (2003). "Fuzzy Concepts, Scanty Evidence, Policy Distance: The Case for Rigour and Policy Relevance in Critical Regional Studies." *Regional Studies* 37 (6–7): 701–717.

McHarg, I. (1969). *Design with Nature*. Garden City, NY: Natural History Press.

Moroni, S. (2019). "The Just City. Three Background Issues: Institutional Justice and Spatial Justice, Social Justice and Distributive Justice, Concept of Justice and Conceptions of Justice." *Planning Theory* 19 (3): 251–267. doi:10.1177/1473095219877670.

Muzumdar, P. (2012). "Influence of Interactional Justice on the Turnover Behavioral Decision in an Organization." *Journal of Behavioral Studies in Business* 5: 31–41.

Nussbaum, M. C. (2011). *Creating Capabilities: The Human Development Approach*. Cambridge, MA: Harvard University Press.

Rawls, J. (1971). *A Theory of Justice*. Cambridge, MA: Harvard University Press.

Rawls, J. (2001). *Justice as Fairness*. Cambridge, MA: The Belknap Press of Harvard University Press.

Rossi, A. ([1966] 1982). *The Architecture of the City*. (Edited by Peter Eisenman. Translated by D. Ghirardo and J. Ockman). Cambridge, MA: MIT Press.

Rowe, C., and Koetter, F. (1978). *Collage City*. Cambridge, MA: MIT Press.

Sen, A. (2009). *The Idea of Justice*. Cambridge, MA: The Belknap Press of Harvard University Press.

Sitte, C. ([1889] 1945). *The Art of Building Cities: City Building According to Its Artistic Fundamentals*. (Translated by Charles T. Stewart). New York: Reinhold Publishing.

Soja, E. (2010). *Seeking Spatial Justice*. Minneapolis: University of Minnesota Press.

Spirn, A. W. (1984). *The Granite Garden: Urban Nature and Human Design*. New York: Basic Books.

Spirn, A. W. (2005). "Restoring Mill Creek: Landscape Literacy, Environmental Justice and City Planning and Design." *Landscape Research* 30 (3): 395–413.

Stein, C. (1951). *Toward New Towns for America*. Liverpool, UK: Liverpool University Press.

Toderian, B. (2013). "The 100 'Best' Books on City-Making Ever Written?" *Planetizen*, December 13, 2013. https://www.planetizen.com/node/66462.

Trancik, R. (1986). *Finding Lost Space: Theories of Urban Design*. New York: Van Nostrand Reinhold.

Unwin, R. ([1909] 1911). *Town Planning in Practice: An Introduction to the Art of Designing Cities and Suburbs*. 2nd ed. London: T. Fisher Unwin.

Venturi, R., Scott Brown, D., and Izenour, S. (1972). *Learning from Las Vegas*. Cambridge, MA: MIT Press.

Waldheim, C. (2016). *Landscape as Urbanism: A General Theory*. Princeton, NJ: Princeton University Press.

Whyte, W. H. (1980). *The Social Life of Small Urban Space*. New York: Project for Public Spaces.

Wilkins, C. L. (2007). *The Aesthetics of Equity: Notes on Race, Space, Architecture, and Music*. Minneapolis: University of Minnesota Press.

Wright, F. L. (1958). *The Living City*. New York: Horizon Press.

Young, I. M. (1990). *Justice and the Politics of Difference*. Princeton, NJ: Princeton University Press.

Young, I. M. (2011). *Responsibility for Justice*. Oxford Political Philosophy. New York: Oxford University Press.

2

THE SEARCH FOR A SOCIAL JUSTICE AND PUBLIC SPACE FRAMEWORK

THE CASE OF OLDER ADULTS IN NEW YORK CITY DURING COVID-19

Setha Low

PUBLIC SPACE AND DEMOCRATIC PRACTICES

The relationship between public space and democracy is one of the cornerstones of a just city. Indeed, democratic societies allow for the potential of politics and the resolution of inequality (Davidson and Martin 2014). Public space is considered the material location of these activities, but a space becomes "public" when people not only have the right to occupy it but also the right to engage in protest, conflict, and contestation in it (Mitchell 2017). Often it is the visibility of a problem that motivates a public to action; thus, without places where problems can be seen and expressed, the politics of public space might not occur (Terzi and Tonnelat 2017). And this is why, historically, public spaces have been the physical sites of democratic performance, where the right to assembly is guaranteed or demanded, and where the physical occupation of space takes on political meaning (Parkinson 2012).

Urban civic spaces such as Tahrir Square, Cairo; Tiananmen Square, Beijing; Wenceslas Square, Prague; Azadi Square, Tehran; Place de la Bastille, Paris; Plaza de las Tres Culturas, Mexico City; Decembrists' Square, St. Petersburg; Trafalgar Square, London; Syntagma Square, Athens; and Red Square, Moscow have been centers of revolution and protest across the globe. In Bagdad, Iraqis consistently used Liberation Square in 2019–2020 to protest high unemployment, poor basic services, and state corruption. In Hong Kong, university students fought for a more democratic government on the streets. In La Paz, Bolivian citizens united on Plaza Murillo seeking to remove President Morales, who had unfairly claimed the last election, while in Santiago, Chile, workers demanding fair wages and lower transportation fares filled Plaza de Armas. Not all prodemocracy protests have occurred in public spaces; the Occupy Wall Street movement took over the privately owned Zuccotti Park in Manhattan, rendering it "public" during its occupation.

The relationship of civic public space and democratic practices stems from a long history of the association of politics with the ceremonial center of the city—whether marked by religious institutions such as a Cathedral or an Aztec temple, military installations on a Plaza de Armas, a courthouse or town hall on a civic square, or the commercial importance of a marketplace. Even with growing concerns over the shrinkage of collective public action and the simultaneous expansion of the personal private sphere, protests and demonstrations continue to take place in the symbolic heart of the city (Brown 2019).

Democracy is also practiced in the less central and smaller public spaces of neighborhoods, towns, and cities. It is not just reflected in the monumental protests or formal parades but also in the daily contact of people, the renewal of friendships and associations, and the formation of new affiliations and social relationships—even with strangers. Public spaces of all sizes and types provide the infrastructure and physical setting for these everyday encounters and assemblages that underlie social solidarity and cohesion. Without these places of contact and communication, where face-to-face interactions can occur and a public culture can flourish, democratic practices become limited and ultimately contracted, providing a voice to only some groups and individuals while excluding others.

But not all public spaces—civic or local—allow for, much less promote, social interaction and solidarity or provide safe places for people to come together. Instead, many spaces physically and symbolically signal exclusion for some and inclusion for others, often along racial, social, gender, sexual orientation, and ableist lines. As chapters in this volume document, public spaces face serious challenges to their "publicness" through restrictive rules, gating, policing, surveillance, privatization, aestheticization, commercialization, and the financialization of everyday life. And yet, in the midst of the COVID-19 pandemic, public spaces became even more important for their potential to counteract isolation and allow for healthy, socially distanced interactions. At the same time, crowded streets and large groups coming together in "super-spreader events" made it hard to even use neighborhood public spaces because of the fear of contracting the disease.

To counteract and push back against these deleterious developments and historically segregationist city planning processes (Freund 2007), this chapter identifies public space characteristics that can enhance, rather than limit, inclusivity and equity. I argue that a social justice perspective that includes a clear values orientation, multiple dimensions, and a set of broad evaluation criteria is fundamental to planning, designing, managing, and ultimately producing and sustaining "good" public spaces— and hence, a more democratic and just society. The inequalities that exist have been compounded by the COVID-19 pandemic, thus making it even more urgent to reinforce the links between public space and democratic practices.

A SOCIAL JUSTICE AND PUBLIC SPACE FRAMEWORK

Because social justice and democratic practices are crucial to a flourishing society, it is important to know how to evaluate existing public spaces to build more socially just ones. It is difficult to enhance a social condition—or any phenomenon—without first defining and measuring it. Public space advocates at UN-Habitat are searching for "equity indicators" that can be measured at the city scale (United Nations 2016). As part of this effort, I am working on how to assess people's perception and experience of social justice and how to create spaces that promote democratic practices, belonging, and sociopolitical inclusion.

To start, I propose examining a broad array of factors that can allow for a better basis for public space research and evaluation along multiple dimensions and interrelated variables. These include:

1. *Physical aspects of the space* (e.g., size, shape, location, amenities, etc.)
2. *Ownership of the space* (e.g., public, limited partnership, public-private partnership, private)

3. *Governance or management authority and funding* (e.g., business improvement districts, homeowners' associations, common interest developments, governmental agencies, conservancies, nonprofits)
4. *Control and influence* (e.g., nature of governance)

   Rules and regulations (e.g., strict versus lenient)

   Access (e.g., open versus closed, free versus paid, temporal versus all-day)
5. *Symbolic/historical meaning of the space* (e.g., representation, recognition)
6. *Political activity* (e.g., allowed versus prohibited)
7. *Civil society* (e.g., informal forum for ideas and problem-solving).

This multidimensional definition can be used along continuums, rankings, or gradients that need to be worked out more specifically. For example, Central Park, a large, central, civically important space in Manhattan, is a Frederick Law Olmsted–designed historical site owned by the city of New York. It receives very little public funding; however, it is sustained and governed by a private conservancy composed of wealthy white residents. The Central Park Conservancy makes decisions and implements changes that reflect the funders' exclusionary esthetic and maintenance standards. It is a financially well-endowed park, yet when asked to share a portion of their allotted tax dollars with other neighborhood parks that lack an economic base, the conservancy refused (DiPrinzio 2019). Political activity is often prohibited at Central Park, and permission is required for any gatherings, although the park can be a forum for the arts through free theater and music performances. While the park is highly accessible with many entrances that punctuate its low stone walls, it is heavily surveilled and policed with extensive and strictly enforced rules and regulations. The racial prejudice of some park users was in plain sight when a white female dog walker called the police in May 2020 after a benign encounter with a Black male birdwatcher who had asked her to put her dog on its leash (Nir 2020). Her fearful reaction revealed the racial contours of the strict and well-maintained regime of park policing and surveillance, both formal and informal, that exacerbates social exclusion.

Thus, Central Park is a "public space" in terms of ownership, access, and name, but when examined along other dimensions, it appears not to be "public" in terms of funding, governance, political activity, degree of racist policing, symbolic representation, and recognition of the diversity of users. The example of Central Park clearly shows that publicness is a complex construct and must be characterized by a broader range of variables than those generally used when categorizing public space. The public/private binary has been helpful, but there are other indicators of publicness that tend to be overlooked and that can provide greater nuance when we are searching to improve public space design.

Following the definition of factors that can help us better define the "publicness" of a space, a second objective is to develop a framework that will identify what is a "good" or "just" public space. A good place to start is to consider urban design models used to evaluate the publicness and quality of a public space. These models measure the type of ownership, degree of control, and freedom, inclusiveness, comfort, engagement, and safety that figure into the overall success of the space.

For example, George Varna and Steve Tiesdell (2010) have developed the "star model" to assess publicness by rating five elements that make up a successful public space. They employ two dimensions that I have previously discussed: ownership (public to private) and control (rules and surveillance) but also three additional attributes: (1) physical connection to the city through centrality and visibility; (2) animation through engagement; and (3) civility reflected in maintenance and facilities. They apply the star model to two public spaces in Rotterdam and find that it helps them identify their degree of publicness.

Vikas Mehta (2014) elaborates on the star model and develops what he calls a public space index (PSI). This index assesses the quality of public space by measuring inclusiveness (presence of diverse people), meaningfulness (community gathering and symbols), comfort (benches and facilities), safety (maintenance and lighting), and pleasurability (personalization and variety). Mehta and his urban design students studied four sites in Boston and Tampa and found that the PSI provided detailed information about the spaces and insights into the overall characteristics and quality of downtown areas.

In contrast to measuring the positive aspects of public space design through the PSI, Jeremy Németh and Stephan Schmidt (2011) focus on degrees of control and freedom by rating physical aspects (spatial relations, programming, and location), codes (regulations, norms, and policing), and content (use, behavior, and meaning) of publicly or privately owned urban spaces. They apply this model to New York City sites and determine that private/corporate public spaces have significantly more features that discourage or control use than publicly owned spaces.

These are all excellent models and work well empirically to differentiate the kinds and attributes of well or poorly designed public spaces. They are effectively used for evaluation of public spaces and their sociality. For my purposes, however, these models are not normative. They are design and site-specific, difficult to use at a city-wide scale, and employ a more limited definition of public space than the one I am proposing. Nevertheless, the star model and the public space index help clarify my objectives as I continue to search for a means to make public space better from a social justice point of view.

Planning and geography scholars argue that a "just city" should be the criterion for allocating and evaluating urban space. Susan Fainstein (2010) proposes a planning theory of distributive justice to produce a better city for all citizens within a capitalist economy. Ruth Fincher and Kurt Iveson (2008) recommend three planning goals to achieve social justice ends: (1) redistribution of space and services to address inequalities of wealth, (2) recognition of identities that are systematically devalued, and (3) opportunities for people to break free of fixed identities through encounters with diverse people and practices. Edward Soja's (2010) theory of spatial justice provides an even broader agenda of social justice that includes freedom, liberty, equality, democracy, and civil rights.

These "just city" models propose normative goals but offer little to specify how to accomplish them. Effective at the city-wide scale, they are difficult to apply to a specific site or public space. Fainstein's (2010) model only considers distributive justice, while Fincher and Iveson (2008) persuasively argue that recognition of difference and encounters with diverse people should also be considered. The limitations of the just city models, however, are that they do not reflect the experience of users as revealed by empirical research, such as the data that I have collected in parks, plazas, beaches, and walkways. Asking people what is important and meaningful to their public space experience and listening to their responses certainly include elements of distributive justice, that is, whether there is enough room for everyone and their diverse activities. But people express concern about much more.

Searching for a way to capture this complexity, I turned to Joel Lefkowitz (2017), an industrial-organizational psychologist who suggested considering concepts from organizational justice research to predict the quality of social relations and sense of fairness in the workplace. A meta-analysis of 413 organizational justice studies found that four kinds of justice—distributional, procedural, interactional, and informational—are critical to promoting "social exchange outcomes"—such as trust, helping, courtesy, and positive affect within complex social organizations such as corporations—and also contribute to a sense of organization citizenship and commitment (Colquitt et al. 2013). These four organizational justice constructs include: (1) distributive justice as it pertains to equity of outcomes; (2) procedural justice as it pertains to decision-making processes; (3) interactional justice as it pertains to the quality of interpersonal and intergroup interactions, and (4) informational justice as it pertains to the adequacy of explanations given in terms of timeliness, specificity, and truthfulness.

This expanded social justice construct offers us much more to contemplate and evaluate since it considers how people feel and respond to fairness in the workplace and within large organizations. This justice construct, based on years of psychological research and testing, forms the basis of what I was searching for to apply in the public space context. Additionally, ethnographic work in parks and plazas (Low 2000; Low, Taplin, and Scheld 2005), coupled with the research of Fincher and Iveson (2008) and the theories of Soja (2010), demonstrate that representation and recognition and an ethic of care are also significant. I, therefore, decided to add these important aspects of justice to the four-part organizational justice framework.

This latest version of the public space and social justice framework offers a normative stance on what constitutes a "good" public space that can be employed at both a site-specific and a city-wide scale. It is now composed of six dimensions of social justice that researchers, designers, community members, and activists can use to design, plan, evaluate, and/or improve a public space. Each dimension identifies a relevant and quantifiable indicator of justice.

1. *Distributive justice* is determined through ease of access, physically and financially.
2. *Procedural justice* is the degree to which people can influence the use of public space in substantial ways. It also refers to having a transparent way for accessing limited public facilities such as ball fields and picnic grounds.
3. *Interactional justice* is an indicator of the quality of social interaction experienced.
4. *Informational justice* can be gauged by whether there is adequate information and signage about public space location, activities, rules, and procedures for use, and these are explained in multiple languages.
5. *Representational justice* can be assessed in many ways, including whether people recognize themselves in the interests portrayed and the available activities or histories that exist within a particular public space.
6. *Ethic of care* is the degree to which people are encouraged by other users and management to care for others or the environment.

There are some encouraging signs that this framework is useful and can be applied in practice. Gibson, Loukaitou-Sideris, and Mukhija (2018) identify four preconditions for the usability of a public space, including distribution, physical access, psychological access, and fit. Their evaluation of California state parks found that good access and distribution of parks are critical, but additionally, the inclusion of culturally appropriate programming and facilities and the removal of psychological, cultural, and economic barriers, such as fees, restrictive signage, poor park maintenance, and safety encourage park use. Loukaitou-Sideris and Mukhija (2018) further employ an environmental justice theoretical framework of "riskscapes" and "ecological pathogens," and they use an early version of my social justice and public space model concluding that "park disparities in periurban parks are not only caused because of the suppliers failing to deliver distributive justice, but also procedural and interactional justice" (54). The University City District, a Business Improvement District (BID) in West Philadelphia, has developed a "just spaces" tool employing a mobile technology and internet application to evaluate and improve public spaces based on the first three principles. Rigolon and colleagues (2019) have applied three of the dimensions (distributional, procedural, and interactional justice) to enhance environmental justice outcomes with positive results.

Thus, a preliminary social justice and public space framework appears to be useful to planning practitioners, environmental justice evaluations, and even a BID concerned with providing socially just public spaces for its residents. To clarify further about how this more extended framework would work, I turn to some research that Anastasia Loukaitou-Sideris and I undertook in the spring of 2020 during the beginning of the COVID-19 pandemic. We were concerned about the absence of public space (and access to public virtual space) for older populations in New York City and Los Angeles and cowrote both an op-ed (Low and Loukaitou-Sideris 2020a) and an essay (Low and Loukaitou-Sideris 2020b) to communicate our mutual concerns. I draw upon this work to illustrate how a social justice and public space framework might suggest solutions to what we saw as emerging problems faced by seniors during this unprecedented time.

EVALUATING PUBLIC SPACE FOR OLDER ADULTS DURING COVID-19

Older adults represent the fastest-growing population segment in the United States and many other cities of the Global North (United Nations 2019), thanks to longer life spans and advancements in medicine. But along with longer life expectancy come challenges. Deteriorating physical health, the death of a spouse or partner, and living alone make older adults particularly vulnerable to social isolation and loneliness (Victor and Bowling 2012; Nies and McEwen 2015). Social isolation often leads to deteriorating mental and physical health (Luanaigh and Lawlor 2008), including depression, decreases in cognitive functioning, cardiovascular disease, and even mortality (Courtin and Knapp 2015).

One aspect of counteracting and lessening social isolation is to have opportunities and neighborhood places to go to, to meet, and to communicate with others. Being able to walk to the neighborhood grocery store or park not only helps older adults accomplish activities of daily living but also facilitates social well-being and social needs (Clarke and Gallagher 2013). The built environment—and public spaces and "third spaces"—interacts with the social environment (Kweon, Sullivan, and Wiley 1998; Low 2020) and influences older adults' health and well-being (World Health Organization 2015).

The COVID-19 pandemic had a tremendous impact on older adults by not only taking a disproportionate number of their lives but also increasing the fear among the living of accessing public spaces, thus furthering their social isolation. Both Anastasia Loukaitou-Sideris and I spent time interviewing older people during the first months of the outbreak and heard stories of seniors having a difficult time. One of them was Rebecca, sixty-five, an African American woman who lives in a low-rise building in Brooklyn. She avoided the elevator in case other people used it and took the stairs, but when she arrived at the street, she felt it was too crowded to safely walk to the nearby park. One early morning she ventured out to Prospect Park (figure 2.1) but found it crowded with young people not wearing masks and just turned around and went home. Another New York City interviewee, eighty-year-old Harold, an Irish American who lives near Times Square, where automobile traffic had been rerouted, could not find a place to rest because chairs had been removed to discourage gathering. He lived too far to walk to a park and worried about taking the subway to visit one. One Los Angeles interviewee was Maria, seventy, a Latina house cleaner, who was hoping to restart her job, but she worried about riding the bus that would bring her to the Larchmont neighborhood where she worked.

The plight of the old has been exacerbated by increasing inequities in terms of health and economic security, at the same time that the numbers of people over sixty-five are expanding in the United States and globally. Of course, certain subgroups of older adults witness greater disparities. Sixteen percent of women and 12 percent of men sixty-five or older in the United States live at or below the poverty level. Older people of color experience poverty at significantly higher rates than their white counterparts (Semega et al. 2019). And it is from these individuals—poor, minority, and old—that the COVID-19 pandemic took its highest toll (CDC 2020).

Stories of the decimation of older patients in nursing homes in the United States dominated the media, accompanied by reports of older

2.1   Crowd on the grass in Prospect Park. *Source*: Setha Low.

people living and dying in isolation—one month into physical distancing and lockdown. Many of those who were not infected were afraid to go outside for a walk or to see someone because of the risk of contagion through physical contact. While it is not unusual for older people to experience some sense of greater vulnerability, the impact of the pandemic heightened this awareness and changed everyday behavior and feelings in ways that were paralyzing and stigmatizing, even for the most resilient. Reports of restaurants as hotspots reduced cooked food options so that, even with remediation of public spaces, there remained multiple challenges to reducing isolation and loneliness. While physical distancing protected individuals from infection, it also led to the unintended consequences of social isolation. These effects were even more dramatic for older adults during a period of remote Zoom meetings where the substitution of digital for physical spaces typically does not work well for them.

To better explain the public space and social justice framework discussed previously, I will briefly apply it to the crisis caused by the pandemic and examine how it can help us plan and design more just public spaces for older adults.

DISTRIBUTIVE JUSTICE

The pandemic made it worrisome for older people to take a walk, spend time in their neighborhood parks, or sit and read a book on a park bench. While the beaches, hiking trails, and other nature spaces at the edges of the city have reopened, these are not the spaces that older adults can easily reach or use. Other "third places" where elders could previously socialize—barbershops, community gardens, mall food courts, old-fashioned cafeterias—have also reopened, but many older adults refrain from using them. What about thinking of "distributive justice" in terms of the best use for the most vulnerable? Distributive justice, in this case, would mean thinking through the time and space needs of older people and adding public space or reorganizing urban space in those places where it is most needed.

In response to the pandemic, many cities designated open streets, thus adding public spaces for walking and counteracting sidewalk crowding (figure 2.2). But to encourage walking among older adults, these spaces also need to be retrofitted with benches for resting and comfort and trees for shade. In New York City, streets have been closed for cars in neighborhoods throughout the boroughs and are now heavily used by seniors (figure 2.3) and mothers with children. Another aspect of a fair distribution sometimes means making sure that there are spaces set apart for older adults during difficult times, such as those presented by the pandemic. Designating "seniors only" settings at popular parks and beaches for the exclusive use of older adults, with benches spaced safely apart for socializing, is one possibility. Using a temporal separation, with certain early hours designated for seniors, is another option. In public transportation, such redistribution may mean allocating the first car of every subway train

2.2 Open street, Manhattan's Upper West Side. *Source*: Setha Low.

and the front section near the driver in every bus for vulnerable and older populations.

PROCEDURAL JUSTICE

One important and often forgotten aspect of justice is whether people feel that there is a fair way to access public space and that the same rules apply to everyone. One issue that emerges in situations such as during

2.3 Older women sitting on wheelchairs in Manhattan's Upper West Side. *Source*: Setha Low.

the emergency planning for COVID-19 is that some populations are consulted while others are not. Are older persons' special needs and concerns included in the planning process for public space? Probably not, since they are an often-silenced urban population. Could there be procedures by which seniors are able to apply for more public space for special events or for walking? On Halloween, my Brooklyn block was closed for children to wear their costumes and trick-or-treat outside safely. What about considering this same kind of protected physical and social interaction for older adults? Yet, often getting special permission for the use of public space requires internet skills that older people lack. The principle of procedural justice guides us to make the procedures for accessing public space more transparent and available to a population that is generally less adept at using digital online platforms.

INTERACTIONAL JUSTICE

Interactional justice means a psychologically positive and inclusive atmosphere where older adults can feel safe, welcome, and treated with respect. The stigma of being old and vulnerable has always been a deterrent to using public space. With COVID-19, it has become even more important to signal that public spaces can safely accommodate seniors' needs and sensitivities. A welcoming public space for older adults needs to be physically and psychologically accessible, offering age-friendly design and programming, opportunities for low-impact physical activities, as well as settings for social interaction (Loukaitou-Sideris et al. 2016; Loukaitou-Sideris 2020). Within these settings, interaction with others should be positive and reaffirm that older people are valued. Intergenerational programs often address the disconnect between the young and the old and can foster the kinds of social interactions that enhance lives.

INFORMATIONAL JUSTICE

Informational justice in public space considers whether signage and other indicators of use and access are available to all populations. Of course, this does impact older persons with reduced eyesight and hearing who may find current directional informational strategies unhelpful. Increasingly, public space information is communicated through the use of digital and smart technologies. However, these informational technologies are not necessarily available, much less understandable, for older adults who did not grow up during the digital age. To ensure informational justice, it is important to incorporate digital, physical, and aurally accessible signage to provide information to seniors who want to use public space safely.

REPRESENTATIONAL JUSTICE

Representational justice refers to whether older adults see themselves represented in public space. Are there other older people there? Are there comfortable seats and benches for sitting and resting along a walkway? Are there age-appropriate activities, programs, and equipment that reflect that older people are invited to be a part of the space? Is the space designed in such a way that it is accessible, with ramps instead of steps and gradually graded paths lined with handrails? Universal design guidelines can generate design changes that improve the physical and social environment for seniors, also making public space more accessible and inclusive for everyone.

Another aspect of representation is whether older residents' histories are still in evidence or have been erased by recent urban development. Monuments, plaques, historic sites, houses, and even ruins of what was there before affirm one's presence in a place. Older residents remember the transformation and experience of space over time and relate to its history and symbolic and personal meanings to their everyday lives. A sense of place attachment is reinforced by leaving the remnants of the past in public spaces to keep the sense of belonging and representation alive (Altman and Low 1992). Social justice principles help to remind us of the importance of a "software" of belonging, sociality, place attachment, representation, and recognition, especially in difficult times.

ETHIC OF CARE

During the COVID-19 pandemic, there were many signs of care in public space, including city workers passing out protective masks in New York City parks and food banks offering free menus at park entrances and on closed streets. All essential workers in New York City put in long hours to make the streets, subways, and walkways as safe as possible, while the police gently encouraged people to put on their masks upon entering a park. Grocery stores and supermarkets showed care by establishing early morning hours for senior citizens to shop with fewer people in the aisles and streets. These acts of care help older adults to feel more comfortable about going out of their apartments into public spaces and neighborhood settings.

In my interviews with older adults, I found that there has been a recognition that special care is needed during extraordinary times. Nonetheless, some also reported feeling threatened by the large groups of young adults and teenagers who sometimes take over a park meadow, sidewalk, or area of picnic tables. At least in my observations, it was more common for the youth not to wear masks, gather closely together, and organize parties and other gatherings. More thought about how to promote an ethic of care would go a long way in making public space feel safer and more welcoming for the most vulnerable.

CONCLUSION

This chapter traces the search for a social justice and public space framework that can be used to evaluate, design, and manage public space at both the site-specific and city scales. I offer a more extended definition of public space that can be employed to compare different kinds of public space and briefly review some of the major influences on my current work. I draw upon urban design, planning, geography, and organizational psychology to construct this current version of a just public space framework.

Applying a six-dimensional justice framework—which includes distributive justice, procedural justice, interactional justice, informational justice, representation, and an ethic of care—to the impact of COVID-19 on the use of public space by older adults highlights how each of the six dimensions could improve public space for seniors during the pandemic crisis. At the moment, this is a preliminary and mostly theoretical examination, but I hope that with time it can be more rigorously applied and considered as another tool in our design toolkits.

Even during a pandemic, it is essential to keep in mind the reciprocal relationship between socially just public spaces, democratic practices, and political representation. Without the participation of older adults in public space, their voices become muted, as in the case of those who live as shut-ins and in nursing homes. Their neglect and their disproportionate numbers of deaths could well be attributed to their lack of visibility and loss of representation. Making sure that everyone has access to public space offers not just health or a social benefit but also reaffirms an older person's political participation and human rights.

REFERENCES

Altman, I., and Low, S. (1992). *Place Attachment: An Introduction*. New York: Plenum.

Brown, W. (2019). *In the Ruins of Neoliberalism: The Rise of Antidemocratic Politics in the West*. New York: Columbia University Press.

Centers for Disease Control and Prevention (CDC). (2020). "COVID-19 in Racial and Ethnic Minority Groups." https://www.cdc.gov/coronavirus/2019-ncov/need-extra-precautions/racial-ethnic-minorities.html.

Clarke, P., and Gallagher, N. A. (2013). "Optimizing Mobility in Later Life: The Role of the Urban Built Environment for Older Adults Aging in Place." *Journal of Urban Health* 90 (6): 997–1009.

Colquitt, J. A., Scott, B., Rodell, J., Long, D., Zapata, C., and Conlon, D. (2013). "Justice at the Millennium, a Decade Later: A Meta-Analysis Test of Social Exchange and Affect-Based Perspectives." *Journal of Applied Psychology* 98 (2): 199–236.

Courtin, E., and Knapp, M. (2015). *Health and Wellbeing Consequences of Social Isolation and Loneliness in Old Age*. London: NIHR School for Social Care Research.

Davidson, M., and Martin, D. (2014). *Urban Politics: Critical Approaches*. London: Sage.

DiPrinzio, H. (2019). "Evidence of Growing Need for Capital in the City's Aging Parks." *City Limits*, October 22, 2019. https://citylimits.org/2019/10/22/evidence-of -growing-need-for-capital-in-the-citys-aging-parks/.

Fainstein, S. (2010). *The Just City*. Ithaca, NY: Cornell University Press.

Fincher, R., and Iveson, K. (2008). *Planning and Diversity in the City: Redistribution, Recognition and Encounter*. Basingstoke, UK: Palgrave Macmillan.

Freund, D. M. (2007). *Colored Property: State Policy and White Racial Politics in Suburban America*. Chicago: University of Chicago Press.

Gibson, S., Loukaitou-Sideris, A., and Mukhija, V. (2018). "Ensuring Park Equity: A California Case Study." *Journal of Urban Design* 24 (3): 385–405.

Kweon, B. S., Sullivan, W. C., and Wiley, A. R. (1998). "Green Common Spaces and the Social Integration of Inner-City Older Adults." *Environment and Behavior* 30 (6), 832–858.

Lefkowitz. J. (2017). *Ethics and Values in Industrial-Organizational Psychology*. 2nd ed. New York: Routledge.

Loukaitou-Sideris, A. (2020). "Designing Parks for Older Adults." In Palazzo, D. and Mehta, V. (eds.). *Companion to Public Space*. London: Routledge.

Loukaitou-Sideris, A., Levy-Storms, L., Chen, L., and Brozen, M. (2016). "Parks for an Aging Population: Needs and Preferences of Low-Income Seniors in Los Angeles." *Journal of the American Planning Association* 82 (3): 236–251.

Loukaitou-Sideris, A. and Mukhija, V. (2018). "Promoting Justice for Underserved Groups in Periurban Parks: The Potential of State-Community Partnerships." *Leisure Studies* 38 (1): 43–57.

Low, S. (2000). *On the Plaza: Public Space and Culture*. Austin: University of Texas Press.

Low, S. (2017). *Spatializing Culture: The Ethnography of Space and Place*. New York: Routledge.

Low, S. (2020). "How Cafes, Bars, Gyms, Barbershops and Other 'Third Places' Create Our Social Fabric." *The Conversation*, May 1, 2020.

Low, S., and Loukaitou-Sideris, A. (2020a). "Public Spaces for Older Adults Must Be Reimagined as Cities Reopen." *Next City*, May 22, 2020. https://nextcity.org/daily /entry/public-spaces-for-older-adults-must-be-reimagined-as-cities-reopen.

Low, S., and Loukaitou-Sideris, A. (2020b). "America under Covid-19: The Plight of the Old." In van Melik, R. G., Filion, P., and Doucet, B. (eds.). *Global Reflections on Covid-19 and Urban Inequalities. Volume 3, Public Space and Mobility*. Bristol, UK: Bristol University Press, 97–108.

Low, S., Taplin, D., and Scheld, S. (2005). *Rethinking Urban Parks: Public Space and Cultural Diversity*. Austin: University of Texas Press.

Luanaigh, C. Ó., and Lawlor, B. A. (2008). "Loneliness and the Health of Older People." *International Journal of Geriatric Psychiatry* 23 (12): 1213–1221.

Mehta, V. 2014. "Evaluating Public Space." *Journal of Urban Design* 19 (1): 53–88.

Mitchell, D. (2017). "People's Park Again: On the End and Ends of Public Space." *Environment and Planning* A. 49 (3): 1–16.

Németh, J., and Schmidt, S. (2011). "The Privatization of Public Space. Modeling and Measuring Publicness." *Environment and Planning B: Planning and Design* 38: 5–23.

Nies, M. A., and McEwen, M. (2015). *Community/Public Health Nursing*. 6th ed. St. Louis, MI: Elsevier.

Nir, S. (2020). "The Bird Watcher, That Incident and His Feelings on the Woman's Fate." *New York Times*, May 27, 2020. https://www.nytimes.com/2020/05/27/nyregion /amy-cooper-christian-central-park-video.html.

Parkinson, J. (2012). *Democracy and Public Space: The Physical Sites of Democratic Performance*. Oxford: Oxford University Press.

Rigolon, A., Fernandez, M., Harris, B., and Stewart, W. (2019). "An Ecology Model of Environmental Justice for Recreation." *Leisure Sciences, September 3, 2019*. https://doi .org/10.1080/01490400.2019.1655686.

Semega, J., Kollar, M., Creamer, J., and Mohanty, A. (2019). *Income and Poverty in the United States: 2018*. United States Census Bureau, September 10, 2019. https://www .census.gov/library/publications/2019/demo/p60-266.html.

Soja, E. (2010). *Seeking Spatial Justice*. Minneapolis: University of Minnesota Press.

Terzi, C., and Tonnelat, S. (2017). "The Publicization of Public Space." *Environment and Planning A*. 49 (3): 1–18.

United Nations. (2016). The World's Cities in 2016—*Data Booklet* (ST/ESA/SER.A/392). Department of Economic and Social Affairs, Population Division, New York..

United Nations (2019). *World Population Ageing 2019: Highlights*. Department of Economic and Social Affairs: Population Division, New York. https://www.un.org/en /development/desa/population/publications/pdf/ageing/WorldPopulationAgeing2019 -Highlights.pdf.

Varna, G., and Tiesdell, S. (2010). "Assessing the Publicness of Public Space: The Star Model of Publicness." *Environment and Planning B: Planning and Design* 38: 5–23.

Victor, C. R., and Bowling, A. (2012). "A Longitudinal Analysis of Loneliness Among Older People in Great Britain." *Journal of Psychology* 146 (3): 313–331.

World Health Organization. (2015). *World Report on Aging and Health*. Geneva: WHO Press.

3

URBAN DESIGN PRAXIS
A RESPONSIBILITY FOR JUSTICE

Michael Rios

POLITICS, AESTHETICS, AND THE IMAGE OF THE CITY

Moral arguments in urban design are entangled in the long history of the field in different imaginaries of the city put forth over time, and in an aesthetics that both reveals and conceals power relations. Aesthetic representations convey messages about what is "good" or "bad" about the city and the role of morality as both promise and threat. A historical example can be found in the famous frescoes of Siena's Palazzo Pubblico, created by Ambrogio Lorenzetti, on the *Allegory of Good Government and Bad Government*. They illustrate an ideal city but choose to represent Siena to send a message to the city-state's aristocratic leadership, the Council of Nine (Belting 1985).[1] These frescoes are a pictorial realization of civitas (the social body of citizens) as the fundamental form of human association. By depicting cause-and-effect situations of corrupt, tyrannical governing compared to those of virtuous governing, the frescoes seek to promote morality in government and provide a constant reminder for the Council of Nine to remain just leaders. Justice is depicted in this fresco as a female figure balancing scales held by wisdom with two cords tethered to the people of Siena, representing its political community (figure 3.1). Lorenzetti used a skewed perspective derived from the gaze line of Justice. In late medieval thought, the belief was that sight was not only the act of seeing but of understanding as well (Greenstein 1988).

3.1 *Justice in the Allegory of Good Government* by Ambrogio Lorenzetti. *Source*: https://commons.wikimedia.org/w/index.php?curid=4006740.

The gaze of justice is a haunting reminder of the stakes wagered in the name of the "good city" (Friedmann 2000; Amin 2006). As a field that imagines, produces, and regulates spaces and habitation in cities, urban design identifies what is common to a public, the form of this visibility in the built environment, and its organization through plans and codes. Different images of the city and forms of urbanism serve a political purpose by determining what is made prominent in the urban landscape and which interests are being served. In *The Politics of Aesthetics:*

The Distribution of the Sensible, Jacques Rancière (2004) argues that politics is the struggle of the unrecognized for equal recognition. He identifies the "distribution of the sensible" as a system of self-evident facts of sense perception made visible to the public by those who control power. In urbanistic terms, Henri Lefebvre (1991, 29) calls this "the illusion of transparency," which masks the reality that city spaces are socially produced to serve powerful interests. At stake are the political outcomes emanating from this exclusionary image of the city.

Aesthetics in space and politics play an important role as urban designers produce urban imaginaries that either reproduce and exacerbate injustice or alternatively seek different visions of justice. Elites connect the social order to the spatial order, and it is this ordering and control of space that also regulates populations in ways that serve dominant interests. What can be drawn from this claim is that aesthetics is more than the appearance of space; it helps determine who is included or excluded and ultimately what is just. Urbanism can either repress ways of inhabiting the city or reveal new sensory possibilities that instigate novel forms of political subjectivity. In this respect, urbanism serves an important boundary-making function in maintaining modes of being and forms of visibility. A city, as envisioned by urban designers, may also produce representations and future projections that, although not always intentional, have the effect of concealing the sensibilities of multiple publics and rendering invisible unequal social relations. What urban design considers as the "public" is always partial and incomplete.

Similar to the resistance of the civil rights movement, events within the past decade, such as the Occupy movement, the Ferguson protests, Black Lives Matter, and urban uprisings in response to George Floyd's killing in Minneapolis signal a disruption of spatial order and the demand for a redistribution of the sensible. Calls for the right to the city and urban commons come in response to the "urbanization of injustice," perpetuated by the increasing marketization and privatization of cities, the militarization of urban space, and other urban management schemes aided and abetted by city planning agencies (Merrifield and Swyngedouw 1997). This is against the backdrop of neoliberal urban policies that continue to widen the gap between the wealthy and the poor and a converging set of analytics that link social and economic power through the lens of racial capitalism (Robinson 1983; Pulido 2016). Added to these imbrications is the COVID-19 pandemic that laid bare unaddressed structural injustices and further revealed disproportionate effects on low-income neighborhoods tied to inadequate housing options, lack of access to transportation alternatives, and exposure to poor air quality and toxic chemicals (Ogedegbe, Ravenell, and Adhikari 2020).

As a field, urban design has yet to come to terms with its own complicity that defines the public in universal terms and lacks the capacities to grapple with intersectional injustices. Moreover, a reliance on outmoded conceptions of the public interest helps to conceal power relations that perpetuate social injustice (Campbell and Marshall 2002). Another limiting factor has been a reliance on liberal theories that dominate planning and urban design discourse but are ultimately "more concerned with public morality and control than social transformation" (Winkler 2012, 169). But as Lefebvre (1974) and Rancière (2004) warn us, it is the promotion of public morality and economic freedom in the guise of public interest that reproduces injustice. As a result, urban design is relatively silent when it comes to justice in the city.

The need to reimagine urban design's relationship to multiple publics and the different interests these groups represent is not new and draws comparisons to the mid- and late-twentieth-century era, when slum clearance and central city redevelopment schemes were met with resistance by many city dwellers who took to the streets in protest. However, the profession will need to move beyond liberal conceptions of justice and defining public interest in simplistic terms. It will also need to acknowledge its own history of racist practices that have consistently haunted it (Thomas and Ritzdorf 1997; Williams 2020). Without an intentional focus on structural injustices, this historical moment will simply highlight the profession's complicit role as an instrument of the powerful for the displacement and dispossession of the marginalized. The following section begins with an overview of how justice is theorized in urban design and planning. I then introduce a social connection model of justice as put forth by political philosopher Iris Marion Young (2013). The aim is to identify ways that urban designers might consider Young's "responsibility for justice." The chapter concludes with implications for a just urban design praxis that focuses on modes of being and forms of visibility that

center on antiracism. The hope is that this chapter elicits deeper considerations regarding ethics in urban design praxis, imaginations of insubordinate space, and the gaze of urban justice.

THEORIZING JUSTICE IN THE CITY

As discussed in chapter 1, historical treatises on urban design heralded
by the profession have little to say about the spatiality of (in)justice
other than general references to distributions of power and the public
spheres of decision making. One of the earliest references comes from
Jane Jacobs, who argued that the functionality and publicness of sidewalks can contribute to overcoming segregation and racial discrimination. A central tenet in *The Death and Life of Great American Cities* (1961)
is diversity—of uses, buildings, and blocks—and the presumption that
diversity in the built environment extends to demographic composition
(Talen and Lee 2018). Jacobs criticizes the geography of homogeneity and
sameness promoted by zoning codes and restrictive covenants. However,
goals toward socioeconomic diversity (as an element of justice) remain
undeveloped in Jacobs's work, prompting calls for greater attention to
historical inequalities and relations of domination (Steil and Delgado
2019). Jacobs's generic focus on diversity foreshadowed the concept of
multiculturalism that soon followed, which depoliticized demands for
recognition by placing those who fall outside of white heteronormativ-
ity into a cultural melting pot. Accordingly, legal scholar Kimberlé Crenshaw (2010, 178) has argued that "just as difference has been historically
foregrounded in efforts to rationalize and sustain certain power relations,
assertions of sameness have also been used to suppress the recognition of
and advocacy around certain patterns of exclusion and marginalization."

As also indicated in chapter 1, one of the most explicit statements
about justice in urban design theory emanates from Kevin Lynch (1981),
who set out to theorize what makes a good city and identified justice as
one of two metacriteria—the other being efficiency. For Lynch, justice
must balance the gains among individuals, whereas efficiency must balance the gains among different values. Lynch's notion of justice falls in
line with a liberal view of urban design that draws on the work of John
Rawls (1971) and his concept of "justice as fairness." One outcome is

an urban design that gives priority to functional and utilitarian considerations and a conceptual notion of "neutral urban forms" for the economic exchange of social goods.

Two other urban designers that refer to the concept of justice are Allan Jacobs and Donald Appleyard (1987), who observe the persistence of urban inequality in cities and call for greater distribution of power among social groups. They ask for identification of "different values and cultures of interest- and place-based groups" and acknowledge the presence of plural communities in cities (116). However, they rely on a neutral and "just public arena" consistent with a liberal conception of planning and design that embraces a benign multiculturalism.

A number of planning theorists have called into question the primacy of the liberal model of planning with respect to justice. In *The Just City*, Susan Fainstein (2010) adds a capabilities approach to the distributive model of planning that maximizes the values of equity, diversity, and democracy to direct and evaluate planning policy. Robert Lake (2017) counters that justice is a subject rather than an object of planning. He emphasizes the context in which justice takes place and that it is applied to a specific process in addressing problems and issues, seeking to imagine possibilities and design concordant responses. According to Lake, placing justice at the center of practice creates a dialectic between local and extra-local scales in which justice unfolds. Other scholars have questioned Fainstein's focus on outcome-based principles that originate from a universal conception of social justice. While values and principles matter, more important is that they reveal where individual commitments lay, since values comprise a plural and relational form of ethics, not a singular, universalist position (McAuliffe and Rogers 2019). This relational understanding of values, in contradistinction to universal ethics, allows for competing visions to coexist and negotiations to take place over different values of the just city, drawing a distinction between Enlightenment universalism and indigenous pluraversalism (Mignolo 2011; Kothari et al. 2019).[2]

Jason Steil and Laura Delgado argue that diversity, as put forth by Susan Fainstein (2010) and Jane Jacobs (1961), while necessary, is not sufficient for justice and does not go far enough to confront structural inequities that exist in contemporary cities. They argue for an "anti-subordination approach" that in lieu of a focus on goals or intent expressed in outcome-based principles, looks to the "collective effects of an action" to "address persistent group disparities in a social system in which some are systematically disadvantaged" (Steil and Delgado 2019, 42).

In *Seeking Spatial Justice* (2010), Edward Soja focuses on action in response to the conditions that reproduce structural injustices. He privileges spatial thinking or, in his words, "a socio-spatial dialectic, with social processes shaping spatiality at the same time spatiality shapes social processes" (18). Defining spatial justice as spatially informed practices and politics, Soja critiques liberal variants emanating from the Rawlsian perspective, including the normative formulations of planning theorists, such as Peter Marcuse, Susan Fainstein, and others, which lack a "critical spatial perspective" (29). Drawing from Lefebvre's treatise on the right to the city, Soja views public space as a localized urban expression of the commons and as "democratic spaces of collective responsibility" (45). However, he also points out that much of the right to the city discourse "seems to be little more than a slightly different way of speaking about human rights in general or merely a generic reference to the need for more democratic forms of planning and public policy" and reduces justice to "softer liberal egalitarianism or normative platitudes" (107).

Some scholars fault Soja's work for a view of space and spatiality as structurally determinant. For example, Francesca Ansaloni and Miriam Tedeschi (2016) argue for a "new ethics of spatial justice" and offer a view of space as indeterminate and becoming; they call into question the viability of planning as a course of action to address injustice. Their theorization draws parallels with other post-structural planning theorists, notably Jean Hillier (2009), and they conclude that there are two choices for planners. One is staking out a neutral position where a planner's role is to offer assessments and analysis but comes to terms with the fact that decisions lie with the state apparatus. The other is an activist stance that abandons any universal ideas of justice and acts outside the boundaries of formal planning. This conclusion calls into question any singular idea of planning or urban design but draws attention to individually situated practices rather than a reliance on the state, institutions, or other organized bodies as sites of action.

A RESPONSIBILITY FOR JUSTICE IN URBAN DESIGN

The aforementioned debates about space, justice, and the city inform moral and ethical dimensions of urban design. However, they do not speak to the aesthetic and sensory elements that obscure structural injustices. The following considers how urban design praxis can offer a way to conceptualize urban design in relationship to justice. This includes a conceptualization of public space as a socio-spatial-political realm, critical analyses of urban processes that (re)produce structural injustices, and linking design to political action. Praxis also entails the freedom to put forth different imaginaries of the city and reveal new urban sensibilities with a view of space and place as sites of worldmaking. Thus, praxis becomes an ongoing dialogue between theory and practice, reflection and action.

A focus on praxis aligns with the ideas of Iris Marion Young as put forth in her posthumously published *Responsibility for Justice* (2013). According to Young, "[Unjust] structures are produced and reproduced by large numbers of people acting according to normally accepted rules and practices, and it is in the nature of such structural processes that their potentially harmful effects cannot be traced directly to any particular contributors to the process" (100).

This observation provides a way to think about structural injustices and the role of urban designers that act according to "accepted rules and practices" but are rarely in a position to attribute blame to a specific individual or group in professional settings. At the same time, Young argues that individuals assume a level of responsibility because individual actions are embedded in larger processes that produce unjust outcomes and proposes a "social connection model" of responsibility to address structural injustices (2013, 105).

The relationship between individual and collective responsibility is a central characteristic of the social connection model as are the interrelationships between diagnosis, assessment, transformative strategies, and collective action. These qualities draw parallels to urban design inasmuch practice often centers on processes that begin with problem-framing and analysis of conditions that lead to envisioning futures and identifying mechanisms for coordinated implementation. However, each element of the social connection model poses significant challenges for contemporary practice and requires a paradigmatic shift in the way planning and urban design are conceived vis-à-vis justice. According to the first element, structural injustices are not isolating, and accountability is attributed to each of us given our embeddedness in institutions and practices that produce injustices (Young 2013). Urban design mostly represents an ameliorative response to the combined effects of economic, social, health, and environmental problems that cloud the ability to assign blame for unjust outcomes. However, this inability does not mean we should gloss over the field's complicit role in giving physical form to policies that have had horrific consequences for many low-income and racialized communities. A social connection model emphasizes interdependencies that exist and identifies ways to create accountability in our everyday activities that go beyond idealizing justice "out there" or further the illusion that urban design serves the public interest. This localized accountability identifies specific predispositions, behaviors, and actions that bring awareness to our silence about what we see (i.e., Rancière's distribution of the sensible) but do not say.

Doing nothing and staying within the norm of acceptable rules and practices is complicit in reproducing structural injustices. Therefore, the second element of a social connection model requires an assessment of the conditions that lead to structural injustices (Young 2013). Such evaluations are often beyond the scope of typical urban design analysis, which constrains itself to site and location without considering larger political or economic questions or whether unintended consequences may further structural injustices. This is reinforced in urban design education, which often propagates the status quo through aestheticized maps and visual representations that depoliticize the spatial and despatialize the political. For example, proposals and designs to improve a commercial corridor may accentuate precarity, gentrification, and displacement of residents. Critical analyses that expand the scope beyond the built environment to account for larger social forces at play are needed. This countermapping to normative representations of space serves a heuristic purpose by raising questions that are site-specific, structurally relevant, and expose the distribution and order of things in the city.

Third, a social connection model emphasizes forward-looking remedies to address the structural nature of injustices that are ongoing, and to transform processes accordingly (Young 2013). This suggests an understanding of how past injustices have come about. In many ways, equity-based planning has been a progressive response to the profession's historical participation in structural injustices (Krumholz 1982; Zapata and Bates 2015). However, equity's migration to urban design has proved difficult. This is because neoliberal practices that dominate capital investment in the built environment have narrow economic interests and masquerade as public interest. Moreover, if it is challenging to assess structural injustices due to urban design's narrow scope, most responses would fail to meet Young's analytical criteria to interrogate background conditions. By contrast, critical analyses of urban processes provide an important diagnostic framing function from which to imagine alternative worlds beyond the present urban order. Forward-looking designs have both spatial *and* social dimensions inasmuch as they provide a framework for collective action.

Fourth, a social connection model rests on a shared responsibility that each individual bears personally, but not in isolation (Young 2013). Young is quick to point out the difference of shared responsibility from collective responsibility, which is neither distributive nor accounts for individual obligation. This is a challenging proposition for a professional field such as urban design, which privileges technical knowledge vis-à-vis the public and rests on a binary relationship between expert and client that upholds a professional identity of neutrality and disinterestedness. This is congruent with a neoliberal logic that treats political problems as a technical matter to be resolved by auditing outcomes based on metrics that are structured by the dominant class. To meet Young's challenge of shared responsibility requires problematizing these and other professional relationships and rules of inference to contradistinctively create a level of critical consciousness that emplaces urban designers in solidarity with others toward dismantling structural injustices manifested in city spaces.

Lastly, shared responsibility rests on the ability of individuals to work in concert with one another through collective action. Young identifies politics as "public communicative engagement with others for the sake of organizing our relationships and coordinating our actions most justly" (2013, 112). She makes a point that politics is not reduced to government action alone; it involves the advocacy and support of civil society and communities that bring injustices to light and compels changes in the policy arena. Young identifies the need for those in less advantaged positions to also have a shared responsibility, as they have a unique vantage point from which to propose remedies. The formation of justice-based polities surpasses conventional procedures and practices that privilege formal and government-led processes over informal planning and community-driven initiatives. A role for urban design is to include in its decision-making and design process new types of coalitions that extend beyond built environment experts and other elites who hold a disproportionate amount of political power. This is in contrast to the use of such processes to manufacture consensus via unreflexively performative methods of participatory design.

THE PLACE OF RACE: IMPLICATIONS FOR A JUST URBAN DESIGN PRAXIS

The gulf that exists between a social connection model and current practices is not trivial and raises important ethical questions about how urban design practitioners, educators, and scholars think about their own responsibilities in relation to social justice. Young's model poses a challenge to adequately respond to structural injustice, given various emphases and scales of intervention in urban design. (Banerjee and Loukaitou-Sideris 2019). This further highlights the need to distinguish among different types of urban design and aesthetic practices, make explicit those modalities that aim to advance justice, and render transparent its political commitments.

Young (2013) identifies a gap within classical and contemporary theories of justice, which do not account for the relationship between individual and collective action, ethics, and practice. While their aspirational dimensions of justice are laudable, flawed assumptions about a universal public realm or public interest and the omission of race as a defining feature of urban injustice in the United States are problematic. Another flawed assumption is that diversity—in uses, building types, and public spaces—can foster social integration. In practice, this has proven difficult and problematic as evidenced in many new urbanist projects (Rios 2008). Additionally, the belief in a distributive model of justice and the presumption of a public arena and civic life, where diverse communities negotiate differences fairly (Anderson 2011), are also problematic. Diversity, used as proxy for justice, aestheticizes difference to avoid redress to structural inequalities. Moreover, a distributive model rests on a supposition that power relations are neutral or can be ameliorated by public policy or government intervention. However, a distributive model of justice, even in a plural society such as the United States, is undergirded by white supremacy and a legal system that has injustice baked into it (powell and Menendian 2011; Rios 2020).

A central theme ignored by many urban design theorists is the racialization of space as a historic and contemporary practice that reinforces social hierarchies. Scholars in other disciplines have studied the connections between race-making and space-making (McKittrick 2006; Lipsitz 2007; Omi and Winant 2014; Pulido 2016). According to George Lipsitz (2007), who links space, place, race, and power through a spatial imaginary of whiteness and Blackness, a "white spatial imaginary . . . functions as a central mechanism for skewing opportunities and life changes in the United States along racial lines." Whiteness is therefore "an analytic category that refers to the structured advantages that accrue to whites because of past and present discrimination" (13). Lipsitz's work is one of the first to call on designers and planners to decouple narratives of racial dominance from spatial imaginaries and to "write and draw the under-represented and the disenfranchised into . . . schemes and plans rather than ignoring or excluding such groups" (20). In an ironic twist, Brandi Thompson Summers demonstrates how capital uses a "Black aesthetic emplacement" to create symbols of Blackness and renegotiate meaning through the "incorporation and exclusion of blackness" that foster investment toward a neoliberal spatial order (2019, 3 and 4). She uses the case of Washington, DC, to document the shift to a "post-chocolate city" that markets racial authenticity to make Blackness palatable for consumption.

Complementary to but distinct from these critical analyses are representations of space as sites of struggle, resistance, and liberation, and an associated Black imagination centered on an ethics of freedom and inclusivity, improvisation and belonging (Kelley 2002; McKittrick 2006; Tomlinson and Lipsitz 2019; Rios 2020). Robin Kelley (2002) tells the stories of the Black radical tradition and struggles for social change, which enabled artists and intellectuals to imagine new worlds through a desire for "something else" centered on love and freedom as counter-points to lived experiences. Earl Lewis (1991) tells the story of twentieth-century Norfolk, Virginia's Black community that reimagined segregation through empowerment strategies centered on social, cultural, and political institutions as an expression of "congregation." James Tyner (2006) documents the importance of Black radicalism in creating an alternative spatial conception to urban politics and social justice, including "their desires to claim and reimagine the city." (Tyner 2007, 219). Similarly, McKittrick (2006, 146) in discussing Black women's geographies, emphasizes the importance of space and place that is "useful in signaling the alterability of the ground beneath our feet" beyond that of containment and enslavement. In these examples, Blackness is viewed not only as a signifier and experience of racialized abjection and vulnerability but, more importantly, Blackness transcends race and identities attached to people of African descent and becomes a liberating practice of freedom available to those who suffer under the violent logics of whiteness.

The coexistence of domination and liberation is explored by Jodi Rios in *Black Lives and Spatial Matters* (2020). Drawing from the accounts of Black queer women at the center of the Ferguson protests, she counters the epistemic violence associated with the Black experience with an "ethics of lived blackness" that centers on "living fully and visibly in the face of forces intended to dehumanize and erase" (23). The case of Ferguson illustrates what Lipsitz has identified as a "Black spatial imaginary" that "can function as a key resource in struggles for social justice, for fair housing, and fair hiring, school desegregation and affirmative action, equal opportunity and democracy" (2011, 255). Building on this theme, Barbara Tomlinson and George Lipsitz (2019, 7) identify the struggles for self-determination and social justice and how people are "envisioning and enacting new identities, identifications, affiliations, and alliances in many different kinds of insubordinate spaces." Rather than an end goal, they see insubordination as a tool against injustices and the hierarchies that exploit people.

In contrast to planning's historical focus on racial disparities and discrimination associated with land use and zoning, housing and economic development, health and the environment (Thomas and Ritzdorf 1997; Raja, Ma, and Yadav 2008; Allen 2011; Yu, Zhu, and Lee 2018; Solis 2020), the scholarship on race and space not only highlights critical analyses of racialized spaces but also identifies sites of resistance and liberation. I draw on this brief overview of scholarship on race and space to conclude with concepts for an "antiracist praxis" (Brand and Miller 2020) for urban design. The scholarship provides a context for urban design praxis to consider politico-ethical questions centered on the role of urban design in advancing justice—as a process of becoming rather than an end state—and vigilance in the pursuit of dismantling spatial injustices. A just urban design praxis identifies what is common or uncommon to a public by making visible forms of social life that are not equally represented in the city. By revealing the structures of injustice, this praxis instigates an awakening of the city's ghostly past in order to challenge complacency and imagine other worlds beyond the present. This requires a redistribution of the sensible in response to Rancière's conception of politics as the struggle of the unrecognized for equal recognition and a shift from a singular vision of the "good city" toward supplementary images of the city as a plurality of good and bad, each expressive of different values of justice. A just urban design praxis draws from the diagnostics and imaginaries of communities that occupy the undercommons of the city while resisting the temptation to codify and professionalize this knowledge into policy (Harney and Moten 2013). The production and use of space derived from these contrapuntal imaginaries include interventions such as the Project Row Houses in Houston, Project Rebuild in Chicago, and the Jackson Plan in Mississippi.

Focusing on Young's social connection model on matters of race and space challenges urban designers to think transversally about ways of being, knowing, and doing to address urban injustices. *Ways of being entail the freedom to imagine* cities and city-making in configurations that do not impose a white spatial imaginary or other oppressive logics. The freedom to imagine is a creative act comprised of ontological designs that suspend the present to enact other worlds. This futuring is vital to open new sensory possibilities through an aesthetics of the possible, which instigates forms of political subjectivity that aim to disrupt the present social and spatial order of things.

Ways of knowing are based on the idea of epistemic repair. This politics of knowing reveals the epistemic injustices that refuse to bear witness to the truth-speaking found in the stories and voices of the marginalized. A critical assessment of the conditions that racialize space produces counter-cartographies to dominant and accepted narratives to come to terms with difference not as an urban anxiety but as a form of grounding in place.

Lastly, *ways of doing speak to our relationships and responsibilities to others through acts of individual and collective insubordination.* Insubordination acknowledges our own embeddedness in systems and institutions that produce injustice and an unwillingness to comply with directives that cause harm or injury. The co-creation of inclusive spaces where listening, sharing, and learning unfolds also acts as insubordination. These are important as we endeavor to foster a larger sense of belonging that gives rise to new associations, alliances, and polities.

ACKNOWLEDGMENT

I would like to thank Jodi Rios and George Lipsitz for providing comments on an earlier draft of this chapter.

NOTES

1. The Council of Nine were a mercantile-banking oligarchy that ruled the Italian city-state of Siena from 1287 to 1355 AD.

2. Universalism believes in one universal truth, which is usually represented by the dominant thinking; in contrast, pluraversalism believes in multiple truths, multiple universes, and different ways of thinking about the world.

REFERENCES

Allen, R. (2011). "The Relationship between Residential Foreclosures, Race, Ethnicity, and Nativity Status." *Journal of Planning Education and Research* 31 (2): 125–142.

Amin, A. (2006). "The Good City." *Urban Studies* 43 (5–6): 1009–1023.

Anderson, E. (2011). *The Cosmopolitan Canopy: Race and Civility in Everyday Life*. New York: W. W. Norton.

Ansaloni, F., and Tedeschi, M. (2016). "Ethics and Spatial Justice: Unfolding Non-Linear Possibilities for Planning Action." *Planning Theory* 15 (3): 316–332.

Banerjee, T., and Loukaitou-Sideris, A. (eds.) (2019). *The New Companion to Urban Design*. New York: Routledge.

Belting, H. (1985). "The New Role of Narrative in Public Painting of the Trecento: Historia and Allegory." *Studies in the History of Art* 16: 151–168.

Brand, A. L., and Miller, C. (2020). "Tomorrow I'll Be at the Table: Black Geographies and Urban Planning: A Review of the Literature." *Journal of Planning Literature* 35 (4): 460–474.

Campbell, H., and Marshall, R. (2002). "Utilitarianism's Bad Breath? A Re-Evaluation of the Public Interest Justification for Planning." *Planning Theory* 1 (2): 163–187.

Crenshaw, K. (2010). "Close Encounters of Three Kinds: On Teaching Dominance, Feminism, and Intersectionality." *Tulsa Law Review* 46 (1): 151–189.

Fainstein, S. (2010). *The Just City*. Ithaca: Cornell University Press.

Friedmann, J. (2000). "The Good City: In Defense of Utopian Thinking." *International Journal of Urban and Regional Research* 24 (2): 460–472.

Greenstein, J. M. (1988). "The Vision of Peace: Meaning and Representation in Ambrogio Lorenzetti's *Sala Della Pace* Cityscapes." *Art History* 11 (4): 492–510.

Harney, S., and Moten, F. (2013). *The Undercommons: Fugitive Planning & Black Study*. Wivenhoe, NY: Minor Compositions.

Hillier, J. (2009). "Assemblages of Justice: The 'Ghost Ships' of Graythorp." *International Journal of Urban and Regional Research* 33 (3): 640–661.

Jacobs, A., and Appleyard, D. (1987). "Toward an Urban Design Manifesto." *Journal of the American Planning Association*. 53 (1): 112–120.

Jacobs, J. (1961). *The Death and Life of Great American Cities*. New York: Vintage Books.

Kelley, R. (2002). *Freedom Dreams: The Black Radical Imagination*. Boston: Beacon Press.

Kothari, A., Salleh, A., Escobar, A., Demaria, F., and Acosta, A. (eds.) (2019). *A Post-Development Dictionary*. New Delhi: Tulika Books.

Krumholz, N. (1982). "A Retrospective View of Equity Planning: Cleveland 1969–1979." *Journal of American Planning Association* 48: 163–174.

Lake, R. W. (2017). "Justice as Subject and Object of Planning." *International Journal of Urban and Regional Research* 40 (6): 1206–1221.

Lefebvre, H. ([1974], 1991). *The Production of Space*. Cambridge, MA: Blackwell.

Lewis, E. (1991). *In their Own Interests: Race, Class, and Power in Twentieth-Century Norfolk, Virginia*. Berkeley: University of California Press.

Lipsitz, G. (2007). "The Racialization of Space and the Spatialization of Race: Theorizing the Hidden Architecture of Landscape." *Landscape Journal* 26 (1): 10–23.

Lipsitz, G. (2011). *How Racism Takes Place*. Philadelphia: Temple University Press.

Lynch, K. (1981). *Good City Form*. Cambridge, MA: The MIT Press.

McAuliffe, C., and Rogers, D. (2019). "The Politics of Value in Urban Development: Valuing Conflict in Agonistic Pluralism." *Planning Theory* 18 (3): 300–318.

McKittrick, K. (2006). *Demonic Grounds: Black Women and the Cartographies of Struggle*. Minneapolis: University of Minnesota Press.

Merrifield, A., and Swyngedouw, E. (eds.) (1997). *The Urbanization of Injustice*. New York: New York University Press.

Mignolo, W. (2011). *The Darker Side of Western Modernity: Global Futures, Decolonial Options*. Durham, NC: Duke University Press.

Ogedegbe, G., Ravenell, J., and Adhikari, S. (2020). "Assessment of Racial/Ethnic Disparities in Hospitalization and Mortality in Patients with COVID-19 in New York City." *JAMA Network Open* 3 (12): 1–14.

Omi, M., and Winant, H. (2014). *Racial Formation in the United States: From the 1960s to the 1990s*. 3rd edition. New York: Routledge.

powell, j. a., and Menendian. S. (2011). "Beyond Public/Private: Understanding Excessive Corporate Prerogative." *Kentucky Law Journal* 100: 83–164.

Pulido, L. (2016). "Flint, Environmental Racism, and Racial Capitalism." *Capitalism Nature Socialism* 27 (3): 1–16.

Raja, S., Ma, C., and Yadav, P. (2008). "Beyond Food Deserts: Measuring and Mapping Racial Disparities in Neighborhood Food Environments." *Journal of Planning Education and Research* 27 (4): 469–482.

Rancière, J. (2004). *The Politics of Aesthetics: The Distribution of the Sensible*. London: Continuum International.

Rawls, J. (1971). *A Theory of Justice*. Cambridge, MA: Belknap Press of Harvard University Press.

Rios, J. 2020. *Black Live and Spatial Matters: Policing Blackness and Practicing Freedom in Suburban St. Louis*. Ithaca, NY: Cornell University Press.

Rios, M. (2008). "The Limits of New Urbanism in Post-Disaster Planning: The Case of East Biloxi." *Batture: The LSU School of Architecture Journal* (4): 12–23.

Robinson, C. (1983). *Black Marxism*. Chapel Hill: University of North Carolina Press.

Soja, E. (2010). *Seeking Spatial Justice*. Minneapolis: University of Minnesota Press.

Solis, M. (2020). "Conditions and Consequences of ELULU Improvement: Environmental Justice Lessons from San Francisco, CA." *Journal of Planning Education and Research*, July 27, 2020. doi:10.1177/0739456x20929407.

Steil, J., and Delgado, L. H. (2019). "Limits of Diversity: Jane Jacobs, the Just City, and Anti-Subordination." *Cities* 91: 39–48.

Summers Thompson, B. (2019). *Black in Place: The Spatial Aesthetics of Race in a Post-Chocolate City*. Chapel Hill: University of North Carolina Press.

Talen, E., and Lee, S. (2018). *Design for Social Diversity*. London: Routledge.

Thomas, M. J., and Ritzdorf, M. (eds.) (1997). *Urban Planning and the African American Community: In the Shadows*. Thousand Oaks, CA: Sage.

Tomlinson, B., and Lipsitz, G. (2019). *Insubordinate Spaces: Improvisation and Accompaniment for Social Justice*. Philadelphia: Temple University Press.

Tyner, J. A. (2006). *The Geography of Malcolm X: Black Radicalism and the Remaking of American Space*. New York: Routledge.

Tyner, J. A. (2007). "Urban Revolutions and the Spaces of Black Radicalism." In McKittrick, K., and Woods, C. (eds.). *Black Geographies and the Politics of Place*. Toronto and Cambridge: Between the Lines and South End Press.

Williams, R. A. (2020). "From Racial to Reparative Planning: Confronting the White Side of Planning." *Journal of Planning Education and Research*, August 5, 2020. doi:10.1177/0739456X20946416.

Winkler, T. (2012). "Between Economic Efficiency and Social Justice: Exposing the Ethico-Politics of Planning." *Cities* 29: 166–173.

Young, I. M. (2013). *Responsibility for Justice*. Oxford: Oxford University Press.

Yu, C-Y., Zhu, X., and Lee, C. (2020). "Income and Racial Disparity and the Role of the Built Environment in Pedestrian Injuries." *Journal of Planning Education and Research, October 31, 2018*. doi:10.1177/0739456x18807759.

Zapata, M., and Bates, L. K. (2015). "Equity Planning Revisited." *Journal of Planning Education and Research* 35 (3): 245–248.

II

WHAT IS THE PUBLIC CITY AND INCLUSIVE URBANISM?

4

RETHINKING URBAN PUBLICS THROUGH THE LENS OF SOVEREIGNTY
MATERIAL ASSEMBLAGES FOR INCLUSIVE URBANISM

Diane E. Davis

In recent years, struggles over inclusion in the United States have intensified, fueled by the emergence of rights-based claims. Such claims are advanced by citizens who have gathered in the streets to challenge historical patterns of systematic racial oppression, xenophobic nationalism, and exclusion. Although "struggle[s] over who has the right to citizenship and who belongs has been at the heart of American life over centuries" (Schuessler 2018), globalization and the normalization of white nationalism are intensifying struggles over belonging. Such concerns have not only been revealed in national political conflicts over whether to build a wall at the US-Mexico border, but they also manifest in mobilizations such as the Black Lives Matter (BLM) movement. For centuries, questions over who belongs to what "public," with what rights and guarantees under the law, have been addressed constitutionally in the US and elsewhere, thus relegating the adjudication of rights, recognition, and distribution of justice typically to national-level authorities. Even so, acts of citizenship—defined in terms of political rights and responsibilities associated with belonging to a given political community—are increasingly unfolding at the urban scale and in ways that may challenge national-scale sovereignty. This is precisely why scholars argue that it may be time to "imagine . . . new territories at which state sovereignty might be fixed" (Purcell 2003, 571; see also Kofman 1995; Sassen 1996).

Building on such possibilities, in this chapter, I privilege the terrain of the city as a critical point of departure for both analyzing and proactively responding to fundamental questions of belonging, rights, and justice. The rationale for doing so is twofold. First, for most citizens, the lived experience of (in)justice is decidedly local, felt in everyday interactions that reveal citizenship in ways that do not always align with the national imaginary. Second, much of the civic activism against oppressive forms of exclusion based on identities, such as race, is now taking place on city streets. Cities not only host high degrees of diversity, but they are also sites where belief in a shared political community of equals is sought after yet extremely difficult to sustain.

I argue that the city is as critical as the nation in producing, revealing, and potentially mitigating extreme patterns of exclusion (Davis and Libertun de Duren 2011). This, in turn, means that the materiality of the urban experience should be the starting point for addressing contemporary conflicts over belonging. Building on recent writings by Sasha Constanza-Chock (2020, 15), who argues that "design justice" is a way of actively engaging with the world to align progressive visions and desires with everyday tensions, conflicting values, and physical and temporal constraints on action, I focus explicitly on interventions that strengthen an inclusive community of allegiance at the city level. The cosmopolitanism and diversity of cities lay the demographic foundation for a public sphere where citizens can engage with each other more tangibly than is possible at the national scale. Yet, most cities' stark sociospatial segregation patterns readily belie such actualization, making clear that the promises of substantive inclusion routinely remain unfulfilled. The question that concerns us here is: What can urban planners and designers do about this? Can cities be reconfigured in ways that might counter the excesses of discriminating nationalism and identity-based exclusion? How, in short, can we achieve what Jacques Derrida (2001, 9) heralded in his classic treatise on cosmopolitanism—a city whose meaning or identity "elevates itself above nation-states" to become a place of refuge, forgiveness, and freedom itself?

SOVEREIGNTY AND THE URBAN QUESTION

To answer these questions, in this chapter, I examine how the urban built environment might provide a material pathway for the formation of a more tolerant and inclusive public sphere. I do so by reflecting on spatial patterns and practices in two "conflict" cities, where struggles over racial, ethnonational, or religious exclusion have been common—Jerusalem and Belfast. I then apply these insights to contemporary American cities, asking whether measures undertaken to heal division in intractably conflicted cities might have relevance for US urban planners and designers.

In theoretical terms, this chapter situates these empirical aims in the context of debates over publics and how a strengthening of bonds of allegiance at the scale of the city might produce a territorial rescaling of sovereignty arrangements historically monopolized by nation-states. I use Benedict Anderson's (1983) concept of "imagined community" to understand bonds of allegiance that strengthen the public sphere. However, rather than focusing on national bonds, as he does, I examine these relationships within cities and by so doing place the concept of urban sovereignty at the center of analysis. Since the Westphalian era, the theory and practice of citizenship and inclusion under the law have unfolded in tandem with a focus on national sovereignty in a process that historical sociologist Charles Tilly (1993) documented as emerging from conflict among cities, states, and empires. Such research reminds us that cities have always been central to sovereignty—in no small part because they have served as sites where citizenship practices first emerged, thus contributing to the sociopolitical construction of a shared national identity. Even today, concerns with the presence or absence of toleration and inclusive sociospatial justice at the scale of the city continue to focus on citizenship (Baubock 2010; Blokland et al. 2015; Yiftachel 2018). I take this research one step further and introduce the notion of *sovereignty* to address the limits and possibilities of citizenship and to advance a design justice agenda geared toward building a more inclusive urban public (see also Davis 2020).

Although definitions of sovereignty have varied historically, the term fundamentally implies supreme authority within and over a given territory. At the scale of the city, this requires a focus on governance and not just citizenship. Despite activist efforts, without interventions from municipal actors empowered to transform urban space and policies, even mobilized citizens will have limited capacity to change the structural contours of the urban built environment or unequal treatment at the hands of local authorities. And although private sector actors are often responsible for spatial interventions that transform the built environment, such as those generated by real estate developers, even those projects cannot happen without the actions (or inaction) of local authorities responsible for advancing justice. In order to hold them accountable, both authorities and citizens must unite behind a shared agenda. This is precisely where urban sovereignty—built on shared ideals and commitments between local governing authorities and citizens—comes in.

In conceptualizing urban sovereignty as a starting point for understanding an "imagined community" of allegiance uniting citizens and governing authorities at the scale of the city, I build on Ash Amin and Nigel Thrift's (2016) and Warren Magnusson's (2011) claims that progressive politics come from "seeing like a city" rather than seeing like a state. I also draw inspiration from political theorist Bonnie Honig's (2017) discussion of "public things," defined as the material objects and physical spaces that hold the potential to produce a sense of shared identity, which will enable citizens to act collectively in pursuit of inclusive democratic ideals. With these theoretical and analytical foundations, my aim is to identify the material conditions under which we might see coexistence, equal justice, and sociospatial inclusion as opposed to conflict, unequally distributed oppression, and exclusion at the scale of the city. I not only ask whether certain spatial conditions will enable or constrain shared community of allegiance in urban spaces but also consider how urban planning principles, design practices, or governance policies might be configured to generate trust between residents and local authorities, thus producing urban sovereignty arrangements imbued with sufficient legitimacy to countervail exclusion and injustice embedded in nationalist governance agendas. Allegiances to equal justice ideals are tested when local authorities, including the police, abuse their power to determine who is "allowed" to be in what part of the city, at what hours, and with what behavior. Likewise, when planning officials restrict or monitor certain populations more than others, through measures like zoning, affordable housing location, or lack of transportation services, they also create fissures and exclusions among urban citizens assumed to have the same national rights and recognitions, thus eroding the social contract and reducing the likelihood of a shared public sphere.

MATERIALITIES AND DISCURSIVE MODALITIES OF EXCLUSION: LESSONS FROM THE USUAL SUSPECTS

To understand how planning, design, or other space-based patterns of exclusion and injustice intersect with questions of sovereignty to narrow rather than widen the public sphere, I begin with a focus on quintessential conflict cities. Cities like Belfast and Jerusalem have been recognized worldwide for their divided city statuses and spatial separation of populations based on religion and ethnicity at the hands of national authorities. Through zoning regulations, policing strategies, or the literal construction of barriers (Bollens 2007; Anderson 2008), local authorities have reinforced what some scholars have called fragmented sovereignty (Gazit 2009)—a situation where clear political distinctions and unequal treatment of diverse urban subgroups are materially represented and reinforced in physical space through actions and interventions intended to politically exclude certain populations. Such practices not only prevent the formation of a unified community but also result in ongoing contestation and active claim-making about who has access to certain city services and spaces (Varsanyi 2006; Yiftachel 2015). Complicating matters, the distinction between those included and those excluded or marginalized in one such community of urban citizens is often a product of informal or unspoken governance arrangements. In these cities, spatial patterns and practices, rather than formal citizenship rights, may tell us more about who holds political and economic power (Chatterjee 2004). Some architectural and design theorists conceive of the city as a political project whose built form establishes political inclusion or exclusion. Aureli (2013, 10) argues that "if the essence of political action is the attempt to project a form of co-existence among individuals, it can be said that architectural form—through patterning, framing, and representing the space of coexistence—inevitably implies a political vision. Far from being just an aesthetic category, physical form represents the political understanding of the city as a constant dialectic process between inclusion and exclusion."

In understanding such elements of city form, barriers to mobility play a critical role. Certain infrastructures—say, transport systems—are routinely structured to (dis)advantage certain social, ethnic, or class groups by making free movement and mixing of residents more or less difficult, either by route design or through the financial metrics of fares (Caldeira 2013; Davis 2019). That the materiality of mobility is used to guarantee or deny equal rights to the city is an observation not lost on riders of Jerusalem's relatively new light-rail system or on its public buses, which reflect the not-so-veiled political project of privileging Israeli over Palestinian residents (Shlomo 2017) (figure 4.1). The same can be said about the location and character of housing, the erection of parks and highways as sociospatial barriers, the gating of communities, or the distributional patterns of other basic urban services, including the authorities' willingness to recognize certain settlements or land occupations.

For years, cities like Belfast and Jerusalem controlled Catholic and Arab populations by physically isolating them from Protestant and

4.1 Palestinians protesting the exclusionary nature of the new light-rail in Jerusalem, July 2, 2015. *Source*: Faiz Abu Rmeleh/ActiveStills.

Jewish residents, using lethal force to maintain separations. Transgression of such boundaries is almost impossible without violence, and the likelihood of a shared public sphere—both physically and socially—is almost nil. The relative routineness of the authoritative exclusionary spatial practices in contested cities is what drives Yiftachel (2018) to highlight the relative routineness of what he calls " 'creeping apartheid' where people and groups constrained by rules, statuses, norms and power relations find themselves . . . 'separate and unequal' in their rights and capabilities under the same regime." When neighborhoods of a city are not all serviced equally by governing authorities, and when the physical form and nature of the city precludes equitable free movement, shelter, and service access, legitimate rule and/or citizenship comes under question, as does the robustness of urban sovereignty (figure 4.2).

This combination of factors suggests we examine two broad categories of urban conditions in order to ascertain the extent to which a shared imagined community of allegiance in the city is possible. One focuses on

4.2 A mural in Bethlehem in the Israeli-occupied West Bank depicting George Floyd, who was killed by a Minneapolis police officer in May 2020. *Source*: Yumna Patel/Mondoweiss.

materialities, such as the spatial, infrastructural, and institutional conditions that have separated subgroups and produced conflict within and between urban residents and local authorities. A second focuses on *discursive modalities* or narrative framings built on historical and cultural memories as well as normative assumptions about who belongs and how sociospatial inclusion is both imagined "from below" and recognized "from above." In Jerusalem, for example, invocations of history or religious justifications for physically dividing a city based on Christian, Muslim, or Jewish architectural iconography can be understood as fueling discursive modalities of exclusion. As such, in order to understand the possibilities for an inclusive urban public sphere, we must examine not just the grounded material realities that enable or constrain substantive inclusion but also the socially constructed and communicative means through which horizontal loyalties among city dwellers and vertical loyalties between them and local authorities might emerge (or not).

Discursive and material conditions are often interconnected in ways that produce sociocultural tensions over belonging. Some of this may owe to histories of urbanization and city form and the ways such patterns may negatively impact certain populations by producing differentiated citizenship and unequal governance repertoires within one city. Architectural forms, monumental traditions, and their semiotics also play a role—particularly those linked to memory, culture, and other representational iconographies. However, perceptions and realities of inclusion or exclusion are not only determined by efforts to link material to discursive conditions; they also depend on something as straightforward as who has access to institutions of governance, planning, and design so as to challenge such conditions. All of this suggests that there are three action domains that must be addressed by planners and designers who seek to construct a more inclusive public sphere at the scale of the city.

First, a city where residents have unequal access to urban public goods—from schooling to healthcare to safety to transportation—will reinforce differentiated citizenship and reflect biased governance practices. If all areas are not serviced equally by governing authorities and planning institutions, and if the city's physical form precludes access for all, then legitimate rule and/or citizenship is questioned. Second, cities need a wide array of spaces to which all residents have open and equal access, no matter their race, class, religion, or ethnicity. Those without are less likely to unite a divided populace. The materiality of mobility directly affects this larger political project of guaranteeing or denying equal rights to inhabitants of a city, as do government or resident biases, implying that such shared spaces could also be conceived institutionally and not merely infrastructurally. Third, cities seeking to foster shared allegiance within and between citizens and authorities need to project both material and cultural semiotics of inclusion—something that can be achieved through the narrative or symbolic construction of shared identity and realized through physical interventions intended to dismantle prior barriers to population mixing.

BEYOND AMERICAN EXCEPTIONALISM: HOW US CITIES CAN LEARN FROM CONFLICT SETTINGS

American cities are replete with discriminatory regulations, land-use restrictions, policing practices, and racialized discourses of belonging that have isolated and disadvantaged communities of color, immigrants, and indigenous populations, denying them public spaces, public services, and equal rights to the city. The American sociologist Elijah Anderson (2015) has gone as far as to argue that city spaces in the US are coded by racial or other normative orders, producing what he distinguishes as "white space," "black space," and "cosmopolitan space." This raises the possibility that a shared public sphere among urban residents may be just as elusive in American cities as in Jerusalem and Belfast.

To be sure, most urban planners and designers understand that there is race and immigrant-based inequality and injustice in American cities, but rarely are such realities framed through the lens of intractable sovereignty conflicts or divided city narratives. Most urban planners and designers have focused their attention on the mounting of participatory processes unfolding on a localized community scale as the pathway toward inclusion. Yet, in the context of the BLM movement, pandemic statistics, and other recent developments in American cities, targeted interventions at the microscale cannot address the larger divisions that have emerged with respect to differential treatment at the scale of the city as a whole. For this reason, it is no longer possible to ignore the commonalities between quintessential conflict cities and American cities.

BLM activists frame the oppressive and unequal urban experiences of African Americans in US cities within the context of white nationalism, historically linked to legacies of slavery and racial oppression, which derive from sovereignty battles during the US Civil War (Hesse 2017). They also use languages of decolonization and occupation to inform their claims for more substantive citizenship (Sharpe 2016; Curley et al. 2018). Some of this debate has focused on racial policing and how contemporary police practices can be understood as legacies generated during the pre- and post-emancipation period to control Black bodies (Hesse 2017). Both developments offer an opportunity to proactively learn from cities historically embroiled in sovereignty conflicts and to apply insights drawn from urban planning and design strategies developed to foster a more inclusive public sphere in conflict cities, with the hope that such strategies can be used to sustain urban sovereignty built around a shared imagined community of allegiance within contemporary American cities.

In moving forward with such an agenda, Belfast is a good city for comparison. During the "troubles," Belfast was known to be a city suffering from "the legacies of political violence, residential segregation, and communities characterized by mutual fears and suspicion" (Morrisey and Gaffikin 2006, 873). Yet, Belfast is also one of the few quintessential conflict cities that might be considered relatively successful in efforts to move beyond past sectarian divisions. The city has fostered community arts interventions and adopted neighborhood redevelopment strategies intended to redress the unequal treatment of its Catholic and Protestant populations, dismantling infrastructural and symbolic borders dividing their neighborhoods, and including a specialized focus "on the role of public arts and use of shared public spaces to promote social cohesion" (Sawhney, Raed, and Norman 2009, 69) (figure 4.3). It has also used urban planning protocols to reintegrate formally segregated areas by reclaiming low-rent workspaces for community arts organizations and encouraging people "to share creative activities in a safe environment" (69). Design and planning researchers have also innovated new processes for engaging citizens collectively in the imagining of new urban spaces. One successful

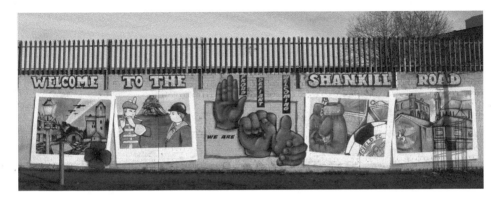

4.3 Shankill Road postconflict mural in Belfast. *Source*: PxHere.

example was a community visual mapping process intended to focus attention on the material effects of sectarian planning decisions of the past. The researchers did so by "integrating the traditional methodology of visual mapping with a tailored taxonomy of elements [revealing former sites] of urban conflict"; encouraging residents to focus attention on "edges, borders, barriers, and doors," among other sightlines that would expose barriers and enable social inclusion at the scale the city (Esposito de Vita, Trillo, and Martinez 2016, 320). Through these various strategies, Belfast has become a laboratory for planners and designers committed to dealing with sectarian conflict (Schar 2016).

Of course, the resolution of Northern Ireland's sovereignty battles through negotiated peace processes—which involved both international and local actors—must also be recognized as an important part of these successes. Without political commitments from the contesting parties to work jointly toward a new future, bitterness would have lingered, and many of these design and planning practices would not have been possible. Moreover, it is important to recognize that not all the planning and design programs introduced in postconflict Belfast have produced an unequivocally inclusive public sphere. In an effort to secure resources to enable urban changes that would reduce sectarian divides, authorities promoted new waterfront developments, new shopping precincts, and invited tech-led industries, which generated new class fissures and uneven spatial development (Murtagh 2018). Yet, observers in Belfast have suggested that such trade-offs may have been necessary to deal with the root of the sectarian problems, arguing that in such settings, planners must emphasize the centrality of economics in peacebuilding. This is a lesson that should not be lost on planners and designers in Louisville, Baltimore, Newark, Kenosha, and other economically depressed or challenged US cities, where support for BLM and race-based inclusion is now on the agenda.

This last observation prompts us to return to American cities today and ask whether similar planning and design interventions might be used to mitigate race-based and other identity conflicts to foster a more inclusive urban public. As in Belfast, economic prosperity and the extent to which income gains are equally distributed are quite relevant to US cities. High income inequality interfaces with high degrees of race and ethnically based spatial inequality. More equitably distributed economic prosperity initiatives could be a starting point for action. Such measures may need to accompany, if not precede, the adoption of targeted planning and design practices that foster inclusion through mapping exercises, housing redevelopment policies, and investments to reduce service inequalities in disadvantaged neighborhoods.

However, in contrast to Belfast, there has not yet been sufficient national reckoning over white supremacy or xenophobic nationalism in the US, suggesting that any advances in fostering inclusion at the local level must be accompanied by local authorities' embrace of the need for "peacemaking." This will thus require revisiting narratives of exclusion on top of infrastructural material realities. Given the stark material inequalities and extended time frame that would be needed to transform the urban spatial structure of American cities, any attempt to foster shared allegiance at the scale of the city will require discourses of inclusion advanced by local authorities, particularly those that generate new forms of trust vis-à-vis urban citizens.

In the American context, one way to start this process is to make room, both literal and figurative, for urban protest and open but peaceful contestation. America has a history of rioting, built on mutual hostility over ethnic and racial differences that have fueled violent conflict between protesters and authorities (Hepburn 2004). Yet, rioting is not the same as protest, with the latter being one of the most robust indicators of democratic citizenship and a vibrant public sphere. Unfortunately, many state legislators around the country have initiated efforts to enact legislation hindering protest activities (Rowland and Eidelman 2017). Yet, designing and fostering welcoming spaces for peaceful demonstrations of citizenship should be high on the agenda of cities, contributing to what Chantal Mouffe (2013) has called "agonistic pluralism." To be sure, guaranteeing that these spaces will be safe for conflict around public issues might only be possible if police behavior is reformed or reframed to accommodate contestation without fear of violence. Even so, whether or not a city or country allows protest is both an indicator of how open and inclusive authorities are to a vibrant public sphere and a sign that urban sovereignty may be in question. This proposition allows us to circle back to the quintessential conflict in cities noted earlier. One could even say that the national state's use of coercive forces to control inclusive gatherings in a city, such as the building of a physical barrier and checkpoints to separate Palestinians and Israelis, are indicators that the urban public sphere materializing in Belfast still remains impossible in Jerusalem. Yet, even when exclusive nationalism still hovers over a city, whether in Jerusalem or Richmond, urban design techniques are deployed to produce local spaces for contestation—such as public squares, which have routinely been prioritized in protests against political oppression or ethnonational exclusion (Davis and Raman 2013; Hatuka 2018). The location of these sites must be accessible to all, and they must not deliberately exclude populations who may not have the mobility means to participate.

Finally, in addition to the design of spaces for protest and public deliberation, attention must be paid to the semiotics and symbols of exclusion that generate protest in the first place and undermine a shared imagined community at the scale of the city (Vale 1999). In the US, the violent defense of confederate monuments fueled conflicts over white supremacy and evoked painful memories of the last major sovereignty battle the US fought: the Civil War. The fact that protesters felt compelled to violently topple such statues—or transform them through more artistic means (see figure 4.4)—also speaks symbolically to the unwillingness of many local authorities and residents to recognize or produce alternative narratives of identity and inclusion for their city. One significant challenge for planners and designers in the months and years to come will be to experiment with alternative symbols, discourses, and activities that

4.4   Robert E. Lee statue in Richmond, Virginia, reclaimed by BLM protesters at the center of what is now being called Marcus-Davis Peters Circle. *Source*: Brian Palmer for Reveal.

unite residents around an urban identity more reflective of the present and future, as opposed to the past. American cities are replete with architectural forms that speak to a prior history in which nonwhite voices have been routinely excluded. Alternative renderings of the urban built environment that display the diverse realities of the city will go a long way in advancing the narrative of a more inclusive public sphere.

CONCLUSION

William Avis (2016, 33 and 35) argues that "cities are inherently sites of conflict" and that this may be "an inevitable aspect of development and change in urban settings." Some forms of contestation are necessary to revitalize the urban public sphere. Even so, not all conflicts are alike. The question is whether such contestation unfolds within an inclusive public sphere or whether it operates within contexts of exclusivity. In this chapter, I have tried to suggest that despite the inevitable existence of tensions between communities of difference or the role of history and culture in keeping such tensions alive, purposeful urban design and planning actions can help create spaces for coexistence. In today's increasingly urbanized world, such interventions may be as important as larger democratic processes in producing a shared commitment among citizens and governing authorities.

I have discussed such interventions through the lens of urban sovereignty, working under the assumption that actions at the scale of the city are often more resonant with and meaningful to citizens than abstract laws, regulations, and policies emanating from the national state. Strengthened urban sovereignty does not inevitably produce good urbanism, and even the most robust sovereignty regimes at the scale of the city cannot eliminate all poverty, inequality, discrimination, or injustice. Even so, scholars and activists can direct their attention to the production of new constellations of sovereignties enabled through newly built environment actions that foster sociospatial inclusion and a shared sense of the public to maximize feelings of membership and belonging.

If we end this chapter as we began, thinking about exclusive nationalisms and how they have fueled struggles over urban inclusion in some of the world's most divided and contested cities, the challenges have been enormous. Yet, similar concerns are now on the political docket in many "ordinary" cities around the world, as certain categories of urban residents find themselves devalued by nationalist agendas or other forms of exclusion. Let us think constructively as well as critically about which sovereignty arrangements are responsible for city-based exclusion, oppression, animosity, and outrage both here and abroad. With such knowledge, we will be better prepared to remediate such injustices, with the aim of advancing actionable research about which urban design and planning strategies and tactics will help generate a shared community of allegiance among communities of difference in cities, no matter where they are.

REFERENCES

Amin, A., and Thrift, N. (2016). *Seeing Like a City*. Cambridge, UK: Polity Press.

Anderson, B. (1983). *Imagined Communities: Reflections on the Origins and Spread of Nationalism*. London: Verso.

Anderson, E. (2015). "The White Space." *Sociology of Race and Ethnicity* 1 (1): 10–21.

Anderson, J. (2008). "From Empires to Ethno-National Conflicts: A Framework for Studying 'Divided Cities' in 'Contested States.'" Working paper 1, *Conflict in Cities and the Contested State Programme*.

Aureli, P. V. (2013). "Preface and Means to an End: The Rise and Fall of the Architectural Project of the City." In Aureli, P. V. (ed.) *The City as a Project*. Berlin: Ruby Press, 10–13 and 14–38.

Avis, W. R. (2016). *Urban Governance (Topic Guide)*. Birmingham, UK: GSDRC, University of Birmingham. https://gsdrc.org/topic-guides/urban-governance/.

Baubock, R. (2010). "Studying Citizenship Constellations." *Journal of Ethnic and Migration Studies* 36 (5): 847–859.

Blokland, T., Hentschel, C., Holm, A., Lebuhn, H., and Margalit, T. (2015). "Urban Citizenship and Right to the City: The Fragmentation of Claims." *International Journal of Urban and Regional Research* 39 (4): 655–665.

Bollens, S. A. (2007). "Comparative Research on Contested Cities: Lenses and Scaffoldings." Working paper 17 (2), Crisis States Research Centre, London School of Economics and Political Science.

Caldeira, T. (2013). "Sao Paulo: The City and Its Protest." *Open Democracy*, July 11, 2013. https://www.opendemocracy.net/en/opensecurity/sao-paulo-city-and-its-protest/.

Chatterjee, P. (2004). *The Politics of the Governed: Reflections on Popular Politics in Most of the World*. New York: Columbia University Press.

Costanza-Chock, S. (2020). *Design Justice: Community-Led Practices to Build the Worlds We Need*. Cambridge, MA: MIT Press.

Curley, S., Rhe, J., Suberi, B., and Subreenduth, S. (2018). "Activism as/in/for Global Citizenship: Putting Un-Learning to Work Towards Educating the Future." In *The Palgrave Handbook of Global Citizenship and Education*, London: Palgrave Macmillan UK, 589–606.

Davis, D. E. (2019). "New Mobility Paradigms and the Equity Question." In Mostafavi, M., Doherty, G., Correia, M., Durán Calisto, A. M., and Valenzuela, L. (eds.). *Ecological Urbanism in Latin America/ Urbanismo Ecologico en America Latina*. Mexico: Gustavo Gili Publishers.

Davis, D. E. (2020). "Exploring the Material Foundations for Imagined Communities of Allegiance in Conflict Cities." In Goldhill, S. (ed.) *Being Urban: Community, Conflict and Belonging in the Middle East*. Oxford: Routledge.

Davis, D. E., and Libertun de Duren, N. (2011). *Cities and Sovereignty: Identity Politics in Urban Spaces*. Bloomington: Indiana University Press.

Davis, D. E., and Raman, P. (2013). "The Physicality of Citizenship: The Built Environment and Insurgent Urbanism." *Thresholds*, no. 41 (Spring): 60–71.

Derrida, J. (2001). *On Cosmpolitanism and Forgiveness*. London: Routledge.

Esposito De Vita, G., Trillo, C., and Martinez-Perez, A. (2016). "Community Planning and Urban Design in Contested Places. Some Insights from Belfast." *Journal of Urban Design* 21 (3): 320–334.

Gazit, N. (2009). "Social Agency, Spatial Practices, and Power: The Micro-Foundations of Fragmented Sovereignty in the Occupied Territories." *International Journal of Politics, Culture, and Society* 22 (1): 83–103.

Hatuka, T. (2018). *The Design of Protest: Choreographing Political Protests in Public.* Austin: University of Texas.

Hepburn, A. C. (2004). *Contested Cities in the Modern West.* London: Palgrave Macmillan.

Hesse, Ba. (2017). "White Sovereignty (. . .), Black Life Politics: "The N****r They Couldn't Kill." *South Atlantic Quarterly* 116 (3): 581–604.

Honig, B. (2017). *Public Things: Democracy in Disrepair.* New York: Fordham University Press.

Kofman, E. (1995). "Citizenship for Some but Not for Others: Spaces of Citizenship in Contemporary Europe." *Political Geography* 14 (2): 121–137.

Magnusson, W. (2011). *Politics of Urbanism: Seeing Like a City.* Florence: Routledge.

Morrissey, M., and Gaffikin, F. (2006). "Planning for Peace in Contested Space." *International Journal of Urban and Regional Research* 30 (4): 873–893.

Mouffe, C. (2013). *Agonistics: Thinking the World Politically.* London: Verso.

Murtagh, B. (2018). "Contested Space, Peacebuilding and the Post-Conflict City." *Parliamentary Affairs* 71 (2): 438–460.

Purcell, M. (2003). "Citizenship and the Right to the Global City: Reimagining the Capitalist World Order." *International Journal of Urban and Regional Research* 27 (3): 564–590.

Rowland, L., and Eidelman, V. (2017). "Where Protests Flourish, Anti-Protest Bills Follow." ACLU, February 17, 2017. https://www.aclu.org/blog/free-speech/rights-pro testers/where-protests-flourish-anti-protest-bills-follow?redirect=blog/speak-freely /where-protests-flourish-anti-protest-bills-follow.

Sassen, S. (1996). *Losing Control? Sovereignty in an Age of Globalization.* New York: Columbia University Press.

Sawhney, N., Raed, Y., and Norman, J. (2009). "Jerusalem and Belfast." *Jerusalem Quarterly (Institute of Jerusalem Studies* 39: 62–80.

Schar, A. (2016). "Adaptive Urban Governance in Northern Ireland: Belfast Planning Issues." *Dublin: Geographical Society of Ireland* 14: 64–69.

Schuessler, J. (2018). "How Black Citizenship Was Won, and Lost." *New York Times*, November 1, 2018. https://www.nytimes.com/2018/11/01/arts/design/black -citizenship-jim-crown-new-york-historical-society.html.

Sharpe, C. (2016). *In the Wake: On Blackness and Being.* Durham, NC: Duke University Press.

Shlomo, O. (2017). "The Governmentalities of Infrastructure and Services in Urban Conflict: East Jerusalem in the Post-Oslo Era." *Political Geography* 61: 224–236.

Tilly, C. (1993). *Capital, Coercion, and European States, AD 990–1992.* Oxford: Basil Blackwell.

Vale, L. J. (1999). "Mediated Monuments and National Identity." *Journal of Architecture* 4 (winter): 391–408.

Varsanyi, M. (2006). "Interrogating 'Urban Citizenship' *vis-à-vis* Undocumented Migration." *Citizenship Studies* 10 (2): 229–249.

Yiftachel, O. (2015). "Epilogue-from 'Gray Space' to Equal 'Metrozenship'? Reflections on Urban Citizenship." *International Journal of Urban and Regional Research* 39 (4): 726–737.

Yiftachel, O. (2018). "Creeping Apartheid? Regime, Space, and Citizenship in Israel/Palestine." *Public Space* 13: 139–167.

5

OPENING UP THE PRIVATE CITY
REMAKING SINGLE-FAMILY ZONING NEIGHBORHOODS

Vinit Mukhija

Conventional wisdom emphasizes adequately designed public spaces to enable democratic engagement and enhance public and inclusive city life. While progressive urban design scholars and practitioners often focus on public spaces—as many of the chapters in our book attest—I posit that private dwellings, including unpermitted or informal housing, contribute significantly to a city's publicness. Public and inclusive cities, I argue, must offer a wide range of housing options to accommodate the diversity of their residents, foster relationships of sharing among them, and provide residents, particularly disadvantaged community members, with democratic opportunities to participate in institutional decisions about land use and housing. To fully participate in public life, residents must be able to change or transform their housing's spatial and institutional arrangements to address their needs. Governments must be able to direct public investments into private and informal living arrangements that underpin public life. I call such a city an open city. Similar to the concepts of the public city and inclusive urbanism that this volume focuses on, the concept of the open city highlights my emphasis on a just urban design strategy that focuses on the private realm of housing.

I develop the open city concept by drawing from existing ideas about openness, diversity, and change in the urban planning and design literature (Turnbull 1988; Brueckner 1990; Friedmann 2002; Sennett 2017,

2018). Openness makes cities inviting and welcoming to migrants and immigrants and fosters their cosmopolitan character (Sandercock 1998). Cities around the world, including American cities, have played this pivotal role. However, the lack of housing affordability in many of these cities counteracts openness. Most US and Canadian cities have grown in population and prominence in the postwar era and are defined and dominated by detached single-family housing, limiting housing supply, and segregating residents by income. Nonetheless, immigrants worldwide have embraced the American Dream—and the Canadian Dream—of private minicastles, although often after transforming them without permits (Mukhija 2014). As urban housing has become increasingly expensive, it is difficult to add additional units unless single-family neighborhoods transform and accept housing diversity. However, many single-family housing owners typically oppose changes to their neighborhoods' physical and social character, and their parochial perspective receives preferential treatment in urban policy.

The urban design and planning challenge is to open up single-family housing neighborhoods to a diversity of housing alternatives and residents. The growing conventional wisdom is that top-down preemption at the state government level, or state intervention in local land-use regulations, is the key pathway for reforming single-family zoning (Glaeser 2017; Infranca 2019; Lemar 2019). However, I argue that urban design, spatial thinking, and local initiatives can be central to transforming and opening such neighborhoods to change and diversity. Local decision making can provide opportunities for residents to collaborate and weigh in. For their part, local governments should also invest in improving informal housing and the shared amenities of upzoned neighborhoods.

I illustrate these arguments through a case study of single-family zoning transformation in Vancouver, Canada.[1] I show how Vancouver's zoning changed to allow second units, locally called secondary suites, in the 1970s and 1980s through small-scale, subneighborhood-level plebiscites and opinion polls. Planners and policymakers intentionally structured public meetings and voting in Vancouver to encourage renters, including residents of unpermitted secondary suites, to deliberate and participate in land-use decision making. This emphasis on the democratic process played an essential role in allowing additional density and more residents and tenants in single-family-zoned neighborhoods. The city incrementally instituted these locally driven, neighborhood-based changes. However, affordable housing is still a challenge in Vancouver. There is an acute need for nonmarket or social housing alternatives and public investment to improve housing conditions in unpermitted units. Additionally, there is a need to accompany land-use deregulation with investment in social infrastructure. Without such investments, Vancouver can only claim to be a neoliberal open city—open to deregulation and private investment but not to less affluent residents.

OPENING UP THE PRIVATE CITY

Urban studies and planning scholars criticize the increasing emphasis on market-based institutions in cities and the privatization of urban life (Squires 1991; Glasze, Webster, and Franz 2004). Similarly, urban design scholars criticize public spaces' privatization in cities, including privately owned plazas in downtowns, corporate campuses, gated communities, shopping malls, and theme parks (Sorkin 1992; Loukaitou-Sideris 1993; Blakely and Snyder 1997; Loukaitou-Sideris and Banerjee 1998). The privatization of public space epitomizes contemporary cities' regressive and unfair character. Contrastingly, progressive scholars interested in inclusive urbanism prefer to focus on shared public spaces as an antidote to the exclusion inherent in privatization (Banerjee 2001; Low and Smith 2006; Hou 2010).

With a caveat, I agree with the thrust of the above sentiment. A progressive critique of the privatization of public life must paradoxically include the everyday private realm of housing. Cities play an important role in fostering and developing a cosmopolitan culture of openness, pluralism, sharing, tolerance, and spatial justice. However, the struggle for public city life cannot focus only on public spaces. It must actively consider and include the private realm of housing. Though cities are admired for their public and communitarian nature, they are shaped by private interests and opportunities (Gans 1968; Warner 1987). A public city needs a diversity of residents, and they need a variety of housing options.

As a political counterpart to the privatization and parochialism of cities, an open city's theoretical construct has epistemological advantages. In contrast to calls for a public city, it more readily conveys that achieving just and inclusive urbanism is likely to involve urban design and planning of both the public and private realm of cities. Moreover, several writers have explicitly used the designation "open city" (Turnbull 1988; Brueckner 1990; Pope 1996; Friedmann 2002; Sennett 2018). The concept can critically build on existing ideas about openness in the planning and urban design literature and scholars' emphasis on pluralism, acceptance of difference, receptiveness to change, the centrality of housing and dwelling, and a conviction in design strategies and processes.

John Friedmann (2002) asked for New York City to remain an open city after the 9/11 attacks had increased sentiments of xenophobia and Islamophobia. While others had called for extreme security measures and restrictions to civil liberties in response to the terrorist attacks, Friedmann called for privileging freedom and tolerance. He recognized the significance of openness in the city to its progressive culture and acceptance of global immigrants. In a similar vein, Teju Cole also used New York City to inspire his profound novel *Open City* (2011). He highlighted the inclusive qualities of the city's urbanism for tolerantly accommodating his Nigerian immigrant hero. Cole used the city's settings to show how great cities, with their diversity of cultures and people, are always conversing and changing with their residents and can be sources of promise.

Many scholars see openness in cities as antithetical to the high modernist dream of master planning and control. For example, Richard Sennett (2018), inspired by Jane Jacobs (1961), criticizes overdetermination in planning and pushes for buildings to be adapted instead of destroyed in response to new needs. He defines open cities as cities that embrace differences and encounters with strangers and have urban forms that are incomplete and can transform. Like Sennett, Albert Pope (1996) advocates for cities that can readily grow, change, and adapt. He focuses on the city's spatial structure and highlights the everyday grid with its ability to expand in multiple directions as the supporting infrastructure of open cities. He contrasts grids with the more closed-off suburban form of cul-de-sacs and superblocks. Pope argues that simple design decisions about street networks and their organization significantly determine cities' open or closed nature and corresponding urbanism.

Scholars have explicitly focused on access to housing while thinking about and describing open cities. Urban economists have characterized cities and regions with housing markets that can dynamically adapt and respond to changing demand as open cities (Turnbull 1988; Brueckner 1990). John Turner, who focuses on housing and community development in the Global South, argues for open housing systems where inhabitants control their housing decisions (1976). Turner's (1972) insightful invocation of housing as both a noun and a verb, or both an outcome and a process, highlights residents' critical role in decision making about their housing. Thus, housing as the symbol of openness in cities can help focus design and policy attention on both access to housing as a desirable outcome and the ability to participate in decision-making processes as a democratic goal.

However, there is a gap in the existing literature on open cities. Previous scholars have privileged more libertarian, anarchist, deregulation-oriented, and market-based ideas in their theories, without much attention to the public sector's contributions and role. For example, Turner, respected and criticized for his anarchist-inspired scholarship and advocacy (Burgess 1978; Harris 2003), was skeptical about governments' role in housing provision. He saw more opportunities for empowerment in autonomy with less government involvement and control. In contrast, I see a much more direct role and responsibility for governments in ensuring access to affordable and livable housing. The Vancouver case, which I will discuss next, illustrates the strengths and weaknesses of prevailing government approaches to actively building and defining the architecture and institutions of openness in cities.

REMAKING VANCOUVER WITH MORE HOUSING UNITS

Canadians share the (North) American Dream of owning a house on its lot (Condon 2010). Detached single-family housing has played a crucial part in Vancouver's development. Planners reserved over 60 percent of the city's zoned land for "RS Zones," namely single-family use (City of Vancouver 2009b, 2019b). Vancouver, however, has an interesting history of radically remaking single-family housing in the postwar era from one to two units, subsequently from two to three dwellings, and since 2018 from three to four units by allowing duplexes with their separate secondary units on the same lot (City of Vancouver 2019a).

Vancouver's context is somewhat unusual due to the city's relatively high density and the widespread prevalence of informal secondary suites in single-family neighborhoods. Lot sizes are comparatively small, making Vancouver's single-family neighborhoods denser than in other cities (Berelowitz 2005; Hirt 2014). Moreover, unpermitted secondary suites are ubiquitous and help further increase the city's density (City of Vancouver 2009b). Most of the city's single-family houses are built above a space for storage, heating equipment, and moisture protection (figure 5.1). It is easy to use the additional space as an unpermitted secondary unit, and single-family houses informally function as duplexes (Lauster 2016; Suttor 2017). According to the city's estimates (Vancouver City Council 2017), there were over thirty thousand secondary suites, including around twenty five thousand without permits, in Vancouver's almost seventy thousand single-family houses.

Housing affordability is a polarizing issue in Vancouver politics (Bula 2018; Fumano 2018). The city's policy focus has been on increasing the

5.1 Shallow basements for storage and protection from the frost line characterize Vancouver's detached single-family houses. *Source*: Vinit Mukhija.

supply of housing through deregulation and upzoning. Scholars argue that the emphasis on redevelopment and densification leads to loss of affordable units, displacement, and gentrification (Blomley 2004; Moos and Mendez 2015). Less attention has been paid to how the city has allowed informal housing and its role in zoning changes. In the following subsections, I describe how planners and urban designers accepted unpermitted secondary suites, built on their prevalence, and increased the allowed density in the city's single-family neighborhoods.

LEGALIZATION OF SECONDARY SUITES AT THE NEIGHBORHOOD LEVEL

During the Second World War, the Vancouver City Council (hereafter council) temporarily suspended zoning requirements. It encouraged residents to share their accommodations, particularly basements of single-family houses, with those who lacked shelter (Wartime Prices and Trade Board 1949). Postwar, the council made secondary suites in single-family zones illegal but created a temporary moratorium for shutting down units constructed before 1956 (City of Vancouver 2004). The council also developed policies for granting "hardship" exceptions on suites occupied by parents, grandparents, or children of owners, which were called family suites, and time extensions for continuing suites without family members based on the owners' or tenants' financial or medical needs (Cheng 1980; City of Vancouver 2009b). The secondary units housing nonfamily members were called nonfamily or revenue suites.

Faced with the ongoing challenge of unpermitted housing, the council decided to get community input on secondary suites through a survey of eligible resident homeowner voters in a limited section of Vancouver neighborhoods with secondary suites—Eastside's Cedar Cottage and Westside's Kitsilano and Grandview-Woodland (Cheng 1980). After a series of public meetings, planners asked property owners in November 1975 if they favored allowing self-contained secondary suites in their subareas (Vancouver City Council, February 5, 1976, Vol. 122, p. 328).

Based on the outcome of the survey, the council rezoned subareas in Cedar Cottage and Kitsilano and created a new zoning type, RS-1A, to allow the conditional creation of secondary suites in all buildings already constructed at the time of the amendment's passage. The additional unit had to have at least one off-street parking space and receive the planning director's approval. Owners would receive a development permit for five years (Vancouver City Council, February 22, 1977, Vol. 125, pp. 319–320).

In the 1980s, judicial courts began to question the fairness of the hardship appeals process. The council decided that it was necessary to increase public engagement and make decisions citywide about secondary suites (City of Vancouver 2009b). It agreed to start with a pilot program of neighborhood review in Joyce Station (Eastside). Notably, unlike the previous survey, the council decided to proceed more democratically, surveying both owners and renters on whether the city should only allow family suites or permit revenue suites also. The program was approved in October 1986 and was slated to commence activity in March 1987, including an eleven-week public review process with two public meetings (Vancouver City Council, March 12, 1987, Vol. 177, p. 765). The Joyce Station Review Committee, consisting of community members and delegates from community and business associations, met weekly during this time.

Planners circulated a final questionnaire presenting all residents with two choices of handling suites: option A, permitting one family suite per house, and option B, allowing one family or nonfamily suite per house. In total, they distributed 1,707 questionnaires to owners and renters in single-family housing zones. Only 36 percent of those receiving surveys responded, with 39 percent favoring option A and 56 percent favoring option B (Vancouver City Council, October 10, 1987, Vol. 180, p. 2767). By the winter of 1987/1988, the council approved the rezoning of portions of Joyce Station as RS-1S (Thomsett n.d.).

THE LEGALIZATION OF SECONDARY SUITES AT THE CITY LEVEL

Given the prevailing policy of hardship exceptions and residents' positive response in Joyce Station, the council decided to allow family suites by-right in all single-family neighborhoods in the late 1980s (City of Vancouver 2004; Thomsett n.d.). It also decided to hold public engagement meetings and conduct a citywide plebiscite as part of the 1988 municipal election and ask all residents if they favored a neighborhood review to discuss revenue suites (City of Vancouver 2009b, Thomsett n.d.).

The council launched a multilingual community engagement process in English, Cantonese, and Punjabi across the city (Vancouver City Council, August 25, 1988, Vol. 187, p. 2612, and September 23, 1988, Vol. 187, p. 2788–2789). The public meetings were contentious. Many homeowners protested the extension of the vote to all residents. At one meeting, 150 people publicly commented, and 148 opposed the voting structure. A resident complained, "Why do 10 illegal people get a vote and only one neighbour who owns his house?" (Kavanagh 1988). Residents of unpermitted suites were afraid to speak out, though. Despite the city's multilingual outreach, most Chinese- and Indo-Canadian occupants of informal suites felt too intimidated to attend meetings. When they participated, they were subjected to sexist and racist remarks (Fayerman 1988).

Vancouver officials conducted the plebiscite on secondary suites as part of the November 1988 civic election. Out of 76,600 respondents, 76 percent (representing the majority of respondents in about three-fourths of the neighborhoods) voted in favor of discussing and being open to considering secondary suites (Vancouver City Council, February 7, 1989, Vol. 189, p. 232; Thomsett n.d.). The "yes" vote drew more heavily from Eastside neighborhoods—the less affluent and more immigrant-heavy half of the city.

The planning department prioritized neighborhoods for area review by their percentage of "yes" votes. Neighborhood planners notified residents that there would be an opinion poll following the area review that they would use to determine rezoning action. If residents voted "no," then owners would have ten years to phase out their nonfamily suites. If residents voted "yes," city staff assured them that property owners with suites would pay their fair share of taxes and that the city would phase out buildings not brought up to code (City of Vancouver 1990a).

Neighborhood reviews of the nine areas that voted affirmatively began following the plebiscite in the 1988 civic election. The nine areas were further divided by subarea, indicating that if a subarea opposed legalizing secondary suites, there would be room to leave it out of the rezoning. Figure 5.2 shows a copy of an opinion survey and a public information announcement from 1990. About two-thirds of the neighborhoods that voted in favor of considering secondary suites supported allowing them. Subsequently, the council rezoned 47 percent of all single-family

City of Vancouver
PLANNING DEPARTMENT

Renfrew / Collingwood
Secondary Suites Opinion Survey

Public Information Meeting

AREAS 1, 2 & 3

TIME: 7:30 p.m., Tuesday

DATE: May 29, 1990

PLACE: Windermere School
              School Auditorium
              3155 E. 27th Ave.,
              Vancouver

THE OPINION SURVEY

The City is carrying out neighbourhood reviews in single-family (RS-1) zoned areas to consider either phasing out or permitting secondary suites.

By answering the question on the enclosed ballot, you can voice your opinion on this important matter. Your opinion will help City Council decide what to do.

When you have answered the question, return the ballot to the Vancouver Planning Department using the enclosed self-addressed envelope. No postage is needed.

**To Have Your Opinion Count, You Must Return
The Ballot In the Enclosed Envelope by June 20, 1990.
Your Response is Completely Confidential.**

THE PUBLIC INFORMATION MEETING

The Planning Department will explain the Renfrew / Collingwood neighbourhood review on secondary suites and the opinion survey. Staff will also explain and answer your questions about typical building code and parking requirements for suites, the difference between RS-1 and RS-1S zoning and the ten-year phase-out program for existing suites under certain conditions.

INFORMATION ABOUT SECONDARY SUITES

A **SECONDARY SUITE** is a second dwelling unit, with its own kitchen, in a house. Single-family (RS-1) zoning permits only one dwelling unit per house. However, the Planning Department estimates that about 30% of all houses in Renfrew / Collingwood contain secondary suites. Most of these suites have not been created legally.

There are two types of secondary suites: Family Suites and Revenue Suites

A **FAMILY SUITE** is a secondary suite which is occupied by immediate family members (parents, children,

5.2 An opinion survey and public information meeting announcement from 1990 for changing the zoning to allow secondary suites in Vancouver. *Source*: City of Vancouver (1990b). "Renfrew/Collingwood: Secondary Suites Neighborhood Survey." Vancouver Planning Department.

residential neighborhoods as RS-1S to allow nonfamily secondary suites (Thomsett n.d.; Whitlock interview 2013).

In July 1999, the ten-year phase-out period enacted following the first neighborhood reviews came to a close, and so-called phase-out suites started becoming eligible for a shutdown. However, since these units provided an important housing stock for the city, the council decided to withhold enforcement for another three years (City of Vancouver 2004). Meanwhile, planners responsible for soliciting input from Vancouver's residents through its CityPlan (1995–2006) and City Vision (1998–2010) programs found citywide support for increasing housing choices, including secondary suites for tenants (McAfee 2013). The city's incremental legalization reforms and its democratic process had helped erode the opposition against them. Also, some reluctant homeowners likely realized that revenue suites helped increase property values and became in favor of allowing them in their neighborhoods. During two public hearings in March 2004, most participants spoke in favor of allowing revenue suites citywide, and the council legalized them in all single-family neighborhoods (Vancouver City Council 2004; City of Vancouver 2009b).

FROM SECONDARY SUITES TO MAKING ROOM FOR DUPLEXES WITH SECOND UNITS

In 2008, the council adopted the EcoDensity charter to promote sustainable growth practices and address climate change. The charter committed Vancouver to promote "gentle" (e.g., rowhouses), "hidden" (e.g., lane-oriented housing), and "invisible" (e.g., secondary suites) forms of densification. The strategies drew from the feedback planners and urban designers received during the CityPlan and City Vision public engagement programs (McAfee 2013).

The council asked the planning department to explore regulations for laneway housing—a detached dwelling built at the rear of a lot facing an alley or lane, where a garage would typically go (figure 5.3). The department recommended allowing laneway housing on 94 percent of the city's single-family lots, specifically on parcels "10 meters (33 ft.) and wider, with access to an open lane, or on a corner site with lane dedication, or a double fronting lane" (City of Vancouver 2009a, 7). In July 2009,

5.3 Infill of a single-family-zoned lot with a laneway house in Vancouver. *Source*: Vinit Mukhija.

the council approved the recommendation and allowed laneway housing of up to 750 square feet with one additional off-street parking space in most of the city's single-family neighborhoods (City of Vancouver 2013; Bula 2009). After reviewing projects from the first one hundred permits, planners recommended eliminating the enclosed parking requirement and increasing the permitted floor area to a maximum of 900 square feet (City of Vancouver 2013). The council accepted the recommendations. By 2018, the city had approved over three thousand permits for laneway houses (City of Vancouver 2018a).

High housing prices, however, continued to be a challenge in Vancouver. In November 2017, the council approved the Housing Vancouver Strategy (HVS) for exploring zoning changes in single-family neighborhoods to allow duplex, triplex, and multifamily buildings (City of Vancouver 2018b). HVS set a ten-year target of seventy-two thousand new homes (City of Vancouver 2018c). As a quick start action for implementing the housing strategy, in September 2018, the outgoing council approved duplexes in 99 percent of Vancouver's single-family neighborhoods (Larsen 2018; Lee-Young and Padgham 2018). The zoning reform, named Making Room, did not change the allowed intensity of development on single-family lots but increased the permitted density of development by allowing owners to build duplexes with secondary suites or lock-off units (City of Vancouver 2018c). With duplexing, owners could build four units on their lots and sell the duplex units (along with their accessory units) separately. In December 2018, a new council agreed to retain the policy and continue to allow duplexes with accessory units in the city's single-family neighborhoods (City of Vancouver 2019a).

HOUSING THE OPEN CITY

Vancouver's remaking of single-family housing provides a useful illustration of the possibilities and challenges of inclusive urbanism through housing. After initially attempting to ban secondary suites in single-family neighborhoods, the city's policymakers and planners adopted supportive upzoning policies to formalize informal housing. They created acceptance of informal housing and upzoning by extending public participation to renters, including occupants of unpermitted housing units. In this chapter, I use the example of Vancouver's transformation of single-family zoning and acknowledgment of informal secondary suites to make a case for inclusive urbanism through attention to housing.

I call cities that enable housing diversity by supporting changes to their housing stock, amendments to zoning regulations, and participation of disadvantaged groups in housing and land-use decisions open cities. I suggest that cities' public and inclusive nature, particularly their tolerance and openness toward immigrants and migrants, depends on housing's private realm. My focus on housing as a defining characteristic of inclusive urbanism builds on the preeminent scholarship of Catherine Bauer (1934), Gwendolyn Wright (1983), Dolores Hayden (1984), and Anne Vernez Moudon (1986), among others. In addition to housing being economically affordable, appropriately designed, safe, and livable, it needs to be adaptable. The unaffordability and inflexibility of housing limits who can access it, where residents with fewer resources or different needs can live, how easily they can participate in the economic opportunities that cities offer, and how readily they can engage in the public life of cities.

Extending opportunities to participate in decision making about housing and land-use policies to disadvantaged groups is an important aspect
of open cities. In Vancouver, the city council decided to democratically
solicit input from all single-family neighborhood residents, including
renters. Many homeowners strongly opposed the decision, particularly
voting by residents of unpermitted secondary suites. The council, however, persisted with the approach. Implementing the democratic process
took four years, from 1988 to 1992, and several contentious public meetings and neighborhood review sessions, but it positively affected the outcome. For many residents, it was the first opportunity to participate in a
significant decision about their city.

Policymakers and planners need to make efforts to understand the
diversity of opinions within their cities, particularly the perspective of
the less affluent, more vulnerable, and more marginalized. Policy decisions about housing affect all city residents. All of them know about the
topic, care about it, and should have the opportunity to participate in
decisions about it. Yes, there are likely to be conflicts and differences, but
this is not a reason to avoid deliberation and input. Disagreements and
differences of opinion are the essence of urban living and contribute to
the publicness of cities.

How cities respond to informal housing is an important aspect of their
openness too. In addition to supportive land-use policies and zoning
changes, cities need to provide loans, grants, and technical assistance for
improving informal housing units. While Vancouver's policymakers tried
to direct private resources to make the city's informal housing units safe
and livable, they did not directly support their upgrading. If they provided public financial resources for improving informal housing, they
could impose conditions and obligations on homeowners to protect vulnerable tenants' rights.

Urban designers understand spatial possibilities and have an important role in open cities. First, they may be able to find creative strategies
for adding more infill housing without losing existing affordable units.
Vancouver's laneway apartments are an example of increasing housing
options in existing neighborhoods. Second, urban designers have an
important role in transforming neighborhoods. As neighborhoods get
denser and more diverse with additional housing, including informal

additions, they need more shared infrastructure and amenities. The COVID-19 pandemic has highlighted the value of neighborhood-level open spaces, playgrounds, and community gardens. Other useful social infrastructure in neighborhoods can include childcare centers, senior centers, community kitchens, healthcare facilities, and language and learning centers for immigrants and adult learners. Such design interventions can signal to homeowners with informal housing that their informal additions are acceptable. Homeowners will likely feel more comfortable investing in their informal units and improving their livability because they are less concerned about potential enforcement actions.

Finally, Vancouver's case illustrates the challenges of focusing on housing in urban design and social justice. Despite the efforts explained here, the city has Canada's most expensive housing market. Local, provincial, and federal policymakers have not devoted enough financial resources to expanding the social housing supply. Moreover, the city's approach of upzoning for housing supply makes it likely that some existing affordable units will be lost in demolition and redevelopment. If Vancouver's policymakers want a city with just housing outcomes and processes, it will not be enough to be creative and opportunistic about market-based infill housing. They will need to actively spend public resources for adequately housing all city residents and enhancing the city's inclusiveness and openness.

NOTE

1. My research is based on two fieldwork visits in Vancouver and follow-up phone interviews and email communication with informed stakeholders. The evidence I share in the chapter is primarily from publicly available government documents, including planning reports and minutes of city council meetings, previous scholarship, and newspaper reports.

REFERENCES

Banerjee, T. (2001). "The Future of Public Space: Beyond Invented Streets and Reinvented Places." *Journal of the American Planning Association* 67 (1): 9–24.

Bauer, C. (1934). *Modern Housing*. Boston: Houghton Mifflin Company.

Berelowitz, L. (2005). *Dream City: Vancouver and the Global Imagination*. Vancouver: Douglas & McIntyre.

Blakely, E. J., and Snyder, M. G. (1997). *Fortress America: Gated Communities in the United States*. Washington, DC: Brookings Institution Press.

Blomley, N. (2004). *Unsettling the City: Urban Land and the Politics of Property*. New York: Routledge.

Brueckner, J. K. (1990). "Growth Controls and Land Values in an Open City." *Land Economics* 66 (3): 237–248.

Bula F. (2009). "The Laneway House: A Novel Solution to Vancouver's Real-Estate Crunch." *Globe and Mail*, July 27, 2009.

Bula, F. (2018). "Vancouver Mayor Gregor Robertson Pushes to Allow Multiunit Housing in Low-Density Neighborhoods." *Globe and Mail*, July 9, 2018.

Burgess, R. (1978). "Petty Commodity Housing or Dweller Control? A Critique of John Turner's Views on Housing Policy." *World Development* 6 (9–10): 1105–1133.

Cheng, Lai-Sum L. (1980). "Secondary Suites: Housing Resource or Problem, the Vancouver Case." MA Thesis, University of British Columbia.

City of Vancouver. (1990a). "Memorandum: South Cambie/West Riley Park—Neighbourhood Review on Secondary Suites." July 4, 1990.

City of Vancouver. (1990b). "Renfrew/Collingwood: Secondary Suites Neighborhood Survey." Vancouver Planning Department.

City of Vancouver. (2004). "Secondary Suites." Policy Report, Development and Building, Rob Whitlock, Director of the Housing Centre, January 13, 2004.

City of Vancouver. (2009a). "Implementing Laneway Housing in RS-1 and RS-5 Single Family Areas." Policy Report, June 9, 2009.

City of Vancouver. (2009b). "The Role of Secondary Suites: Rental Housing Strategy—Study 4." Social Development—Housing Policy, Community Services Group, December.

City of Vancouver. (2013). "Amendments to the Laneway Housing Regulations and Guidelines and Expansion of the Laneway Housing Program." Policy Report, Development and Building, May 6, 2013.

City of Vancouver. (2018a). "Amendments to the Zoning and Development By-law—Laneway Home Regulations." Policy Report, June 5, 2018.

City of Vancouver. (2018b). "Making Room Housing Program: Overview and Quick Start Action." Administrative Report, June 5, 2018.

City of Vancouver. (2018c). "Amendments to the Zoning and Development By-law for Most RS Zones to Allow Two-Family Dwellings (Duplexes) to Increase Housing Choice." Policy Report, June 27, 2018.

City of Vancouver. (2019a). "Amendments to the Zoning and Development By-Law to Revise Design Regulations for 'Outright' Two-Family Dwellings (Duplexes)."

From General Manager of Planning, Urban Design and Sustainability, February 6, 2019.

City of Vancouver. (2019b). "Housing Choice in Low-Density Neighborhoods." Housing Vancouver, Backgrounder, Summer. https://vancouver.ca/files/cov/making-room -backgrounder.pdf.

Cole. T. (2011). *Open City: A Novel*. New York: Random House.

Condon, P. M. (2010). *Seven Rules for Sustainable Communities: Design Strategies for the Post-Carbon World*. Washington, DC: Island Press.

Fayerman, P. (1988). "Acrimony, Racism Deplete Suites Committee." *Vancouver Sun*, November 18, 1988.

Friedmann, J. (2002). "City of Fear or Open City." *Journal of the American Planning Association* 68 (3): 237–243.

Fumano, D. (2018). "Growth, Density Lead the Debate in Most Council Races in Metro Vancouver." *Vancouver Sun*, September 16, 2018.

Gans, H. (1968). *People and Plans: Essays on Urban Problems*. New York: Basic Books.

Glaeser, E. (2017). "Reforming Land Use Regulations." *Brookings*, April 24, 2017.

Glasze, G., Webster, C., and Franz, K. (2004). *Private Cities: Local and Global Perspectives*. New York: Routledge.

Harris, R. (2003). "A Double Irony: The Originality and Influence of John FC Turner." *Habitat International* 27 (2): 245–269.

Hayden, D. (1984). *Redesigning the American Dream: The Future of Housing, Work, and Family Life*. New York: W. W. Norton.

Hirt, S. A. (2014). *Zoned in the USA: The Origins and Implications of American Land-Use Regulation*. Ithaca, NY: Cornell University Press.

Hou, J. (ed.) (2010). *Insurgent Public Space: Guerilla Urbanism and the Remaking of Contemporary Cities*. New York: Routledge.

Infranca, J. (2019). "The New State Zoning: Preemption amid a Housing Crisis." *Boston College Law Review* 60 (3): 823–887.

Jacobs, J. (1961). *The Death and Life of Great American Cities*. New York: Random House.

Kavanagh, J. (1988). "Planners Predict Prolonged Fight over Illegal Suites." *Vancouver Sun*, November 2, 1988.

Larsen, K. (2018). "Vancouver's New Duplex Rules Explained." *CBC News*, September 20, 2018.

Lauster, N. (2016). *The Death and Life of the Single-Family House: Lessons from Vancouver on Building a Livable City*. Philadelphia: Temple University Press.

Lee-Young, J., and Padgham, M. (2018). "Vancouver Council Votes to Rezone Most Single-Family Areas for Duplexes." *Vancouver Sun*, September 19, 2018.

Lemar, A. S. (2019). "The Role of States in Liberalizing Land Use Regulations." *North Carolina Law Review* 97 (2): 293–254.

Loukaitou-Sideris, A. (1993). "Privatisation of Public Open Space: The Los Angeles Experience." *Town Planning Review* 64 (2): 139–167.

Loukaitou-Sideris, A., and Banerjee, T. (1998). *Urban Design Downtown: Poetics and Politics of Form*. Berkeley: University of California Press.

Low, S., and Smith, N. (eds.) (2006). *The Politics of Public Space*. New York: Routledge.

McAfee, A. (2013). "Tools for Change: CityPlan—Vancouver's Strategic Planning Process." *Built Environment* 39 (4): 438–453.

Moos, M., and Mendez, P. (2015). "Suburban Ways of Living and the Geography of Income: How Homeownership, Single-Family Dwellings and Automobile Use Define the Metropolitan Social Space." *Urban Studies* 52 (10): 1864–1882.

Mukhija, V. (2014). "Outlaw Inlaws: Informal Second Units and the Stealth Reinvention of Single-Family Housing." In Mukhija, V., and Loukaitou-Sideris, A. (eds.). *The Informal American City: Beyond Taco Trucks and Day Labor*. Cambridge, MA: MIT Press, 39–57.

Pope, A. (1996). *Ladders*. Architecture at Rice; 34. Houston: Rice University, School of Architecture, New York: Princeton Architectural Press.

Sandercock, L. (1998). *Towards Cosmopolis: Planning for Multicultural Cities*. London: John Wiley.

Sennett, R. (2017). "The Open City." In Haas, T., and Westlund, H. (eds.). *The Post-Urban World: Emergent Transformation of Cities and Regions in the Innovative Global Economy*. New York: Routledge.

Sennett, R. (2018). *Building and Dwelling: Ethics for the City*. New York: Farrar, Straus and Giroux.

Sorkin, M. (ed.) (1992). *Variations on a Theme Park*. New York: Noonday Press.

Squires, G. D. (1991). "Partnership and the Pursuit of the Private City." In Gottdiener, M., and Pickvance, C. (eds.). *Urban Life in Transition: Critical and Comparative Perspectives*. Thousand Oaks, CA: Sage, 196–221.

Suttor, G. (2017). "Basement Suites: Demand, Supply, Space, and Technology." *The Canadian Geographer* 61 (4): 483–492.

Thomsett, D. (n.d.). "Secondary Suites Neighbourhood Review Program." Unpublished manuscript.

Turnbull, G. K. (1988). "Residential Development in an Open City." *Regional Science and Urban Economics* 18 (2): 307–320.

Turner, J. F. C. (1972). "Housing as a Verb." In Turner, J. F. C., and Fichter, R. (eds.) *Freedom to Build: Dweller Control of the Housing Process*. New York: Macmillan Company, 148–175.

Turner, J. F. C. (1976). *Housing by People: Towards Autonomy in Building Environments*. New York: Pantheon Books.

Vancouver City Council. 1961–1989. "Meeting Minutes."

Vancouver City Council. (2017). "Motion on Notice: Reporting Data on Secondary Suites." December 12, 2017.

Vernez Moudon, A. (1986). *Built for Change: Neighborhood Architecture in San Francisco*. Cambridge, MA: MIT Press.

Warner, S. B. (1987). *The Private City: Philadelphia in Three Periods of Growth*. Philadelphia: University of Pennsylvania Press.

Wartime Prices and Trade Board. (1949). "Order No. 200." Canadian war orders and regulations.

Whitlock, R. (2013). Interview (in-person), former Director of the Housing Centre, City of Vancouver, October 1, 2013.

Wright, G. (1983). *Building the Dream: A Social History of Housing in America*. Cambridge, MA: MIT Press.

6

REINSTATING LANDSCAPES OF URBAN RESISTANCE

Alison B. Hirsch

REFLECTIONS, 2020

The events of 2020, specifically the nine minutes and twenty-nine seconds caught on video of George Floyd's killing, forced me to revisit questions I had begun to ask five years earlier and had temporarily set aside. My earlier research was about place memory in marginalized communities and its suppression and erasure by hegemonic forces. Acts of resistance and the claiming of the city as public in the face of institutions of exclusion were equally significant to that research. This chapter builds on that earlier work to argue that a spatialized reinscription of symbolic claims to the right of the city is critical to a truly *just* urban design.

The video of George Floyd dying under the Minneapolis police officer's knee outside the corner market on Chicago Avenue and East Thirty-Eighth Street in South Minneapolis was nationally and internationally catalytic. Yet, viewing this state-sponsored violence was not unfamiliar to the global public. Video footage of Eric Garner's killing in 2014 in Staten Island and Rodney King's brutal beating in 1992 in the San Fernando Valley of Los Angeles are visual testimonies to the crimes of the systems in which so many of us are complicit (see also Sturken 1997). In a recent article titled "America's Cities Were Designed to Oppress," architect and design justice advocate Bryan Lee (2020) responded to this ceaseless cycle,

"When it comes to violence against Black people in America, history repeats itself so precisely that it can be hard to place any given moment into context." Until we start addressing the realities of our history with truth and reconciliation, it is impossible to move forward. Embedded in this history are the systems of oppression, stories of resistance to those systems, and moments of rupture when those systems have the potential to be overturned or radically transformed.

The first part of this chapter focuses on urban design or the physical formation of the city as an arena for justice and a platform for mobilization emergent from such historically symbolic claims to space and rights. The second part looks to specific urban design proposals as testing grounds for playing out new narratives of justice in South Los Angeles.

URBAN UPRISING, 1992

The urban unrest following the Rodney King verdict was a turning point for the city of Los Angeles. Specific "flashpoints," such as the intersection of Florence and Normandie Avenues in South Central Los Angeles, triggered violent expressions of protest in a wider urban geography (see *Los Angeles Times* 2002; Chandler, Glick Kudler, and Barragan 2020). While the systems of injustice that led up to the events have been well-documented (see especially Davis 1990; Soja 1996; see also Dear and Flusty 1998; Dear 2003), I began examining the city for physical traces of the 1992 uprisings as haunting reminders of specific regimes of power. Only a few of the most consequential sites retain a palpable reminder of the historical events that momentarily brought visibility to long-standing inequities and indelibly transformed the city. My research questioned how to recognize and confront difficult or conflicted pasts in the built environment while addressing the urban needs and dreams of today.

By inventorying the sites along the Vermont Avenue corridor most physically impacted by the unrest in 1992, this work considers the potential of reinstating the uprisings' spatial inheritance as restored sites of resistance and the advancement of collective liberties. It features designed propositions for the future of these sites in South Central Los Angeles, developed in a graduate research studio in landscape architecture conducted at the University of Southern California. While my students generated the proposals without a community engagement process and in a format too limited to respond to the complexity of questions asked in this chapter, they started a conversation about how to restore space once claimed as public through performative appropriation and how we might physically interpret histories of the built environment as a form of reckoning over racial and spatial justice, even as these areas experience a demographic shift.

THEN

As documented by Soja (1996), two decades of conservative policy at the federal level, an oppressive and discriminatory police force and inequitable criminal justice system, macroeconomic processes of deindustrialization, the influx of Latinx immigrants and Korean merchants competing for jobs and opportunities in South Central, and a media infusing public imagination with misconceptions about people and place, propelled these culminating acts of anger and revolt.

Just as the Los Angeles Police Department (LAPD) patrolled and controlled Black and Chicano neighborhoods from the aerial distance of constant helicopter surveillance, "helicopter journalism" brought the "riots" into the living rooms of the American public who saw only the fires, violence, and looting, completely severed from what was happening on the ground and the complex sociospatial dynamics leading to the unrest (Tice 1992; see also Sturken 1997). With only the sounds of the chopper and the sensationalized commentary of the news agency, rather than the voices of community spokespeople or citizens in the streets, the public remained disconnected from the complexities of need, hope, fear, and anger of communities historically silenced.

In a more recent interpretation of the events of 1992 and the range of cultural responses, which interrupted the rhetoric of what she calls "civil racism," scholar Lynn Mie Itagaki (2016, 26–27) claims: "How threatening the violence was to the status quo is signaled by the powerful institutions and narratives arrayed to invalidate the political and economic claims made by the participants, journalists, politicians, observers and victims. Because nonwhite bodies were conspicuously involved and were not perceived as civil, any actions performed by such bodies cannot but be uncivil, any claims made cannot but be illegitimate." The delegitimizing of any such political or economic agenda—especially through the media's construction of the events—has perpetuated this popular narrative. The use of the term *riot* rather than *uprising*, or the more neutral *unrest*, also reinforces the criminalization of actions rather than acknowledges them as political reactions to compounded systemic failures, including the failure of the criminal justice system to fairly serve all people (Wick 2019).[1]

The rebellion came as little surprise to those who tracked the mechanisms of the state, market, and media, which controlled, exploited, and suppressed multiethnic minority populations in the city. Resisting the urban disenfranchisement caused by neoliberal globalization and systemic racism, the uprisings became a true claiming of "the right to the city" in Lefebvrian terms (Lefebvre 1996) and a means through which to challenge institutional forces that denied these rights.

The uprisings, therefore, revealed the potential power of the underclass to occupy, appropriate, and claim spaces of the city. While the brutal beating of white truck driver Reginald Denny at Florence and Normandie—as we witnessed in edited form through the camera of the helicopter above—was an act of seemingly senseless brutality, the intersection and the act came to represent much more (Sturken 1997).[2] The flashpoints became symbolic of a demand for justice and a population asserting its voice.

SINCE

This research began with the discovery of photographer Joel Sternfeld's book, *On This Site: Landscape in Memoriam* (1997), which pictures places of tragic or traumatic events that exist without palpable traces of these pasts. The sites—including spreads of Florence and Normandie and the location of the Rodney King beating (figure 6.1)—appear as ordinary everyday spaces yet have extraordinary histories. The images in the book are juxtaposed with a neutrally written account of those histories. The vacuity and anonymity of these once potent sites of symbolic claims to sociospatial justice in the city triggered this consideration of how to bring legibility to these powerful places and initiate discourse about the complexities of issues that prompted the unrest.

Spatializing or geocoding violence against racial minorities and police killings of unarmed Black men, women, and children "reveals the lack of

6.1 The northwest corner of Florence and Normandie Avenues, Los Angeles, California, October 1993. *Source*: Joel Sternfeld.

innocence in the landscape," as artist Josh Begley (2016) suggests in his media work *Officer Involved*, which collates locations of police brutality in images taken from the "neutral" gaze of Google Earth and Street View.[3] The Equal Justice Initiative (2017) released a report of the "terror lynchings" that took place in the US between 1880 and 1940 to advocate for marking these sites (see also *New York Times* 2015). In the case of the LA uprisings, we can similarly ask whether and how urban designers and policymakers might physically and fairly recognize histories of resistance to violence and inequality where they occurred. The fact that many of the sites hardest hit by the unrest were the result of looting or arson rather than obvious activism complicates this question, but, as Itagaki (2016) argues, we might alternatively consider these acts as part of broader political claims on the state.

Pulling from Foucault's notions of an oppositional "counter-memory"—a resistance against official versions of historical continuity—scholar Erika Doss introduces the "counter-memorial," which "ideally encourages public agency and articulates the complexities of modern history" (2010, 256) rather than the traditional "symbolic memorial" (2002, 73), which typically promotes healing through abstracted forms and metaphorical references. A hybrid program that activates particular sites significant to the unrest and provides equity of access and inclusion might address pressing environmental needs and improvements while offering platforms for continued debate and negotiation.

In parallel, landscape theorist Elizabeth Meyer takes on the issue of contaminated industrial landscapes and landscape architects' too-prompt instinct to mitigate without a critical interpretation of the processes of production and consumption that contributed to the site's "disturbed" condition. Meyer's opposition to disguising or masking the "uncertainty and risk" associated with disturbed sites as "places of anxiety and discomfort" is actually quite relevant for socially contested urban sites. She states, "Witnesses who encounter landscapes of disturbance, doubt, uncertainty, and beauty in their everyday experiences . . . might be bewildered, moved to wonder and recentered. . . . What might happen if that experience of beauty within risk caused a collectivity of individuals to act differently in their everyday lives? We might truly know what the cultural agency of landscape could be" (Meyer 2007, 82). While we might argue that these South LA sites lack *beauty*, this same form of "recentering" or "destabilizing" the limits of our comfortable expectations (while carefully avoiding risks of retraumatization), may provoke us to think more critically about the social, cultural, political, and economic processes that impact the built world around us— and who it includes or oppresses. This may, in turn, stimulate public discourse and *reckoning*, as well as heighten human compassion.

NOW

Most of the affected sites exist in areas that continue to suffer from disinvestment, environmental burdens, and lack of quality public space (Wolch, Wilson, and Fehrenbach 2005; Ong et al. 2017; on vacancies since uprisings, see Reyes and Jennings 2017). We might thus question: For such cultural landscapes, how do we follow the utilitarian mandate of addressing dire needs while asking the public to think critically about their past and future (rather than perpetuate cultural amnesia or appeal to the common insistence on forgetful "healing")?

One primary challenge of such a physical intervention is how to respond to the vast magnitude of people and property impacted by the uprising and its effects in the context of South Los Angeles' dramatic demographic shifts. While Los Angeles initially embarked on ambitious plans to address the physical damage caused by the unrest, as well as the injustices particularly affecting the Black communities of South Central Los Angeles, most institutional efforts fell short of projected aims. Examples include Rebuild L.A., an initiative instigated by Mayor Tom Bradley and Governor Pete Wilson; the federal Empowerment Zone; and the L.A. Revitalization Zone (Sides 2012c). Areas of moderate success included liquor store abatement, although South Los Angeles continues to have a higher proportion of liquor stores than other city neighborhoods (Sides 2012b; see also Park 2004 and Sloan 2012). While it is easy to dwell on the city's failures in physical rebuilding, planning, and policy (largely related to its inability to incentivize investors to areas "perceived to be rife with crime and prone to riots" [Sides 2012c]), authors, including Robert Gottlieb focus on the unrest as a stimulus for social movements that target housing and transportation inequities and gang intervention "[becoming] the basis for a reconstituted Progressive L.A." (Gottlieb et al. 2006, 68). Intended to provide an alternate vision of a city long characterized by dystopic narratives, this sense of positive social transformation is indeed palpable in some once-marginalized districts, yet with repercussions like gentrification and displacement (Sides 2012c; on investment and gentrification in LA, see, for example, Sonksen 2017).

The transforming population of South Los Angeles has contributed to a shift in perceptions about the area. A historically Black area, it is now predominantly Latinx. In his book *Post-Ghetto*, historian Josh Sides (2012a) argues, "The Latin Americanization of South Los Angeles was an economically advantageous development," as the population has a high labor force participation rate and thus purchasing power. He concludes, "If the demographic trends of the past two decades continue . . . [by 2020] there may no longer remain any visible legacies of the riots of 1992. One might find instead an extraordinarily diverse and highly integrated community of Californians for whom the anger, despair and violence of 1992 seem as antiquated as the days of Jim Crow."[4]

Thus, one might question the relevance of interpreting an event that did not have a direct or immediate impact on the shifting populations that now reside in the area (even though 51 percent of those arrested during the unrest were Latinx and 38 percent were Black). It begs the question of whether the lack of visible legacies is a positive reflection of a city moving away from a shameful past or whether some tangible reflection, particularly in the form of truly public space, might be a productive reminder to consistently evaluate conditions for spatial justice.

Along the Vermont Avenue corridor, neighborhoods like Vermont Knolls, Manchester Square, Harvard Park, and Vermont Square are still largely African American and are majority low-income.[5] These areas continue to be affected by high foreclosure rates and an abundance of liquor stores (*Los Angeles Times* 2014). Quality of environment and access to park or recreational space, as well as nutritional food options and other basic retail needs, are extremely limited, so efforts to mitigate such conditions could be deemed as positive opportunities (Park, Watson, and Galloway-Gilliam 2008). At the same time, marking sites critical to histories of oppression and resistance to stimulate conversation about the city's progress in addressing social and environmental inequities has the opportunity to lead to a more just public realm.

JUST URBAN DESIGN

In the weeks after the uprisings, the then major LA gangs—the Crips and the Bloods—formed a historic truce and generated a proposal for the reconstruction of the city. Called "Give Us the Hammer and Nails, We Will Rebuild the City," the proposal recommended job-generating opportunities, small business financing options, educational, healthcare, and social service funding and policy, police reforms, and physical infrastructure upgrades—including retrofitting burned buildings and lots, upgrading streetscapes, sanitation, lighting, and improving and developing programming at parks and recreation centers (Gangresearch.net. n.d.). The comprehensive plan sent to Mayor Bradley aimed to mitigate poverty, racism, and gang violence. Despite its reasonable cost, the proposal was generally ignored. Sociologist Melvin Oliver and his coauthors suggested a similarly comprehensive plan styled after the Works Progress Administration (WPA) initiatives during the Great Depression, with an emphasis on job creation and infrastructure. They noted, "Only when South Central Los Angeles is perceived as a public space that is economically vibrant and socially attractive will the promise of this multicultural community be fulfilled. Thus far, private-sector actions and federal-government programs and proposals have done nothing to bring us nearer to reaching this goal" (Oliver, Johnson, and Farrell 1993, 135).

Rather than serve exclusively as a critique of cultural amnesia and ceaseless cycles of structural violence, reinstating publicness, where it was forcibly claimed by symbolic acts, might be one element of a just urban design. Through design inquiry and urban design pedagogy, the primary task became how to conceive of ways to reinstate the flashpoints of the rebellion—specifically the intersections of Florence and Normandie, and Vermont and Manchester Avenues—as discursive arenas for public debate, negotiation of identities, new forms of collectivity, and persistent spaces of disruption and resistance to the notion that the state is "the only legitimate source of citizenship rights, meanings and practices" (Holston 1998, 157). By focusing on two intersections, my students contended with both the memory of rebellion against institutional powers and the everyday practices and appropriations of space on these sites today—as a smaller-scale form of insurgency. Both objectives are particularly relevant now with the increasing rise of organized civil society and civic mobilizations, where city inhabitants assert new forms of citizenship that destabilize the old.

FLORENCE AND NORMANDIE

A ubiquitous example of a Los Angeles intersection in a marginalized neighborhood, Florence and Normandie, hosts a liquor store, an auto repair shop, and a gas station (the still-standing Tom's Liquor has become the symbolic reminder of the events that occurred in 1992). It is a tall task to consider this intersection as a memory infrastructure that reflects on the violence that occurred there; the legacies of oppression, trauma, and tragedy that led to the eruption; and the collective claiming of space on April 29, 1992, while addressing the urban needs and dreams of the communities that exist there today. My graduate design-research studio challenged students to contemplate one or many of these considerations as a way to begin changing the conversation around urban design, cultural memory, and spatial justice.

This intersection prompted response to decades of helicopter surveillance and the detached gaze of news helicopters capturing a version of the events taking place there in 1992. Giving the intersection aerial legibility, particularly for police surveillance that still hovers over large swaths of LA—a marking made as a reminder of what can occur in reaction to state-sanctioned oppression and brutality—entered the discussion. Yet, clearly, this has little direct impact on the communities that continue to suffer from the perpetuation of these systems. Thus, the intersection—as the initial and catalytic flashpoint—also inspired an evaluation of how the street was "claimed" on April 29, 1992. For instance, by sinking vehicular circulation, one proposal reappropriates the street as a public arena—as it operated on that fateful day. The proposed sectional change interrupts the relentless gridded streets that define the area's homogenous flatlands and co-opts elevation—a vantage typically afforded in LA's landscapes of privilege among the hills and by the ocean (figure 6.2). The intersection thus becomes visible—as an "X"—from above and below, breaking down the street grid in both plan and section and forcing the driver and pedestrian off the path of habitual movement. At the same time, pedestrians are visibly lacking along both commercial streets because of disinvestment manifest in vacant storefronts and the lack of shade or any sort of appeal to one's sense of safety and comfort. Recognizing the lack of human occupation of the street except for the weekend churchgoers

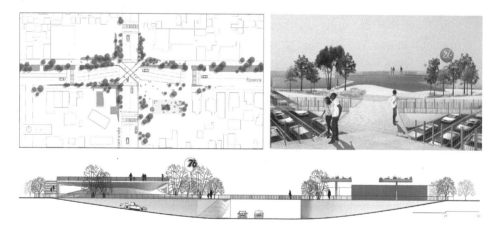

6.2 Sinking vehicular circulation to reclaim the site as the domain of the people. Its aerial imageability is intended to reference decades of overhead surveillance as well as helicopter journalism on April 29, 1992. *Source*: Jonathan Froines.

attending the sixteen storefront churches that exist along this half-mile stretch of Florence Avenue, the proposal additionally exaggerates their frontages (figure 6.3). These "churchyards" introduce an undulation to the street that slows traffic and narrows Florence Avenue from seven to four lanes. The churchyards provide amenities as shaded spaces for parishioners and the general public and thicken the pedestrian domain of the now uninviting intersection and street.

The lack of shade as a symbol of disinvestment and neglect (see Bloch 2019) is made even more flagrant by the cell tower next to Tom's Liquor that is poorly disguised as a tree on this otherwise barren corridor. As a communication infrastructure, its looming vertical presence might also be

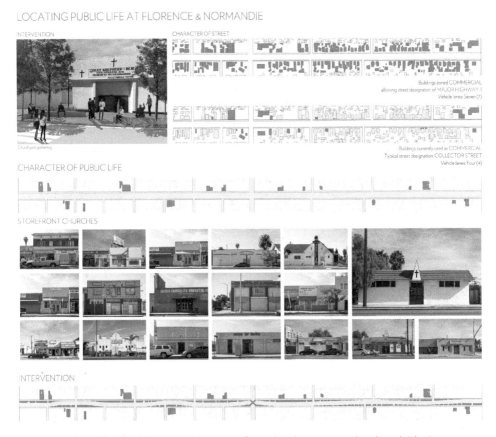

6.3 The thickened frontages of the storefront churches create "churchyards" by introducing an undulation to the street that breaks the grid, slows traffic, and narrows Florence Avenue. *Source*: Jonathan Froines.

reconceived as a beacon for new forms of communicative or media activism and organizing. For instance, one proposal started with four potential scenarios for the intersection, each cued by the presence of Tom's Liquor and the cell tower as communications infrastructure and one of the only "trees" along either Florence or Normandie Avenues. The scenarios introduced a "memorial ecology," programming aimed at overcoming the digital divide, a stage for public debate, and improved access to fresh and healthful food and transit. The composite scheme, pictured both as an everyday space and a space of event or rupture (figure 6.4), aims to bring together

6.4 Composite scheme, pictured both as an everyday space and a space of events, brings together many of the aims of the individual scenarios. *Source*: Yao Yao.

these multiple goals and restore the site as a public space for performative appropriation. These hybrid infrastructures thus not only contain symbolic content evoking memories of historical claims to space and justice, but they also respond to today's compounded injustices by providing spaces for educational attainment, community health, and mutual aid. Many of these designs for a just city likewise aim for the institution of new public rituals that both recognize the tragedies and triumphs of the uprisings and provide opportunities for rallies, demonstrations, and other forms of community organizing to ultimately affect change.

VERMONT AND MANCHESTER

The buildings around the Vermont and Manchester intersection were decimated by fire during the three days of unrest in 1992. Ironically, some who lived in the area considered this clearance an opportunity to replace what had devolved into a landscape of swap meets, auto shops, and vacant lots from its heyday in the 1940s and 1950s when it was "a community of striving and prosperous Black families . . . a community of Black-owned businesses and world-class entertainment" (Sides 2012a, see also Santa Cruz and Schwenke 2014). Yet, despite numerous plans to redevelop the area, two massive lots scorched in the uprising remain vacant today, increasing perceptions of blight, abandonment, and neglect. Modest acts of insurgent citizenship have reappropriated these symbolic spaces—particularly forms of informal entrepreneurship that line the chain-link fence and scaffolding (figure 6.5). On April 29, 2015 (twenty-three years from the day the Rodney King verdict was handed down), ground was broken to transform these vacancies into the $200 million Vermont Entertainment Village—a flashy outdoor mall seemingly unresponsive to the immediate community. Renderings of the project picture a white clientele and stores such as Gucci, Chanel, Armani, Abercrombie and Fitch, and the Hard Rock Café (Sassony Group, "Vermont Entertainment Village"). But construction did not proceed, and the county finally seized the property by eminent domain in 2017, something the local residents had wanted for decades.[6] This site thus offers the opportunity to imagine multiple ways to achieve a just urban design.

Many proposals attempted to design and enhance the fencing to increase the small-scale economic opportunities it provided as an informal "swap

6.5 Informal vending along the fence of 8500 block of Vermont Avenue, 2015. *Source:* Alison Hirsch.

meet." Others sought larger-scale economic opportunities and more comprehensive access to basic amenities sorely lacking in this area. The discovery of "ethnic edges" or places of historic transcultural conflict along the Vermont Avenue corridor (from Koreatown to South Los Angeles—a transect that cuts through many of the areas most affected by the events of 1992) inspired a proposed intervention at these edges at three intersections including Vermont and Manchester. The proposal (figure 6.6) introduced multiple programs situated in thickened edges to create hybrid spaces for renewed forms of social interaction. These spaces not only enforce some accepted landscape architecture norms but also tackle questions of collective memory, spaces of conflict and resistance, and the needs of the current population—in this case, quality recreational and community gathering space that subtly enhances economic opportunity and provides a platform for new forms of occupation.

Other proposals used urban policies as design tools to reclaim the site. In contrast to the Vermont Entertainment Village proposal, they proposed community anchors to catalyze design and placemaking within public and private spaces to respond to residents' retail, service, and recreation needs and desires. Precedents underpinning their study included architect Teddy Cruz's "Living Rooms at the Border"—a proposal for iterative modular programs that respond to the largely Mexican population in San Ysidro,

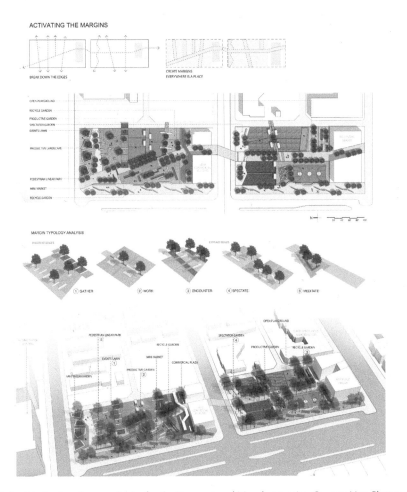

6.6 "Activating the margins"—for the Vermont and Manchester site. *Source*: Nan Cheng.

a San Diego suburb north of the US/Mexico border, conducted in collaboration with community development agency Casa Familiar (Estudio Teddy Cruz n.d.). Cruz's proposal presents the possibility of "neighborhood-driven equitable urban development," with Casa Familiar acting as the mediating agency between the municipality, a microfinancing institution, and locals investing in the site. One student team likewise developed a plan for financing to ultimately create long-term community control. While the city would ideally purchase the land from its owner/developer, the Sassony Group, and a mediating agent—similar to Casa Familiar—would ensure its future, the students recognized the decades of resistance by the developer and proposed a Community Benefits Agreement (CBA) between the Sassony Group and a combination of local nonprofits. The CBA includes tax credits and other subsidies and would work in partnership with community-based microfinancing agencies to offer microcredits to small businesses and organizations to initiate projects onsite.

Finally, directly addressing the question of memory through the treatment of this site as a cultural landscape offered a possible path toward community healing. For instance, one proposal took an archaeological approach to the site's renewal (figure 6.7). Aerial images of these scorched blocks just after the unrest show still-standing walls defining vacuous spaces open to the sky. Restoring the spatial diversity of these footprints while integrating what evidence still exists from the 1930s structures that burned in 1992 recognizes this cultural landscape as one that evolved

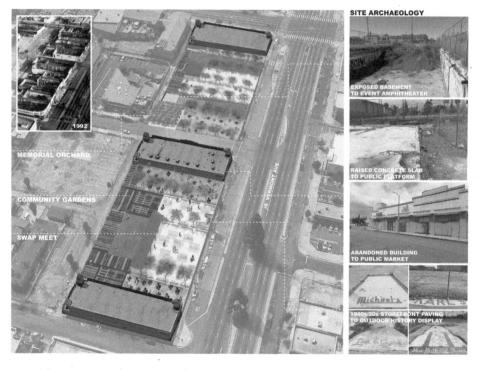

6.7 Vermont and Manchester from a thriving commercial site to the spatial voids that remained in 1992 to a multiuse public space reminiscent of the past while providing investment and amenities for the future. *Source*: Jade Orr and Rachel Ison.

from the premier shopping district of southwest Los Angeles, with Charleston's Department Store, J. J. Newberry Co., M & V Market, and F. W. Woolworth Co., to the "proud product of dozens of ethnic hands" in 1992, consisting of forty-two businesses including two large swap meets. The proposed transformation of this site, which has become a symbol of institutional abandonment and neglect, into a diverse park with memorial space and local retail, recognizes the unequal distribution of public green space across Los Angeles (Wolch, Wilson, and Fehrenbach 2005; Park, Watson, and Galloway-Gilliam 2008) while simultaneously restoring the site's commercial vibrancy.

CONCLUSION: LOOKING FORWARD

The speculative design process aspired to create discursive places where, in the words of geographer Ash Amin (2002), "engagement with strangers in a common activity disrupts easy labelling of the stranger as enemy and initiates new attachments. They are moments of cultural destabilization, offering individuals the chance to break out of fixed relations and fixed notions, and through this, to learn to become different through new patterns of social interaction." Yet, while elements of the ideas above might challenge conventional expectations of urban landscape design and planning, the proposals remain relatively tentative in their efforts to destabilize and recenter the public into new patterns of social interaction. They largely sustain the frameworks of state and market institutions that ultimately provoked the uprisings, while only some include new policies and programs for transferring (and restoring) power to local citizens. Yet, this exercise in *designing* the commons or an enhanced public sphere in spaces of historic conflict highlights an obvious tension—as these spaces can never be truly designed by the professional designer or planner without the voices, stories, experiences, and leadership of those that live in their daily reality. However, the hope is that such proposals and the questions that prompt them begin to change the conversation about urban design to how we might prioritize justice and reconciliation through the agency of cultural memory and find the truths the city has to tell—bringing them to the surface as a form of collective cultural reckoning. Histories of struggle, resistance, and claims to space, justice, and forms of liberation must not be erased or buried under the rhetoric of incivility and criminality. Instead, they can contribute to the process of restorative truth-telling and confronting the continued challenges of racial inequality today and provide pathways to community healing, so essential to people and places who have suffered from generations of oppression and violence.

On May 2, 1992, after three days of uproarious unrest, thousands of citizens from all over the city armed themselves with brooms and shovels to clean up the charred ruins of South Central Los Angeles. While the urgency of the unrest could not be swept away by this collective act, the common effort was the first symbolic performance of hope. Yet, hope for meaningful change was largely thwarted until perhaps 2020, during the protests in the wake of George Floyd's killing, when demands for change were made not in the neighborhoods still scarred from years of disinvestment and neglect, but in neighborhoods of white wealth and privilege, including Beverly Hills, Santa Monica, and Hollywood. Instead, in South Los Angeles, residents and organizers held a cleanup as a "peaceful protest" to signal that change can come from within (Brown 2020).[7]

These symbolic acts of resistance, hope, and change are memorials in and of themselves. Whether a just urban design comes in to facilitate these claims to space and rights, expressions of anger and hope, and celebrations of life, culture, and love for one's community is an essential question to ask today and is integral to the path for restorative justice. Cities across the world are being transformed into spaces of resistance; the hope is that designers and planners support, enable, and enforce the perpetuation and renewal of public space and work to dismantle the systems that perpetuate spatial injustice.

NOTES

1. Wick (2019) quotes UCLA African American Studies professor Brenda Stevenson, who addresses the word *riot* and USC law professor Jody Armour, who reminds us that even though the video of Rodney King being beaten was so pervasive and infuriating, the Black and Brown communities of L.A. did not immediately take to the streets but waited for the verdict, assuming justice would be served.

2. Sturken (1997) notes that what was edited out of the footage of the events of Florence and Normandie were the heroic actions of four Black strangers who saw what was happening on TV and came out to Denny's aid.

3. See also: Collective Punishment n.d.

4. Since Sides (2012a) references 2020, it is worth acknowledging that while South L.A. is much more diverse now, anger and despair are still recognizable and palpable in the area following the isolation and economic collapse from the global pandemic, as well as a reckoning over racial justice following the killing of George Floyd, and the conviction and sentencing of Minneapolis police officer, Derek Chauvin.

5. These neighborhood designations are coming from "Mapping L.A. Neighborhoods" (*Los Angeles Times* n.d.), which is based on the 2000 census.

6. Ground was broken in October 2020 on the Vermont Manchester Transit Priority Project, which will transform the two blocks into the SEED School of LA County, the state's first public boarding high school targeting at-risk youth from the area, as well as 180 units of affordable housing, Metro Job and Innovation Center, and community-serving retail stores. See: https://thesource.metro.net/2020/10/21/metro-county-of-l-a-and-seed-foundation-hold-groundbreaking-for-seed-school-of-l-a-county-in-south-los-angeles/ (accessed December 28, 2020).

7. Three years earlier, on April 29, 2017, organizers staged Future Fest as a rally, march, and arts festival recognizing the twenty-fifth anniversary of the uprisings.

REFERENCES

Amin, A. (2002). "Ethnicity and the Multicultural City," *Report for the Department of Transport, Local Government and the Regions and the ESRC Cities Initiative,* January 2002.

Begley, J. (2016). "Officer Involved." Intercept, accessed August 17, 2016. https://theintercept.co/officer-involved/.

Bloch, S. (2019). "Shade." *Places Journal.* https://placesjournal.org/article/shade-an-urban-design-mandate/?cn-reloaded=1.

Brown, K. (2020). "South L.A. Still Bears the Scars of 1992. One Resident Held an Event to Beautify It." *Los Angeles Times,* June 7, 2020. https://www.latimes.com/california/story/2020-06-07/south-l-a-devastated-by-previous-rioting-resident-holds-cleanup/.

Chandler, J., Glick Kudler, A., and Barragan, B., (2020). "Mapping the 1992 LA Uprising," *Curbed Los Angeles,* May 1, 2020. https://la.curbed.com/maps/1992-los-angeles-riots-rodney-king-map.

Collective Punishment (website). (n.d.) "Collective Punishment: Mob Violence, Riots and Pogroms against African American Communities (1824–1974), Interactive Map." Accessed August 17, 2016. https://collectivepunishment.wordpress.com.

Gangresearch.net. (n.d.). "Crips' and Bloods' Plan for the Reconstruction of Los Angeles." Accessed January 7, 2015. http://gangresearch.net/GangResearch/Policy/cripsbloodsplan.html.

Davis, M. (1990). *City of Quartz: Excavating the Future in Los Angeles*. London: Verso.

Dear, M. (2003). "The Los Angeles School of Urbanism: An Intellectual History." *Urban Geography* 24 (6): 493–509.

Dear, M., and Flusty, S. (1998). "Postmodern Urbanism." *Annals of the Association of American Geographers* 88 (1): 50–72.

Doss, E. (2002). "Death, Art and Memory in the Public Sphere: The Visual and Material Culture of Grief in Contemporary America." *Mortality* 7 (1): 63–82.

Doss, E. (2010). *Memorial Mania: Public Feeling in America*. Chicago, University of Chicago Press.

Equal Justice Initiative. (2017). *Lynching in America: Confronting the Legacy of Racial Terror*. Montgomery, AL: Equal Justice Initiative. http://eji.org/reports/lynching-in -america.

Estudio Teddy Cruz. (n.d.) "Designing Political and Economic Process." Vimeo, accessed June 10, 2015. https://vimeo.com/16778067.

Gottlieb, R., Freer, R., Vallianatos, M., and Dreier, P. (2006). *The Next Los Angeles: The Struggle for a Livable City*. Los Angeles: University of California Press.

Holston, J. (1998). "Spaces of Insurgent Citizenship." In Holston, J. (ed.) *Cities and Citizenship*. Durham, NC: Duke University Press, 155–173.

Itagaki, L. M. (2016). *Civil Racism: The 1992 Los Angeles Rebellion and the Crisis of Racial Burnout*. Minneapolis: University of Minnesota Press.

Lee, Jr., B. (2020). "America's Cities Were Designed to Oppress." *Bloomberg CityLab*, June 3, 2020. https://www.bloomberg.com/news/articles/2020-06-03/how-to-design -justice-into-america-s-cities?utm_medium=website&utm_source=archdaily.com.

Lefebvre, H. (1996). *Writings on Cities*. Cambridge, MA: Blackwell.

Los Angeles Times. (n.d.). "Mapping L.A. Neighborhoods." Accessed June 15, 2016. http://maps.latimes.com/neighborhoods/.

Los Angeles Times. (2002). "Charting the Hours of Chaos." December 28, 2002. https://www.latimes.com/archives/la-xpm-2002-apr-29-me-replay29-story.html.

Los Angeles Times. (2014). "Interactive: Foreclosed Properties Still Dragging Down Neighborhoods." June 10, 2014. http://www.latimes.com/business/realestate/la-fi-g -foreclosure-registry-map-20140609-htmlstory.html.

Meyer, E. (2007). "Uncertain Parks: Disturbed Sites, Citizens, and Risk Society." In Czerniak, J., and Hargreaves, G. (eds.). *Large Parks*. New York: Princeton Architectural Press, 59–86.

New York Times. (2015). "Map of 73 Years of Lynchings." February 9, 2015. http:// www.nytimes.com/interactive/2015/02/10/us/map-of-73-years-of-lynching.html.

Oliver, M., Johnson, J., Jr., and Farrell, W., Jr. (1993). "Anatomy of a Rebellion: A Political-Economic Analysis." In Gooding-Williams, R. (ed.). *Reading Rodney King, Reading Urban Uprising*. New York: Routledge, 117–141.

Ong, P., Cheng, A., Pech, C., and Gonzalez, S. (2017). *1992 Revisited: Divergent Paths*. Los Angeles: UCLA Center for Neighborhood Knowledge, Luskin School of Public Affairs.

Park, A., Watson, N., and Galloway-Gilliam, L. (2008). *South Los Angeles Health Equity Scorecard*. Los Angeles: Community Health Councils, Inc.

Park, K. (2004). "Confronting the Liquor Industry in Los Angeles." *International Journal of Sociology and Social Policy* 24 (7–8): 103–136.

Reyes, A. E., and Jennings, A. (2017). "'It Looks Bad. It's Dangerous.' Vacant Lots Dotting South L.A. a Painful Reminder of L.A. Riots." *Los Angeles Times*, April 29, 2017. https://www.latimes.com/local/lanow/la-me-ln-vacant-lots-20170423-story.html.

Santa Cruz, N., and Schwencke, K. (2014). "South Vermont Avenue: L.A. County's 'Death Alley.' " *Los Angeles Times*, January 19, 2014. http://homicide.latimes.com /post/westmont-homicides/.

Sassony Group. "Vermont Entertainment Village." Accessed June 1, 2018. http:// sassonygroup.com/vermont/.

Sides, J. (2012a). "Conclusion: How to Get to Post-Ghetto Los Angeles." In Sides, J. (ed.). *Post-Ghetto: Reimagining South Los Angeles*. Berkeley: University of California, 209–212.

Sides, J. (2012b). "Renewal through Retail? The Impact of Corporate Reinvestment in South Los Angeles." In Sides, J. (ed.). *Post-Ghetto: Reimagining South Los Angeles*. Berkeley: University of California, 33–54.

Sides, J. (2012c). "Twenty Years Later: Legacies of the Los Angeles Riots." *Places*, April 2012. doi:10.22269/120419.

Sloan, D. (2012). "Alcohol Nuisances and Food Deserts: Combating Social Hazards in the South Los Angeles Environment." In Sides, J. (ed.). *Post-Ghetto: Reimagining South Los Angeles*. Berkeley: University of California Press, 93–108.

Soja, E. (1996). "Los Angeles, 1965–1992: From Crisis-Generated Restructuring to Restructuring Generated Crisis." In Scott, A., and Soja, E. (eds.). *The City: Los Angeles and Urban Theory at the End of the 20th Century*. Berkeley: University of California Press, 426–461.

Sonksen, M. (2017). "The History of South Central Los Angeles and Its Struggle with Gentrification." *KCET*, September 13, 2017. https://www.kcet.org/shows/city-rising /the-history-of-south-central-los-angeles-and-its-struggle-with-gentrification.

Sternfeld, J. (1997). *On This Site: Landscape in Memoriam*. San Francisco: Chronicle Books.

Sturken, M. (1997). *Tangled Memories: The Vietnam War, the AIDS Epidemic, and the Politics of Remembering*. Berkeley: University of California Press.

Tice, C. (1992). "Helicopter Journalism." In Hazen, D. (ed.). *Inside the L.A. Riots: What Really Happened and Why It Will Happen Again.* New York: Institute for Alternative Journalism.

Wick, J. (2019). "Essential California: In 1992, Was It a 'Riot,' 'Uprising' or 'Civil Unrest?' " *Los Angeles Times*, May 1, 2019. https://www.latimes.com/newsletters/la-me-ln-essential-california-20190501-story.html.

Wolch, J, Wilson, J. P., and Fehrenbach, J. (2005). "Parks and Park Funding in Los Angeles: An Equity-Mapping Analysis," *Urban Geography* 26 (1): 4–35.

7

AIR AND ARTIFICE
BUREAUCRAT URBAN DESIGNERS
IN HARLEM, 1967

Rebecca Choi

In the summer of 1966, Arthur Drexler, curator of architecture at the Museum of Modern Art (MoMA), wrote a letter to Donald Elliott, a legal advisor to John Lindsay, who was then mayor of New York City. "We believe," wrote Drexler, "that the urgency of urban renewal problems in the United States is now so great that they must be admitted to the area of this Museum's interest in modern architecture" (Drexler 1967). Invoking alarmism and opportunism, the letter set into motion plans for an exhibition funded in large part by the mayor's office. Branded as "an exhibition intended to help the public visualize some changes that architectural planning can offer to improve life in New York City," *The New City: Architecture and Urban Renewal* exhibition opened at MoMA in January 1967 (Drexler 1967). Far from blazing new trails, however, Drexler was noticing currents already swirling in uptown circles. Earlier in 1966, Elliott—a lawyer by trade—had organized a task force on urban design, which brought reputable architects together with businesspeople, lawyers, and philanthropists to manage the city's beautification program (*New York Times* 1966). Notably, the task force produced *The Threatened City: A Report on the Design of the City of New York*, which recommended that the city form a council on urban design. The council's responsibilities would include streamlining the city's development programs. The report's authors claimed that the "knowing designer[s]," or the architects and planners on the urban design council, could improve the city's appearance and physical condition by commissioning concept designs for the entire city (Mayor's Task Force on Urban Design 1967, 32). Such power had not lain in the hands of a single entity in the city since Robert Moses had served as parks commissioner in 1960. This time, the consolidation of power into one committee would result in the flooding of Mayor Lindsay's office with design expertise over the subsequent decade. It was through the chatter surrounding *The Threatened City* that Drexler conceived the museum's role. If the city planned to take areas deemed as "national emergencies," such as Harlem, the South Bronx, and Bedford-Stuyvesant (three working-class, largely minority neighborhoods), as test sites for new design-focused urban renewal plans (42), why not use the museum as a further site to exhibit those ideas?

But what were the city's threats? Were the protests in the streets, especially visible in Harlem at the time, perceived as a new type of threat? As it turns out, Drexler and the museum, the architects who participated in the show, and city officials all wrote frankly about their awareness of demonstrators, protestors, and so-called rioters demanding justice in the neighborhoods. Reflecting on the need to target "problem" areas, or New York City's so-called ghettos, Drexler chose Upper Manhattan—Harlem, to be exact—as the ideal site for design's cleaned-up alternatives because it offered "the greatest possible number of problems" (Drexler 1967). Echoing the rhetoric of *The Threatened City* report, which warned of an "overgrown, over-congested, ill-managed and ill-kempt, usually sullen, sometimes violent" city (Mayor's Task Force on Urban Design 1967, 8), *The New City* exhibition also described New York in the throes of a crisis. Both the exhibit and the report idealized an aesthetic rehabilitation of the city through architecture and urban design.

This chapter offers a close reading of *The Threatened City* report and a proposal, "Housing without Relocation," displayed in *The New City* exhibition. In doing so, I not only show how MoMA, city officials, and architects worked together in their response to racial uprisings, protests, and community activism in Harlem, but I also discuss how design expertise was used to promote private development and elite interests while at the same time enabling architects to build space for themselves within city government.

"Housing Without Relocation" (HwR) highlights the intimate role that architects played in reshaping city governance in the late 1960s. Four of the five architects who made up the HwR team (Richard Weinstein, Jonathan Barnett, Jack Robertson, and Giovanni Pasanella) were also consultants for Mayor Lindsay's earlier mayoral campaign and later served (with the exception of Pasanella) as the founding members of the New York City Department of City Planning Urban Design Group (UDG). The UDG was a team of architects working for the city but who primarily promoted private development projects (Mogilevich 2020). Planting the seeds for the public space privatization and corporate center strategy followed by New York and other US cities in the subsequent decades (Loukaitou-Sideris and Banerjee, 1998) from its inception within the Department of City Planning in 1967, the UDG incentivized development projects that contributed to the financialization and privatization of urban design, creating project plans that relied on private investment. For example, their effort to transform Second Avenue by promoting sidewalk eateries, or their plans to build pedestrian street malls on Forty-Second Street, are among the UDG's well-known strategies that centered on private ownership as a spur for pedestrian consumer culture.

Moreover, the UDG orchestrated the sale of one of the city's first banking-air-rights transactions for the historic Seaport district. At the time, the Seaport district, a former center of shipping trade in the nineteenth century, was at risk of being destroyed by a developer who had plans to clear the site and transfer the air rights above it to build an office tower on another parcel of land. For Weinstein of the UDG, Seaport contained important landmarks and historically relevant brick structures from the 1800s in need of preservation (Weinstein 2000, 91). With the intention of preserving the seaport, Weinstein brought the problem to Donald Elliott, the legal advisor to the mayor, who was able to legalize banking air. In this way, air rights were only "scraped off the blocks" they wanted to protect, thus rendering them impossible to legally demolish (Weinstein 2000, 96). Thus, it was under the guise of preservation that banking air was made into policy. The uniqueness of banking air was its invisibility. For the UDG architects, it was a way of patterning city design by manipulating how and where funds were channeled, air and capital becoming aligned such that this newfound liquidity fundamentally changed the way urban form was shaped.

The link between the UDG and HwR, then, is contextualized retrospectively by the seaport banking air transaction in 1973. However, before the seaport transaction, the members of the UDG began their experimentation with air rights with HwR, a proposal that provided a road map for the eventual invention of "banking air." HwR came about in the context of *The New City* exhibition. Here, the architects experimented with and laid the groundwork for the practice of banking air as a new policy innovation by working with air as the main subject of their portion of this group exhibition. In the sections that follow, I show that the UDG's strategies for urban development did not constitute *just urban design* but were racially motivated. Analysis of the institutional correspondence between MoMA and city officials shows that the museum and the city collaborated to narrate racial differences in the city and then worked to "fix" the so-called problems through tactical innovations (such as banking air) with the goal of maintaining whiteness. By supporting a new experimentation of "racially contingent forms of property and property rights," what legal historian Cheryl Harris (1993, 1714) has called the ideological foundations for "whiteness as property," HwR provides an exemplary case study for how whiteness, like property, is invested in. More specifically, close analysis of HwR demonstrates how architecture involved itself in a new bureaucratic framework of urban design in order to innovate the financialization of an otherwise free natural resource—in this case, air.

HOUSING WITHOUT RELOCATION

Upon entering *The New City* exhibition, visitors were greeted by floor-to-ceiling maps, a large-scale model of Upper Manhattan, and stark black and white plans, diagrams, and photographs on the walls. The content of the show included proposals from architecture schools of three Ivy League universities—Columbia University, Cornell University, and Princeton University—and the Massachusetts Institute of Technology. Projects included waterfront revitalization schemes, adding green spaces, parks, and new zoning measures. Of the four teams, the architects involved in HwR were among the only ones who were also working in the mayor's office in New York City. The Columbia team that developed HwR featured five architects: Jonathan Barnett, Jaquelin T. Robertson, Giovanni Pasanella, Myles Weintraub, and Richard Weinstein, along with structural engineer David Geiger. The idea that the team could call the project "Housing without Relocation" when, in fact, they were demolishing close to seventy-four blocks of Harlem stands in stark contrast to the project's purported aims.

The team's proposal, nicknamed "the vault," was essentially a long tunnel-like structure upon which housing blocks could be built (figure 7.1). In theory, the vault would conceal both the noise and "visual blight" of the trains that ran along the elevated tracks of Park Avenue, a long north-south boulevard running parallel to Central Park. At its northernmost section, the vault cut through east and central Harlem. HwR appeared to solve two problems at once: concealing unsightly infrastructure and building housing on top of it. According to the HWR team, the project focused on what the architects perceived to be wounded. They explained, the project's "use of air rights over the tracks would convert this major source of blight into a new building . . . well-ventilated and brightly lighted." The vault was imagined as a concrete shell on which housing, boosted into the air above

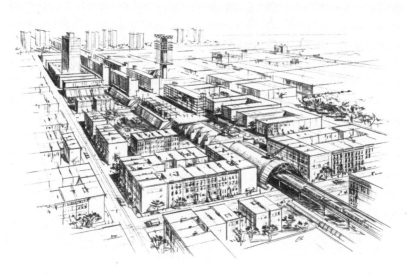

7.1 Page from *The New City: Architecture and Urban Renewal* catalog showing the HwR proposal. *Source*: The Museum of Modern Art/Licensed by SCALA/Art Resource, NY.

Harlem, could be constructed, as if "building on the side of a hill" (*Museum of Modern Art 1967*, 30).

Using the same engineering innovations developed for the construction of dams, the long line, according to the team, was the deliberate product of a machine that could continuously pour concrete along a fixed linear track, rolling on wheels and leaving behind a tunnel structure. The existing tracks, the area's "greatest single source of blight," would be successfully hidden from sight (*Museum of Modern Art 1967*, 30). The intervention appeared to solve two problems simultaneously, hiding the tracks while building new housing.

In plan, the logic of the project presented itself as one that supported the north-south flow of movement along Park Avenue. Built in 1837, the New York and Harlem Railroad that runs along Park Avenue was a relatively porous structure of wrought iron girders and steel beams that allowed plenty of movement for cars and people beneath the tracks. As the diagram suggests, the existing rail line, shown in the plan in figure 7.1, extended past the Harlem River and down Ninety-Seventh Street, beyond HwR's purported site boundaries. Electric bus lines were intended to run alongside the outer sides of the vault at an "intermediate level," where access would be made available from the "streets below and the pedestrian boulevard above." Described as "providing fast and pleasant local transportation," the Columbia team presented an allegory of city life enriched by circulation (*Museum of Modern Art 1967*, 30). It was a rational plan that, when viewed in section, formally resembled Robert Moses's infamous Lower Manhattan Expressway, a template for how to modernize the city through infrastructural development. Viewed in section, the vault read like an assemblage of urban objects: stairs, bridges, tunnels, doors, and successive blocks of apartments.

Yet, when viewed from above, HwR appears to be a linear wall-like project, made up of urban essentials from electric bus lines, housing, and a soundproof shell. Had it been built, it would have separated the white neighborhood to the east from the predominantly Black neighborhood that makes up central Harlem. With only six clear openings for east-west movement along its length, HwR, with its barrel vault train-line tunnel, would bisect two miles of Harlem, cutting off one side from the other. The project both depicts and transforms what was a porous infrastructural zone into a continuous linear tunnel. While the project did propose apartments and townhouses, HwR, not unlike other large-scale urban renewal projects of its time, would create a physical border wall, further deepening the division between east and west Harlem.

HOUSING WITHOUT HARLEM

By 1965, Harlem had emerged as a site of radical resistance and freedom struggle, which was not only visible in the Harlem uprising but also reflected in the sheer number of community coalitions that specifically addressed issues of spatial justice. Organizations included the West Harlem Community Organization and the Community Association of the East Harlem Triangle, which improved neighborhood-serving social resources such as schools, education, and health centers. Among these, the Morningside Renewal Council and the Architect's Renewal Committee in Harlem (ARCH), a Black architecture collective, worked in unison to protest a renewal initiative that would have demolished "20 of the 25.7 acres in West Harlem" (Goldstein 2017, 23–24). It is with some irony, then, that the Columbia team described the areas flanking Park Avenue as "wounded" yet "redeemable" (through their housing proposal) since residents and activists were collectivizing to push for their own vision of Harlem.

In its claim to rethink Harlem through typically modernist design interventions, the HwR team concealed its efforts to recode the problem of the city. Adjacent to the vault itself were the surrounding neighborhoods of east and west Harlem. The vault relied on the air rights above these neighborhoods that made the eight-story vault itself possible. In short, the relationship between the vault and the air that surrounds it would be key to HwR's perceived success. HwR's portrayal of air is illustrated in the section drawing as a vast empty white space (figure 7.2), suggesting how the team of architects abstracted their project as one comprised of buildings rather than a project that gained its form by virtue of its access to, yet ultimate exploitation of, the air above the tracks. Philosopher Luce Irigaray reminds us that part of the uniqueness of air is its invisibility: "Providing us with an invisible dwelling wherever we are or go, air is also a faithful companion for the one who can pay attention to its invisible presence" (Irigaray and Marder 2016, 28–29). Her usage of

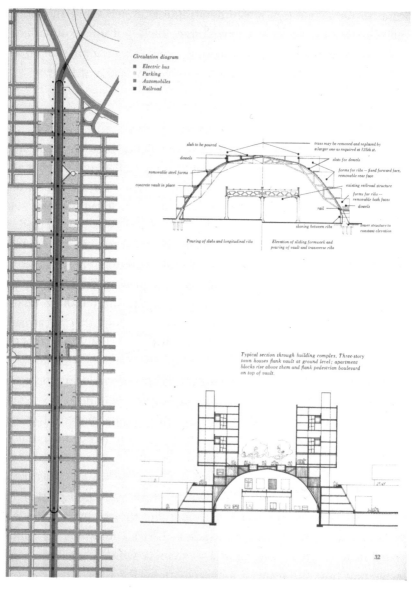

Circulation diagram
■ Electric bus
▫ Parking
■ Automobiles
■ Railroad

Typical section through building complex. Three-story town houses flank vault at ground level; apartment blocks rise above them and flank pedestrian boulevard on top of vault.

7.2 HwR proposal circulation plan diagram on the left, and section drawings on the right. Circulation diagram shows areas for electric buses, automobiles, railroad access, and parking. Section drawings show the architects' strategy for constructing the vault over the railroad tracks, and their vision for building housing above the vault that takes advantage of the air rights around it. *Source*: The Museum of Modern Art/Licensed by SCALA/Art Resource, NY.

the word *pay* helps us to consider, in the context of HwR, the cost of this natural resource.

As the Columbia team explained, "The cost of acquiring the air rights and adjacent property, plus the cost of constructing the vault, is competitive with the total sum that would have to be expended to condemn and clear a comparable land area elsewhere in Harlem" (*Museum of Modern Art 1967*, 30). HwR makes a provocative case for studying the genealogy of banking air rights as an issue of urban design. Banking air included the practice of buying air rights to speculate on their value and manipulate their use for urban design purposes and was ultimately used in development schemes across the city. Through the concept of banking air, the UDG (also the Columbia team), working in city government, expanded notions of property beyond land to "creatively" accumulate air rights and extract value from them. Banking air or accumulating and stockpiling air rights as a speculative maneuver marked the latest tactic of reconsolidating property and power in the hands of the city's white elite. As George Lipsitz (1998, viii) argues, this was "a means of accumulating property and keeping it from others." Banking air, a highly specialized application of air rights transfers, specifically afforded the possibility to organize city space according to a set of creative legal terms dedicated to financializing the air above buildings.

Thus far, the chapter has presented an analysis of HwR and the concept of banking air; but none of these ideas would have been implemented without the help of what I call a "bureaucrat urban designer" who could navigate the sticky terrain of legal and financial procedures and the city's regulatory systems.

DRAWING IN THE DESIGNER

The idea of a bureaucrat urban designer was first put forward in *The Threatened City* report. A new designation for the architect within civil service, the bureaucrat urban designer was provided a privileged position in the city's spatial governance. In the report, an organizational chart visualized this role by placing a group called the Council on Urban Design at the top of a design-making chain, one with the same line of oversight on capital development projects as the mayor (figure 7.3). While the idea of

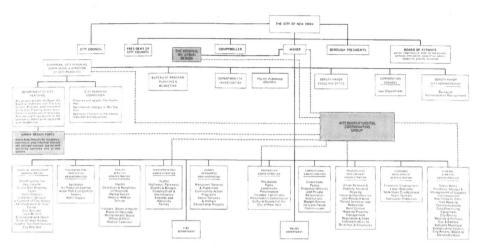

7.3 Organizational chart in *The Threatened City* report shows the Council on Urban Design (toward the top in gray box) placed at the same level of decision-making as the mayor, while the Urban Design Force (left, gray box) occupies its position as part of the city planning department, giving urban designers new powers in municipal governance.

banking air for future sales allowed for the purchase of air to be used at a later time, it was a speculative practice that required predictable demand. Here, the newly established position of the bureaucrat urban designer within city government searched sites to create this demand in the process of rerouting density quotas throughout the city.

On the left side of the chart, a different body from the council was an urban design force that, according to its position within the chart, would exist as its own bureaucratic entity alongside the Department of City Planning (Mayor's Task Force on Urban Design 1967, appendix). Whether positioned as an end node or functioning as the bottleneck of design decisions, the force held unparalleled oversight over decision making. If the proposals in the report were to be accepted, and they eventually were instated, the urban design force would hold the same discretionary power as the mayor, planning commissioner, and planning director and would oversee entire entities of transportation, recreation, housing and development, and public works.

The mayor essentially enacted *The Threatened City* report by passing a motion that instated its proposals; this way, the Council on Urban Design became a part of the bureaucratic structure of the City of New York. This reorganization, or streamlining of the capital development procedures, made actions such as budgeting part of a legible workflow (Mayor's Task Force on Urban Design 1967, appendix). It funneled the design of the city through a pipeline where the urban design council standardized and produced policy to be legalized—preparing program requirements such as building envelopes, floor area ratios, preparing and awarding design contracts, construction contracts, advertising bids, and gaining oversight to rewrite policy around the transfer of air rights. These decisions were previously spread out under the purview of four regulatory agencies: the board of estimates and city council, the city controller, Bureau of the Budget, site selection board and code enforcement agencies.

The council also recommended simplifying decision-making processes that had previously resembled a pinball machine, with all decisions bouncing up and down between the mayor and those beneath. On their own recommendation, all discretion was given to the council itself. The early innovation behind the council's proposal was that bureaucratic processes were made legible, and by making them legible, they became open to manipulation (Scott 1998, 2). In fact, the recommended procedure outlined how the project designer would ultimately control almost every component of new development projects. As architects became incorporated into city planning and development processes through the legislative role of urban designers, their influence on policy became increasingly clear. These bureaucrat designers, located at the point where politics and urban design meet, exemplified a frustrating consolidation between the profession and city governance that paved the way for policy solutions that only further entrenched the status quo.

The charts and diagrams included in the *Threatened City* report tell a clear story of a streamlined planning commission giving greater power and oversight to certain architects. The same architects who produced HwR were also teaching at Columbia, conceiving of HwR, and working in the mayor's office. Across these activities, they developed a form of architectural drawing that was not recognizable through the typical conventions of the architect's drawing toolkit, such as the plan, section, elevation, or even the bird's eye perspective, rendered in a manner that visualized and pointed to a future building scheme. Instead, they diagrammed organizational charts that changed the definition of what constituted an architectural drawing. As an alternative kind of architectural drawing, the charts modeled information rather than visualized future proposals. They provided an example of how to think through urban design as a governmental project concerned with data. Urban design, in this sense, was both a way to model "governmentality"—what Michel Foucault (1979, 20) describes as a set of "institutions, procedures, analysis, and reflections" that make the exercise of a regulatory state power possible—and a way of manipulating it. No longer was the urban designers' role to simply implement policy: now it was to mediate it through techniques that they alone controlled.

The newly established position of the urban designer within the city government would become instrumental in this radical reorientation of architecture's role in city government. In the context of New York City and its newly inaugurated mayor, the architects participating in the HwR, who would later lead the council, invented a new designation: the "credentialed" urban designer, who became the legitimating technocrat and civic instrument in the development of New York (Weinstein 2000, 57). The power of the role that the urban designer would take on in New York City allowed him (most of them were men) to determine urban development projects throughout the city, thus enmeshing urban design's role with an ever-growing speculative economy. Writing in 1975 about the incoming Mayor Beame's administration, *New York Times* architecture critic Paul Goldberger notes that "there was one architect on the staff of the City Planning Commission in 1967. Now there are 48, with 30 more in affiliated agencies. The architects are on the city payroll as urban designers, a new profession that sees its job as providing guidance at the point where politics and architecture meet."

JUST AIR

HwR stands as an example of how an architectural proposal for Harlem was a creative maneuver that demonstrated to developers and public officials how air could be banked. Through architectural and urban visualization methods, it opened the doors for a kind of real estate thinking that was hitherto stuck with the usual constraints of floor area ratio, footprint, and building code regulations. Reconceiving air into a commodity that could be financialized—bought, sold, and speculated on—across the five boroughs, HwR and the UDG advanced the wide-scale implementation of zoning laws through a hypothetical design vision and artifice.

Though the HwR team and the city knew that community organizations were working in Harlem, team members continued with the top-down approach typical of that time (Weinstein 2000). They echoed the rhetoric of the then chair of the city planning commission, who explained that the city had been "trying to do urban renewal without taking down any buildings, moving any people or hurting anybody" (Ballard 1964, as cited in Goldstein 2017). The "empty slums" that Weinstein (2000, 53) suggested tearing down, the very same blocks that the HwR team would propose to "scrape off" (2000, 96) the air rights from, were the same neighborhoods that the Community Association of the East Harlem Triangle and the West Harlem Community Association were trying to turn into social resources that would serve Harlem. In this instance, there was little recourse for a marginalized or segregated population, even as collectively armored as the Community Association of the East Harlem Triangle or the West Harlem Community Association, to survive in a city that used urban design to wield power and circumvent local opinion.

The banking and transfer of air rights was conceived through an architectural proposal, "Housing without Relocation," within the discursive arena of an exhibition, *The New City*, which ultimately laid the groundwork for a tightened way to give developers further control over the conditions and capital accumulation of building. The way in which a relatively discreet architectural proposal projected the creative application of a zoning law exemplifies how policy makers, city managers, architects, and lawyers can perform strategic maneuvers with a natural resource—air—and transform it into a commodity that would be quite literally out of reach of the community groups acting to improve their lives.

The connection between HwR and the UDG raises a number of questions about how a complex latticework of policy, urban governance, and cultural institutions, such as MoMA, interpreted race through the neighborhood of Harlem, a place that the *New City* both identified as a problem site, at the same time as it eradicated any mention of specific "social ills" that it sought to rectify. For those in power, architecture through urban design was cleverly deployed as a corrective agent—not only for the renewal enterprise and the "slums" it created but as a means to contain and silence the range of Black and Puerto Rican voices at the moment when social movements began to resist and refuse these systems operating in Harlem. It is unsurprising, then, that the urban designer, considered the special agent who understood architecture *and* the spatial characteristics of public policy (Weinstein 2000, 56–57), would be the essential weapon against an organizing, and specifically, minority, public. If, in New York, the urban designer did not oversee large renewal projects, highway projects or otherwise, but rather functioned as a policy expert that organized ways to discriminate against minority publics in a fundamentally new way, then rethinking the role of "just design" by revisiting *HwR* and the UDG offers instructive insights into how cities were able to exploit and financialize air rights through architectural means.

REFERENCES

Drexler, A. (1967). Letter to Donald Elliott, June 16, 1966 (1967). Folder 818.23, MoMA Exhibition Records 1960–1969, Museum of Modern Art Archives, New York, NY.

Foucault, M. (1979). "Governmentality." *Ideology & Consciousness* 6: 5–21.

Goldberger, P. (1975). "Urban Design, Entrenched in the City's Bureaucracy, Finds Less Support Under Beame." *New York Times*, January 28, 1975, sec. Archives.

Goldstein, B. (2017). *The Roots of Urban Renaissance: Gentrification and the Struggle over Harlem.* Cambridge, MA: Harvard University Press.

Harris, C. I. (1993). "Whiteness as Property." *Harvard Law Review* 106 (8): 1709–1745.

Irigaray, L., and Marder, M. (2016). *Through Vegetal Being: Two Philosophical Perspectives.* New York: Columbia University Press.

Lipsitz, G. (1998). *The Possessive Investment of Whiteness: How White People Profit from Identity Politics.* Philadelphia: Temple University Press.

Loukaitou-Sideris, A., and Banerjee, T. (1998). *Urban Design Downtown: Poetics and Politics of Form.* Berkeley: University of California Press.

Mayor's Task Force on Urban Design. (1967). *The Threatened City: A Report on the Design of the City of New York.* New York: Mayor's Task Force on Urban Design.

Mogilevich, M. (2020). *The Invention of Public Space: Designing for Inclusion in Lindsay's New York.* Minneapolis: University of Minnesota Press.

Museum of Modern Art. (1967). The New City: Architecture and Urban Renewal Catalog. MoMA Exhibition Records 1960–1969, Museum of Modern Art Archives, New York, NY.

New York Times. (1966). "Lindsay Picks Paley to Head City Beautification Project." April 15, 1966.

Scott, J. C. (1998). *Seeing Like a State: How Certain Schemes to Improve the Human Condition Have Failed*. New Haven, CT: Yale University Press.

Weinstein, R. (2000). *Inside, Outside Oral History Transcript, 1996–1997: Richard S. Weinstein*. University of California, Los Angeles Oral History Program (interviewed by A. B. Smith).

PARTICIPATION AND ORGANIZING
FOR JUST DESIGN

8

BUILDING COMMUNITY CAPACITY AS JUST URBAN DESIGN
LEARNING FROM SEATTLE'S CHINATOWN INTERNATIONAL DISTRICT

Jeffrey Hou

When the first confirmed case of COVID-19 in the United States was reported outside Seattle in early 2020, the fallout was felt more than thirty miles away in the city's Chinatown International District (CID). Although no case was immediately reported, the CID neighborhood experienced a steep decline in business but growing incidents of racially motivated vandalism (Peng 2020), recalling historical episodes of racial discrimination and assaults against the community. As early as the 1860s, violent outbreaks have repeatedly occurred against Chinese immigrants in Seattle. In 1886, an anti-Chinese riot resulted in the expulsion of virtually all the Chinese civilians from the city of Seattle (Crowley 1999). As an ethnic enclave located next to the city's original skid row, the district was itself the result of racially restricted covenants enacted in many parts of Seattle against people of color, a practice that continued into the twentieth century. Despite these barriers, the district thrived and emerged as a multiethnic neighborhood with Chinese, Filipino, and Japanese immigrants sharing the same streets (Chin 2001; Abramson, Manzo, and Hou 2006).

During World War II, the community suffered another blow, as Japanese residents were uprooted and sent to the internment camps in one of the darkest moments in US history. Many Japanese American residents lost their property and never returned to the neighborhood (Takami 1998). Setbacks for the community continued after the war. Similar to other inner-city neighborhoods in the US, the district became the site of major infrastructure projects. In the 1960s, the construction for Interstate 5 bisected the community, demolishing many apartment buildings that had been home to immigrant residents. In 1972, the construction of the Kingdome, a multipurpose stadium, began right next to the district after policymakers rejected the initial site, located in a more affluent neighborhood. This time, however, alarmed by the threats of noise, traffic, and displacement, residents and community members rebelled. Their protests led to the establishment of a special review district to protect the neighborhood's cultural and historical character and the founding of several community development organizations (Chin 2001; Santos 2002).

In the early 2000s, although racially restrictive covenants and forced relocation were considered things of the past, the community faced new challenges, including the encroachment of office and commercial development from downtown, conflicts within the community concerning priorities for local development, and debates over the identity of the neighborhood. The challenges also included limited forms of community engagement and barriers for participation, dialogue, and consensus-building in the local planning and design process (Hou 2014). It was in this context that we, as faculty and students at the University of Washington, Seattle, began a journey of neighborhood design collaboration with local community organizations in the CID. With these continued barriers and disparities in mind, we made community capacity-building a focus of our work.

This chapter is presented as a retrospective of this two-decades-long work (2002 to 2021), focusing on how community capacity-building can address the challenges of just urban design in a community faced with longstanding biases and barriers. The narrative is written from the perspective of my multiple roles as an instructor of service-learning design studios, a member of many standing committees and task forces in the community, a pro bono consultant on community-initiated projects, and a member of friends' groups for park projects. The materials presented in this chapter draw from my engagement in meetings, workshops, and other community events and activities as a participant, organizer, committee member, and instructor. The observations and reflections are based on my interactions, including formal interviews and conversations, with community members and staff of neighborhood organizations and city departments during this extended period of time.

COMMUNITY CAPACITY-BUILDING

As US cities face the recent racial upheavals, there have been growing reflections on the built-environment professions for being complicit with "racism by design" through zoning and other planning practices (Agyeman 2020) and for being associated historically with serving the privileged (Abendroth and Bell 2016). With this as the context, how can urban design reverse its role and instead serve as a tool for equity and justice in society? Besides dismantling structural barriers and addressing the need for diversity and inclusion, it is also important for urban design to contribute to building community capacity to address longstanding social and institutional barriers as well as disparities of power and resources. But what does capacity-building entail in planning and design practice? How can community capacity bring about just urban design?

The literature in community development, education, and community health offers many definitions of *community capacity*. Dennis Poole (1997, 163) defines community capacity as "the characteristics of communities that enable them to plan, develop, implement, and maintain effective community programs." Steve Skinner (1997, 1–2) characterizes community capacity-building as "development work that strengthens the ability of community organizations and groups to build their structure, systems, people and skills so that they are better able to define and achieve their objectives." Building on the literature on social capital, Thomas Beckley and colleagues (2008, 60–61) define *community capacity* as "the collective ability of a group (the community) to combine various forms of capital within institutional and relational contexts to produce desired results or outcomes."

Specific types or domains of community capacity have been a focus in the literature. Ronald Labonte and Glenn Laverack (2001), for instance, present nine capacity-building domains, each acting as individual building blocks: community participation, leadership, organizational structure, resource mobilization (the ability of a community to mobilize resources

both from within and beyond itself), external linkages, problem assessment, project management, critical assessment, and outside agents. Similarly, Selma Liberato and colleagues (2011) identify nine domains for
assessing community capacity-building: learning opportunities and skills
development, resource mobilization, partnership/linkages/networking,
leadership, participatory decision making, assets-based approach, sense of
community, communication, and development pathway. Natalie Mountjoy and colleagues (2014) propose five primary types of capital-based
capacity: human capital, social capital, organizational capital, economic
capital, and natural capital. In a similar vein, Robert Chaskin (2001, 318)
suggests that community capacity resides in the community's individuals, formal organizations, and the networks that tie them "to each other
and to the broader systems of which they are a part."

Community capacity has been associated with many benefits. Through
a multicase study of citizen planning academies, programs that seek to
build knowledge, skills, networks, norms, and trust for citizens to be
engaged in urban planning, Lynn Mandarano (2015, 174) finds that the
model of public outreach and education programming can lead to "improvements in individual human and social capitals that translate into effective community engagement measured as actions taken by participants to
improve community conditions." Capacity-building and the formation of
social capital are seen as important in achieving more effective, sustained,
and democratic participatory processes at the local level (Docherty, Goodlad, and Paddison 2001) and in meeting community needs (Flora and
Flora 2007; Green and Haines 2008). Capacity-building has been recognized for serving a variety of purposes—improving responses to climate
change (Archer and Dodman 2015); as a prerequisite for neighborhood
regeneration (Banks and Shenton 2001); urban policy, regeneration, and
social development worldwide (Craig 2007); and for health and education (Beckley et al. 2008).

While capacity-building is broadly considered valuable (Simmons,
Reynolds, and Swinburn 2011), the concept also has its share of criticisms.
For instance, Peter Shirlow and Brendan Murtagh (2004, 59) suggest that
capacity-building is often seen as expecting people lacking in resources
"to pull themselves up by their collective bootstraps." Capacity-building
can also be seen as shifting the responsibility of the government to the

community or civil society (Shirlow and Murtagh 2004). It has been criticized for building on a deficit model of communities that "fails to engage properly with their own skills, knowledge, and interests" (Chaskin 2001, 335) and assuming communities as "empty buckets that need to be filled with human and social capital and capacities for collective action" (Fallov 2010, 795). Furthermore, capacity-building has been seen as obscuring "structural reasons for poverty and inequality" (Chaskin 2001, 335). To address these concerns, Chaskin (2001, 295) suggests the need to leverage existing assets and resources within a community to "solve collective problems and improve or maintain the well-being of a given community."

As evident above, the capacity-building processes are complex, expansive, and nuanced. Keeping track of all the associated domains and parameters can be a challenge in adopting a capacity-building approach to urban design. In the following, I take a cue from a question posed by Beckley and colleagues (2008, 56) in their research: "The capacity to do what?" I will focus on three areas of our work in Seattle's Chinatown International District: *capacity to participate, capacity to organize,* and *capacity to collaborate.* Short of a longitudinal analysis, I will focus on capacity outcomes as a way of assessing community capacity-building.

CAPACITY TO PARTICIPATE

As a liberal West Coast city, Seattle is known for its abundance of community processes under what Carmen Sirianni (2007) describes as an ambitious and successful policy design for collaborative planning. But when I began working in the CID in 2002, I was taken aback by practices that did not consider the culture of the immigrant community. Most community meetings at the time consisted of one or more formal presentations followed by audience response. A few vocal individuals would almost always dominate the discussion. It was hard to gauge how the information was received by most of the audience—let alone know how representative the audience was. Later, as the city began a planning process to increase density in South Downtown (including CID), there were many more community meetings, sometimes with top city officials and even the mayor present at the meetings, but surprisingly without language interpretation for the immigrant residents.

In 2002, I was invited by the InterIm Community Development Association (ICDA), based in the CID, to run a design studio in conjunction with an urban design master plan project they were leading. Through the initial meetings, I realized right away the complexity of the neighborhood, including its diverse demographics, multiple cultural identities, and entrenched local politics, as we met with each of the community organizations and their staff and volunteers to solicit their feedback. Specifically, the community was divided on many fronts, including different perspectives on local economic development, territorial boundaries, and development priorities (Abramson, Manzo, and Hou 2006). Because of these differences, the master plan project was stalled for months.

Learning from our experience in the earlier meetings, it occurred to me that a better way to go about community engagement and to build capacity was to initially focus on smaller-scale projects with a limited scope. These smaller-scale projects would provide us with opportunities to work with specific organizations with a subset of stakeholders on focused issues and to build community capacity for them. This approach became an outcome of the urban design master plan project—a series of pilot projects to improve the neighborhood and to recognize its diverse cultural identities. Some of these projects became the focus of our subsequent design studios, as well as projects that involved student interns and me on a pro bono basis. In each of the subsequent projects, we first worked with our partner organization(s) to define the focus, scope, and approach for the project. Based on the nature of the project and the intended audience, we then experimented with appropriate participatory design techniques and methods of engagement.

PHOTOVOICE AND "DESIGN AS SECOND LANGUAGE"

Maynard Avenue Green Street was one of the first focused projects we worked on. In this project, we used the "photovoice" technique to interview the local residents and stakeholders who were primarily older adults (Hou 2005). The technique provided an opportunity for the participants to convey to us what they considered welcoming and unwelcoming aspects of the neighborhood. We then translated the results into a streetscape design that was implemented in 2009. In 2005, we worked on a new project to explore opportunities for creating more community open spaces to address increasing density. During the studio process, we were invited to work with Wilderness Inner-City Leadership Development (WILD), a neighborhood youth leadership program, to explore intergenerational uses of open space through a design workshop. Together with the youths (who also taught a weekly English as a second language class for older adults in the neighborhood), we developed a course lesson/ design game called Design as Second Language (Hou 2013) (see figure 8.1). Through this game, older adults worked alongside high school students to design a park.

"DESIGN BUFFET" AND EVERYDAY ENGAGEMENT

In 2007, we were invited by the WILD coordinator to work with community stakeholders to develop the initial studies and concepts for renovating the International Children's Park, which faced disrepair and

8.1 Using cut-out photos with bilingual labels, residents developed their design of a neighborhood park. *Source*: Jeffrey Hou.

public safety challenges. We worked again with youths to engage older adults who often accompanied their grandchildren to the park. This time around, we developed a new design game called Design Buffet to further leverage the everyday skills and knowledge of the community stakeholders, young and old (Hou 2013). In 2008, in a project to plan for the expansion of Hing Hay Park, we infused participatory design activities with an ongoing free meal program so that the residents could participate within their comfort zones, together with their peers. In other projects, including Street Carts Studio (2010) and Park Here (2012), students interviewed and sometimes shadowed storeowners to better understand their everyday business activities. In almost all projects, we used a community open house format to present our design proposals to the community so they could join us at their convenience and engage with the designers directly.

Through these forms of engagement, which were new to the community at the time, we were able to develop more informed concepts for park and streetscape design based on inputs from the community stakeholders. Today, even without our direct involvement in many community initiatives, these methods of engagement have continued. Community engagement activities in the CID are now often combined with community events, including festivals and alley parties. Design projects frequently involve multiple and more focused gatherings with targeted audiences in addition to the required public meetings. A wider range of activities is designed for direct and active engagement with the community stakeholders. These practices, performed by community organizations, sometimes in collaboration with professional firms, represent the capacity outcomes in community participation.

CAPACITY TO ORGANIZE

Developing more engaging methods of participation was not the sole focus of our work. From my earlier work in environmental activism, I learned that organizational capacity was just as important as the participatory processes (Kinoshita and Hou 2001). With this understanding, we tried whenever we could to partner with and even build organizations in the community. Over the years, we have worked with at least a dozen partners on projects in the CID. They ranged from community development corporations to government agencies. Some have even become longtime collaborators.

After the successful collaboration in 2005, we started regularly working with the WILD program. Building on the outcome of the workshop to activate a park, the youths adopted a project to organize a pilot night market in the CID. Starting with a survey to gauge the support from local businesses, followed by an analysis of possible neighborhood sites, and a visit to the Richmond Night Market (the largest summer night market in the region), the youths successfully organized a pilot night market in Hing Hay Park in summer 2006 (Hou 2010, 2011) (see figure 8.2). The responsibility of sustaining the event fell on the local business chamber the following year. Since then, the annual event has grown exponentially in size and popularity, bringing thousands of visitors to the district every year. Besides the longevity of the event, many of the youths have also stayed involved in the district either as volunteers or as full-time staff working for community organizations after they have completed college. Several WILD staff and interns have further become important organizers in the community.

8.2 Programmed activities at the pilot CID night market in 2006 featuring games for children and adults. *Source*: Jeffrey Hou.

In 2008, with an environmental justice grant from the US Environmental Protection Agency, the Seattle Chinatown International District Preservation and Development Authority (SCIDpda) (a community-based public development authority founded in 1975) launched a community design and resource center called the IDEA Space.[1] Focusing on business assistance, design, public safety, and real estate development, the center's mission complemented SCIDpda's role as a property developer and manager. Over the years, IDEA Space has become one of our most important partners in the neighborhood. Through IDEA Space, we were able to expand the range of projects and involvement in the community, with the staff responsible for coordinating outreach activities, maintaining regular communication with community stakeholders, and applying for grants to support and implement ideas that emerged from the community process. In its first five years of operation, IDEA Space leveraged over $3 million in investments in neighborhood improvement, engaged over two thousand volunteers, and assisted, served, and/or partnered with over 225 businesses and property owners in CID. It has been instrumental in managing many neighborhood projects, ranging from storefront improvements and alleyway activations to park renovation and expansion. Although the personnel at IDEA Space have turned over through the years, many of them continue to serve in other neighborhood organizations and as staff and allies in city departments.

Newly formed friends' groups have also been important to successful project implementation. The Friends of International Children's Park (FICP) was the first such organization established in the neighborhood to lead the renovation of the park after many years of neglect. FICP was instrumental in running a grassroots campaign and received multiple rounds of Neighborhood Matching Funds from the city to support community outreach and site design. Based on the outcomes of community engagement, the campaign succeeded in getting the project listed in the Parks and Green Spaces Levy, approved by Seattle voters in 2008 to provide funding for park development in underserved neighborhoods. FICP played a critical role in the design process through a design subcommittee composed of both professionals and community stakeholders. Throughout the process, the group also engaged in further fundraising and outreach. After the construction was completed, members of FICP continued their involvement through programming of regular activities and events in the park. The successful renovation of the International Children's Park provided a precedent for forming another friends group, the Friends of Hing Hay Park, to support the park's expansion, a project with even greater complexity involving many more community groups.

The sustaining power of the CID Night Market, the accomplishments of IDEA Space, and the successful operation of the Friends of International Children's Park and the Friends of Hing Hay Park represent the capacity outcomes in community organizing and the expanded organizational capacity within the neighborhood.

CAPACITY TO COLLABORATE

In 2002, when our work first started, the CID community was deeply divided on many issues. There were disagreements over the district's name, with the Chinese community preferring Chinatown while some considered International District to be more inclusive. Disagreements also existed on issues ranging from housing to local economic development, with community development corporations considering affordable housing as a priority while many in the business community favored market-rate development. Community stakeholders or representatives would typically join a meeting more to defend their interests than to engage in dialogue. The agenda of community meetings, already limited in their ability to engage the stakeholders, often got derailed by persistent disagreements over issues unrelated to a project.

As mentioned before, working on projects with limited scope and focus was one way to overcome the divisions. The focused scope of projects helped keep the number and range of stakeholders manageable and their attention engaged with the issues at hand. For Maynard Avenue Green Street, the stakeholders were mainly the nearby residents and adjacent property owners. The International Children's Park also had a clear scope, with public safety and expanding opportunities for children's play as the main focus. Before 2002, the focus of the community development corporations in the district was on housing development. Taking on new park and streetscape projects enabled the lead organizations to develop experience and expertise working on projects in the public realm that required negotiating with more diverse stakeholders and interests.

In 2013, with the help of IDEA Space staff, the neighborhood took on one of the most complex public space projects to date—the expansion of Hing Hay Park. Located in the physical heart of Chinatown and the district, the park, with its Chinese-style pavilion (donated by Taipei city government in 1975), has become a symbol of the district and serves as the site for many festivals and events, including the annual Lunar New Year Festival. Because of its location and Chinese name, many in the Chinese community consider it a Chinatown park. However, before the park was created in the 1970s, the property was the site of restaurants and clubs popular with diverse community members, including early Filipino immigrants. As such, how the park could reflect the neighborhood's rich cultural identities became a design challenge. Public safety was another major issue as residents and stakeholders were concerned that the expanded park would invite more unwanted behaviors and transient populations to the neighborhood, which was already a challenge.

To facilitate community engagement in the design process for the park, a friends' group was formed with representatives from different community organizations, including those representing the Chinese and Filipino communities. I was nominated to serve as the group's cochair alongside a respected elder from the Chinese community. After years of working together on several other projects and serving on the same committees, many group members knew each other. Some even had personal ties across ethnic lines. The time spent over the years through many difficult situations seemed to have helped. Specifically, many seemed to accept that despite the differences of opinions, it was important to be involved to move the project forward. Working with the community, the design team developed a design with a terraced landform as a unifying landscape feature shared by all the Asian cultures in the neighborhood. While some Chinese community members insisted on the park being a Chinatown park, they also agreed that the park should welcome everyone. Through regular meetings, the friends' groups worked with the design team to resolve issues of safety, programming, and cultural representation.

8.3 The expanded Hing Hay Park features an iconic gateway inspired by Asian paper-cutting and folding traditions welcoming visitors into the park. *Source*: Jeffrey Hou.

The expanded park opened in the summer of 2017, and a grand celebration was held in early 2018 after the large gateway was installed (figure 8.3). In the same year, SCIDpda received a small Neighborhood Matching Fund grant to conduct a post-occupancy evaluation study for both the International Children's Park and the Hing Hay Park. Surveys found very favorable perceptions toward the two parks by respondents (64 percent very favorable and 27 percent somewhat favorable for International Children's Park; 64 percent very favorable and 33 percent somewhat favorable for Hing Hay Park) (Hou 2019). Although some community members still dislike the modern aesthetic of the gateway, others have embraced it as a new neighborhood landmark. More significantly, the friends group continued to work on a signage project with help from IDEA Space staff. This time, however, rather than debating over the park's sole identity, members agreed to highlight all the languages representing the neighborhood's diverse cultural groups. The result was lantern-shaped signage that projected an image with the park's name in all the languages spoken in the district. The successful completion of the iconic park and the multicultural signage presented a significant milestone in the community. The process also demonstrated the capacity outcomes in the area of collaboration.

CONCLUSION: COMMUNITY CAPACITY AND JUST URBAN DESIGN

Despite its broad application from community development and climate change to health and education, relatively little has been written on community capacity-building in urban design. For urban design to address disparities and injustice in society and the built environment, it is not enough to focus on the physical design and the built environment alone. We must also address the disparities in terms of power and capacity that have hindered underserved and historically marginalized communities in their ability to engage more meaningfully and effectively in the planning and design processes. This includes the ability to identify and define the issues on their own terms, recognize and utilize their knowledge and skills, and mobilize the resources needed to address the issues and challenges. As seen in the case of Seattle CID, urban design (i.e., the design of spaces in the urban public realm) offers a wide range of opportunities to leverage community assets and build capacity in local communities. By building on skills and knowledge that already exist in the community, urban design can be a powerful way of recognizing the agency and assets of the community. Through the engagement process, community organizers and stakeholders can also develop the experience, confidence, knowledge, and organizational networks needed to launch and sustain their initiatives.

This chapter provides a snapshot of our two-decade work in Seattle's CID, focusing on community capacity building. Through the work of many organizations and individuals in the community, the district's conditions have greatly improved over the years. The once boarded-up buildings, empty lots, and surface parking have since been transformed into affordable and market-rate apartment buildings for new and longtime residents. Newly expanded and renovated parks have replaced underutilized open spaces providing residents with better access to social activities, nature, and opportunities for games and exercises. They also attract visitors and customers to the neighborhood. Starting with preserving the housing stock in the 1970s and the improvement of public realms over the past two decades, the transformation of Seattle's CID offers lessons for other similar communities. Specifically, it shows how community capacity-building could be a key to success and how the capacities to participate, organize, and collaborate could work in tandem with one another.

With the recent wave of violent attacks and racial biases against Asian Americans in US cities during the pandemic, it is even more important to revisit and recognize the roots of the historical disparities and disenfranchisement facing the communities. Building community capacity presents a key to addressing such structural disparities. In the case of Seattle CID, community capacity is also a key to addressing other emerging challenges on the horizon. Like many other inner-city ethnic neighborhoods, CID is experiencing forces of development and gentrification. While the local community development corporations and traditional family associations continue to own a significant portion of the district's properties, newly built and proposed hotels and residential towers could still disrupt the community's physical and social fabric. The rising rents and property taxes already present growing burdens for property owners and businesses. Dealing with these challenges will require the community to wield its capacities in participating, collaborating, and organizing. Already, community organizations have exercised their capacity through organized protests and engagement in the mandated review process, as well as participating in the citywide deliberation on affordable housing. These are also lessons for other communities and urban design professionals. What takes place in urban design can impact not just how built environments are shaped today but also the ability of communities to cope with future challenges that affect their social and economic well-being. By helping to build greater community capacity, urban designers can begin to address the fundamental disparities in our society and make urban design a tool for lasting justice and resilience.

NOTE

1. The name was capitalized as a play on the partial acronym of the district name, Chinatown International District.

REFERENCES

Abendroth, L., and Bell, B. (eds.). (2016). *Public Interest Design Practice Guidebook: SEED Methodology, Case Studies, and Critical Issues*. London: Routledge.

Abramson, D., Manzo, L., and Hou, J. (2006). "From Ethnic Enclave to Multi-ethnic Translocal Community: Constructed Identities and Community Planning in Seattle's 'Chinatown-International District.' " *Journal of Architecture and Planning Research* 23 (4): 341–359.

Archer, D. and Dodman, D. (2015). "Making Capacity Building Critical: Power and Justice in Building Urban Climate Resilience in Indonesia and Thailand." *Urban Climate* 14 (1): 68–78.

Agyeman, J. (2020). "Urban Planning as a Tool of White Supremacy—The Other Lesson from Minneapolis." *Conversation*, July 27, 2020. https://theconversation.com /urban-planning-as-a-tool-of-white-supremacy-the-other-lesson-from-minneapolis -142249.

Banks, S., and Shenton, F. (2001). "Regenerating Neighborhoods: A Critical Look at the Role of Community Capacity." *Local Economy* 16 (4): 286–298.

Beckley, T. M., Martz, Nadeau Solange, D., Wall, E., and Reimer, B. (2008). "Multiple Capacities, Multiple Outcomes: Delving Deeper into the Meaning of Community Capacity." *Journal of Rural and Community Development* 3 (3): 56–75.

Chaskin, R. J. (2001). "Building Community Capacity: A Definitional Framework and Case Studies from a Comprehensive Community Initiative." *Urban Affairs Review* 36 (3): 291–323.

Chin, D. (2001). *Seattle's International District: The Making of a Pan-Asian American Community*. Seattle: International Examiner Press.

Craig, G. (2007). "Community Capacity-Building: Something Old, Something New?" *Critical Social Policy* 27 (3): 335–359.

Crowley, W. (1999). "Anti-Chinese Activism—Seattle." History Link, May 2, 1999. https://www.historylink.org/File/1057.

Docherty, I., Goodlad, R., and Paddison, R. (2001). "Civic Culture, Community and Citizen Participation in Contrasting Neighbourhoods." *Urban Studies* 38: 2225–2250.

Fallov, M. A. (2010). "Community Capacity Building as the Route to Inclusion in Neighborhood Regeneration?" *International Journal of Urban and Regional Research* 34 (4): 789–804.

Flora, C. B., and Flora, J. L. (2007). *Rural Communities: Legacy and Change*. 3rd ed. Boulder, CO: Westview Press.

Green, G. P., and Haines, A. (2008). *Asset Building and Community Development*. 2nd ed. Los Angeles: Sage.

Hou, J. (2005). "Speaking Images: A Case Study of Photovoice Application in Community Design. Paper presented at Visualizing Change: Association of Community Design Conference. New York, March 30–April 1.

Hou, J. (2010). "'Night Market' in Seattle: Community Eventscape and the Reconstruction of Public Space." In Hou, J. (ed.). *Insurgent Public Space: Guerrilla Urbanism and the Remaking of Contemporary Cities*. London: Routledge, 111–122.

Hou, J. (2011). "Differences Matter: Learning to Design in Partnership with Others." In Angotti, T., Doble, C., and Horrigan, P. (eds.). *Service-Learning in Design and Planning: Educating at the Boundaries*. Berkeley, CA: New Village Press, 55–69.

Hou, J. (2013). "Transcultural Participation: Designing with Immigrant Communities in Seattle's International District." In Hou, J. (ed.). *Transcultural Cities: Border Crossing and Placemaking*. New York: Routledge, 222–236.

Hou, J. (2014). "Life before/during/between/after Service-Learning Studios." In Bose, M., et al. (eds.). *Community Matters: Service-Learning and Engaged Design and Planning*. London: Earthscan, 315–333.

Hou, J. (2019). *Post-Occupancy Evaluation of Two Chinatown International District Park: Donnie Chin International Children's Park and Hing Hay Park*. Seattle: Seattle Chinatown International District Preservation and Development Authority.

Kinoshita, I., and Hou, J. (2001). "Organized Participation and Community Capacity-Building: Recent Cases of Organized Community Actions in Taiwan and Japan." *Building Cultural Diversity through Participation: Proceedings of the Third Annual Pacific Rim Participatory Community Design Conference*, Matsu, Taiwan. May 27–June 3, 2001. Taipei: Council for Cultural Affairs, III-29–51.

Labonte, R. and Laverack, G. (2001). "Capacity Building in Health Promotion, Part 1: For Whom? And for What Purpose?" *Critical Public Health* 11 (2): 111–127.

Liberato, S. C., Brimblecombe, J., Ritchie, J., Ferguson, M., and Coveney, J. (2011). "Measuring Capacity Building in Communities: A Review of the Literature." *BMC Public Health* 11: 850.

Mandarano, L. (2015). "Civic Engagement Capacity Building: An Assessment of the Citizen Planning Academy Model of Public Outreach and Education." *Journal of Planning Education and Research* 35 (2): 174–187.

Mountjoy, N. J., Seekamp, E., Davenport, M. A., and Whiles, M. R. (2014). "Identifying Capacity Indicators for Community-Based Natural Resource Management Initiative: Focus Group Results from Conservation Practitioners across Illinois." *Journal of Environmental Planning and Management* 57 (3): 329–348.

Peng, S. (2020). "Smashed Windows and Racist Graffiti: Vandals Target Asian Americans amid Coronavirus." *NBC News*, April 11, 2020. https://www.nbcnews.com/news/asian-america/smashed-windows-racist-graffiti-vandals-target-asian-americans-amid-coronavirus-n1180556.

Poole, D. L. (1997). "Building Community Capacity to Promote Social and Public Health." *Health and Social Work* 22 (3): 163–170.

Santos, B. 2002. *Hum Bows, Not Hot Dogs: Memoirs of a Savvy Asian American Activist.* Seattle: International Examiner Press.

Shirlow, P., and Murtagh, B. (2004). "Capacity-Building, Representation and Intra-community Conflict." *Urban Studies* 41 (1): 57–70.

Simmons, A., Reynolds, R. C., and Swinburn, B. (2011). "Defining Community Capacity Building: Is it Possible?" *Preventive Medicine* 52: 193–199.

Sirianni, C. (2007). "Neighborhood Planning as Collaborative Democratic Design: The Case of Seattle." *Journal of the American Planning Association* 73 (4): 373–387.

Skinner, S. (1997). *Building Community Strengths: A Resource Book on Capacity Building.* London: Community Development Foundation.

Takami, D. A. (1998). *Divided Destiny: A History of Japanese Americans in Seattle.* Seattle: University of Washington Press; Wing Luke Asian Museum.

9

MAKING "PUBLIC SPACE" TRULY PUBLIC

IDENTIFYING AND OVERCOMING BARRIERS TO TRULY INCLUSIVE AND EQUITABLE SPACES

Chelina Odbert

Public space has become a term so deeply embedded in the professional and everyday lexicon that it almost risks seeming banal. In professional settings, its definition points, with matter-of-fact authority, to environments that all people can share. Indeed, UNESCO defines public space as "an area or place that is open and accessible to all peoples, regardless of gender, race, ethnicity, age or socio-economic level" (UNESCO 2017). In reality, though, public space is seldom open and accessible to everyone. In communities across the globe, most public spaces are public in name only. They may be designated as public on maps or listed as public in municipal codes, but the experience of public space for far too many people belies the open and democratic intent present in UNESCO's definition. In contrast, public spaces often exclude populations who stand to benefit most from them: women, the unhoused, the poor, and populations in Black, indigenous, and people of color (BIPOC) communities. Far from the neutral definition posited by UNESCO, *public* is something acted upon, contested, questioned, and subject to change—and all too often exclusionary, inequitable, and unjust.

In my work at Kounkuey Design Initiative (KDI), I consistently encounter three common patterns of public space exclusion when we plan, design, and build public spaces around the world:

1. An array of forces, from subtle social signals to overt rules, that invite some populations and exclude others
2. An unequal distribution of public space resources that renders them inaccessible for many disadvantaged communities
3. A disparity in the quality of public space, which correlates with neighborhood income levels and limits public space use by low-income communities of color

In the chapter that follows, I present the manifold ways public space can be made to exclude and draw from three different KDI projects to discuss how we overcame those barriers. By considering public space projects from Mendoza, Argentina, Los Angeles, and the Eastern Coachella Valley, California, I present strategies to make public spaces more equitable and, thus, cities more just.

THE CHALLENGES: EXCLUSION, UNEQUAL DISTRIBUTION, AND POOR QUALITY

EXCLUSION

While contested dynamics have always been present in public spaces, the events of 2020 brought the fact of exclusion into sharp focus. For example, consider the experience of Chris Cooper, a New Yorker and avid birdwatcher, who took his binoculars and a notepad to watch birds in Central Park one morning in May 2020. With public health officials urging people to avoid indoor spaces because of surging COVID-19 cases, Cooper was doing exactly what he was supposed to do. Cooper is Black, and his Blackness became the subject of public space contestation, culminating in multiple 911 calls to report his presence in the park (Closson 2020). Met with suspicion and fear, Cooper was ultimately accosted and threatened with criminalization by a white woman for simply being in that public space. This episode takes place in countless different ways in other public spaces—with more or less dire outcomes—and captures a poignant reality—not everyone has free and fair access to public space.

Policy, planning, and governance can create their own barriers, employing statutory mechanisms to make public space inaccessible. In some cases, the very materials and tools of landscape architecture and urban design can be turned against accessibility and equity, also creating barriers—with fences, benches, plantings, and paving—that exclude certain members of the public. Police presence, too, can make public spaces feel less safe for Black and Brown people, as the events of 2020 made all too clear.

Women are also routinely and broadly excluded from public space. Around the world, women express feelings of discomfort when in public spaces (Ranade 2007; Gondon, Lieber, and Maillochon 2007). As a 2007 study in Mumbai found, women and girls rarely linger in public spaces. Instead, women tend to use public spaces only when they have a reason to be there or to get from one point to another (Ranade 2007).

By its very definition, public space avails itself to multiple and competing uses—and men tend to predominate in that competition. A study in Kampala, Uganda, found that "children and women face special challenges in accessing open spaces for recreational purposes; football takes up much of the space and is dominated by male adults." Respondents in the same study also underlined the lack of amenities, such as toilets, as an issue for women, the elderly, and those with children. Women were 15 percent less likely to use public spaces as a result (Advocates for Public Spaces 2015, 29).

Men who are part of the LGBTQIA+ community also face exclusionary pressures, including threats—perceived and real—harassment, or violence. Across Europe, for example, a full 50 percent of LGBTQIA+ individuals reported avoiding public spaces because of fear of harassment (European Union Agency for Fundamental Rights 2014).

Whereas some members of the public are kept out of public space by way of insidious, often invisible, pressures, cities tend to be more explicit about their actions to exclude people experiencing homelessness from public spaces. They do this through deliberate acts of design. In a study by the National Recreation and Park Association (2017), for example, 46 percent of parks departments around the US reported using design standards and infrastructure that discourage use by the unhoused. In 2016, when San Francisco put forward a proposal to create a reservation system that would charge residents for access to the popular Dolores Park, the city government used law and economics to create exclusions for the unhoused to public space (Woolf and Wong 2016).

UNEQUAL DISTRIBUTION

Even if cities and communities could suddenly make existing public spaces universally accessible to all members of the public, there would still remain this stubborn fact: distribution of public spaces is not equal. As data makes plain, cities do not allocate public space resources equitably. And, in an expected pattern, communities that lack public spaces also include high concentrations of those groups who are less welcome in public spaces: low-income communities of color (Dahmann et al. 2010).

That this pattern is so entrenched and consistent across geographic, cultural, and political contexts is no coincidence. Not simply a byproduct of policies that failed to consider public space equity, this injustice is most often the result of deliberate actions that have historically marginalized low-income communities of color, including patently racist land-use policies, neoliberal governance, and inadequate political representation by marginalized communities (Rothstein 2017).

Many present-day policies continue to exacerbate public space inequity. In the US alone, this inequality has risen in almost every metropolitan area since 1980 (Glaeser, Resseger, and Tobio, 2009). In Los Angeles, for example, where over half of the city residents live in neighborhoods that are classified as park-poor, 82 percent of residents lacking access to public space live in low-income communities of color (Placeworks 2016). This pattern is not limited to major American cities. Around the globe, municipalities show similar trends and statistics. Even in rural communities, in the US and abroad, where land is abundant and less costly than in dense urban centers, public space seems to be an amenity of the affluent (Dahmann et al. 2010).

QUALITATIVE DISPARITY

Those public spaces that do exist in low-income communities of color rarely match the quality, programming, and amenities of those in higher-income neighborhoods. The images of public space that most immediately spring to mind in the popular imagination—strolls in the park, a game of softball, or just a breath of fresh air—do not capture the reality of public space for many people. Walks in the park can be threatening, even dangerous, and the lack of programming can render recreation impossible.

When compared against those in more affluent areas, parks in low-income communities are more often in states of disrepair, have poor quality and availability of amenities and recreational opportunities, and higher-than-average adjacencies to industry and infrastructure, posing public health risks, and making them less accessible for active or passive recreation. In a study that mapped recreational programs in 152 municipalities across Southern California, researchers found that areas with higher population density, lower incomes, and a higher proportion of BIPOC residents had inferior access to public recreational programming (Dahmann et al. 2010). And as Ming Wen and colleagues (2013) demonstrated, if public space is regarded as unsafe or lacking in programs or facilities, its utilization suffers. Even in New York City, where low-income residents have decent spatial access to public space, the fear of crime, environmental toxicity, and park adjacency to industrial uses make access to parks effectively lower in low-income neighborhoods.

Because accessible, high-quality public space promotes mental and physical health, reduces morbidity and mortality, stimulates economic development, builds environmental resilience, and creates social infrastructure vital to our everyday lives, the above three inequities of public space have real and urgent consequences (Braubach et al. 2017; World Health Organization Regional Office for Europe 2017; Klinenberg 2018). The events of 2020—civil uprisings, climate-related risks, and the COVID-19 pandemic—brought these inequities into unavoidable focus. With mandates requiring people to seek shelter at home or keep safely distanced in outdoor areas, the fact that many people lack access to those resources should be recognized for what it is—an urgent public health concern with life-and-death consequences.

LEARNING FROM PRACTICE

To counteract the aforementioned three challenges and carry out the work of creating safe, accessible, equitable, and healthy public spaces for everyone, we need to reconsider how parks and other public spaces are developed, designed, and built. In this section, I draw from three KDI public space projects to discuss how we achieved this.

RETROFITTING PUBLIC SPACE TO EXPAND INCLUSION
IN MENDOZA, ARGENTINA

Because so many public spaces have embedded systems of exclusion, one of the focus areas of KDI's work is to retrofit public spaces to expand inclusivity. In Argentina, where KDI led a planning and design process to set new national standards for public space upgrades in informal settlements, we encountered existing public space infrastructure across the country that worked just fine for most men but failed to deliver for women. Within the informal settlement of La Favorita, in the city of Mendoza, KDI, the World Bank, and the national and municipal governments undertook a process of upgrading a relatively new park at the center of the community. The first time this park was designed, just a decade earlier, the government had failed to solicit input from local residents, so the upgraded park was left underutilized. Those who did use it were almost exclusively men.

When the World Bank commissioned KDI to determine how to move forward from what seemed to be a failed investment, they asked us to pay special attention to the distinct gender imbalance among park users. Our first step was to meet with the women in the community to learn from them what they desired to see in the park and what they perceived as the shortcomings of its original design.

We asked the women to lead KDI, government officials, and other residents (including men) through a discovery process. Working with a group of female resident leaders of varying ages and relationship statuses, we embarked on a week-long process of assessing existing infrastructure through a range of activities. These included group walk audits conducted exclusively by women residents; a "day in the life" mapping exercise, where women leaders were paired with government representatives to allow them to experience and document their daily routes and routines; and, finally, a women-led survey of other residents of all genders to understand popular perceptions about the park and its users.

Through these varied perspectives and collected data points, the answer to the question of "Why doesn't this park work for women?" revealed itself quickly and clearly. The data also showed that the park's problems were already obvious to everyone in La Favorita. For example, the pathways that crisscrossed the park were made of rough, loose stone, making it impossible to push a stroller, walk with a toddler, or wheel a grocery cart through the park, which are mostly activities done by women. Furthermore, the scale of the park was wrong. Covering a full city block, the park was large, which seemed favorable to those people designing it, but its scale left its interior removed from the surrounding sidewalks. This left women visitors vulnerable to sexual harassment, threats, and attacks. Deep in the park, passersby would not notice or hear people in need of help. Park programming had also missed the target. With only one soccer field, a few concrete chess tables, and an attempt at a playground, the park provided places for men to gather and play sports while clearly implying that a woman's place was observing children on the play structure.

The next step was to propose an alternative through a multiphase process carried out in conjunction with a KDI-led design studio at Harvard Graduate School of Design. This process included a workshop where resident women led a decision-making process to prioritize investment and amenities and another creative session where women gave form and aesthetic value to the park through collages and sketches. Students in the studio took these findings as starting points, adding their design and planning expertise to present six concepts to residents and the municipal department. After this feedback, the schemes were finalized and put to the larger community for a vote. The residents of La Favorita selected a new design for the park from the six options produced by the design process they themselves had led. The redesigned park made substantive changes to the existing public space. Hardscaped and lighted pathways now connect market kiosks, a flexible amphitheater, a library grove, a field hockey pitch that can also be used for soccer, and a bus shelter that makes getting to and from the park easier. Vegetation delineates space while ensuring sightlines do not become obscure over time, providing eco-system benefits without compromising safety. The retrofit design changes the park's topography to ensure better connections with the surrounding neighborhoods and provide a range of distinct seating environments that inclusively accommodate couples, individuals, families, or groups of friends (figure 9.1). The new park's construction started in 2021. It will be a better, more usable space not only for women but also for men, the disabled, and sexual and gender minorities. As this and other projects show, places designed to work better for women work better for everyone.

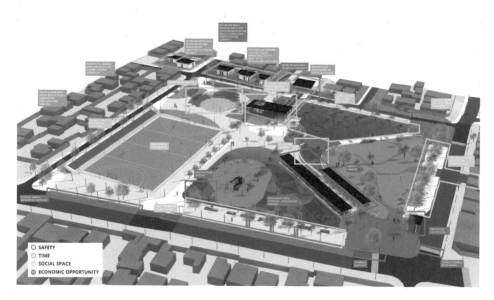

9.1 Plaza Aliar, Mendoza, Argentina. By involving the community as active participants in the planning and design of this public space retrofit, the plaza better and more equitably met the needs of the local community. *Source*: Anne Stack and Mark Bennett.

EXPANDING THE MAP OF PUBLIC SPACE TO IMPROVE ACCESS IN LOS ANGELES

Redesigns and retrofits can make individual public spaces more inclusive, but for most cities, public space inequality exists at a larger scale. As decades of racist policy and real estate pressures pushed low-income communities of color into ever denser urban environments, one of the many deleterious outcomes of that dynamic is the lack of availability of land for new public spaces in these communities.

To design a way around that challenge, KDI looks for places that tend to be written off as waste spaces. In Los Angeles, for example, lower-income neighborhoods across the city tend to include a patchwork of city-owned lots that have long sat vacant. Not only do these empty sites create a stultifying effect on a neighborhood's economic, social, and cultural landscape, they can also become unwanted eyesores. As a matter of policy, when our work started, there was no pathway for any group, individual, or agency to access the vacant land in order to put it to higher and better use. So, under the existing regulatory environment, to occupy those spaces—even if done for the noblest of purposes—would have been a criminal trespassing act.

Seeing opportunities with these vacant sites to address a burden and fill a gap, we partnered with a coalition of policy, advocacy, and development nonprofits to temporarily activate a series of spaces for a weekend at a time to show what was possible and to build the political will and resident base needed to address the issue more permanently. The approach worked; city officials, who supported and visited the temporary installations, immediately saw the need, value, and possibility. Quickly, the Mayor's Office of Budget & Innovation and several Los Angeles City Council members joined our efforts. Together we set out to change municipal policies making it possible for community members to access these lots for community use. In 2018, the city council passed a resolution allowing residents to temporarily adopt a series of city-owned vacant lots. This became what is now known as the Adopt-A-Lot program, which provides a legal pathway for community groups to adopt a city-owned vacant lot for up to two years and transform it into a public space with any number of varying uses. At the end of that adoption period, residents can opt to make the public space permanent, starting with a near-zero cost for land acquisition and support from a range of possible development partners.

One of the lots adopted in 2019 was in the neighborhood of Watts in South Los Angeles. A group of women, known as Brillante Watts, met while living in the Jordan Downs public housing complex. For several years, these women have advanced their mission of unity by leading resident-driven change initiatives in Watts and providing much-needed recreational programming, such as a weekly walking group composed of residents from the many public housing complexes across Watts. As explained in their Adopt-A-Lot application, while Brillante Watts had "a good thing going with their walking group," they also wished to have a central location for their wider network to meet and share. They spoke of this space as a "missing puzzle piece"—something they could not only shape and call their own but also care for and nurture collectively as a group.

The group adopted a small, triangular lot, a leftover space between the end of a rail line and the beginning of a neighborhood. Through a KDI-led design process and with financial support from the Adopt-a-Lot program, the women created a place to dance and exercise together with a Zumba stage, a "community table" to host informal and formal outdoor meetings, and a series of garden beds to collectively cultivate healthy food (figure 9.2).

Since opening this public space, the group has partnered with neighbors adjacent to the site to care for and maintain it, including painting over preexisting graffiti, watering the plants, and adding other finishes. A philanthropic investor in the program has begun conversations with Brillante Watts about next steps to make the community space a permanent feature in the neighborhood after the adoption period is over. Brillante Watts will gather thoughts from users of the park space over time to understand what works and what can be changed or improved in its design features and programming, and these will inform the design of the permanent park.

9.2 Adopt-A-Lot, Los Angeles, California. In Watts, a Los Angeles neighborhood that lacks adequate access to public space, this program transforms vacant city-owned lots into community-run, neighborhood-based public spaces. *Source*: Kounkuey Design Initiative.

ELEVATING THE QUALITY OF PUBLIC SPACE TO INCREASE USE
IN EASTERN COACHELLA

In many of the communities where we work, community leaders and planners understand that quality public spaces attract users and deliver multiple benefits to the largest audience. For this reason, leaders also want to create more of them. However, budget realities and outmoded design processes often forestall that dream.

The Eastern Coachella Valley, where KDI has been planning, designing, and building a growing network of new public spaces since 2012, faces a host of environmental, economic, and political pressures. Dotted by a series of unincorporated towns that are home to low-income agricultural workers, the valley is central to the country's food supply chains, but it lacks even the most basic municipal services, including public space. Prior to 2010, four of these rural farmworker communities had not a single public space or park within a twenty-mile radius.

The regional parks district had long hoped to bring quality parks to the east valley, similar to those found in the affluent western part of the valley, but because of the tax-based formula for funding the district, the reality of doing so expeditiously was grim. One opportunity appeared, however, when a well-intentioned outside organization with charitable aims offered to build a pocket park on a vacant residential lot in the community of North Shore. Wanting to put an amenity in the community as quickly as possible, the district supported the endeavor. However, the well-wishing group engaged only nominally with the community. Thus, even though the pocket park was the only one for miles around, and there was universal consensus across the community about the need and desire for a public space, the one that was built did not work. Without a shade structure, the park was a health risk to use under the desert's intense sun. Lacking a restroom, it was impractical, often impossible, to spend prolonged periods of time there. And without lighting, the playground was not available after sunset, when open spaces are mostly used in the area because of the hot climate.

When KDI began to work in North Shore, we took a fundamentally different approach to both the design and the funding strategy. First, we proposed a community-driven design process to uncover residents' design and programming priorities. Through that process, we arrived at a very different vision for the park. Second, we considered the location. The pocket park was set on a residential lot with very little setback from adjacent lots. As residents shared with us, the pocket park had been a poor location for multiple reasons: for one, the proximity of adjacent houses made sports activities risky, with out-of-bounds balls landing in backyards or, worse, crashing through windows. Plus, the space was too small to have the things the community really needed and wanted. At the top of their list of priorities was a soccer field and a walking path, and neither of those was feasible on a quarter-acre residential lot. Thus, when residents chose a site for their new park, they selected a parcel adjacent to that same residential neighborhood but on an undeveloped street. The five-acre site was surrounded by hundreds of acres of vacant, undeveloped land, leaving plenty of room for errant balls and/or future park growth.

Next was the question of what to put in the park. Residents had a long list of desired amenities, and through a series of activities coordinated by KDI, they weighed options against space and budget constraints and found consensus around certain elements. For example, residents entered the design process very concerned that youth did not have enough extra-curricular opportunities. Through a design process that included the youth themselves, the park came to include a youth-run bicycle repair shop. Another idea the residents brought to the project addressed economic opportunities. Rather than having a single concession stand in the park, they wanted to have a space for an active marketplace, where multiple vendors could sell healthy hot food and fresh farm products. In this predominantly Latinx community, celebrations and gatherings are an important part of community life, so they all agreed that some sort of a flexible performance space was essential.

When all these programmatic elements came together under the theme of "earth, sea, sky" (a theme developed by residents to reflect the geography's essential attributes), each element was rendered in colors, materials, and forms, strikingly distinct from those found in any park within the district. Vibrant hues, varied topographic mounds, and a range of concrete etchings (adapted from drawings local children had made) came together to compose a park made for, by, and with the residents of North Shore.

But even with this high-quality vision in place, there was still the question of cost. The traditional funding model did not allow for the district to pay for a park of this type, so when KDI approached the parks district, we proposed a two-part funding strategy. First, we offered to contribute a participatory design process free-of-charge to the district by allocating KDI "seed" funding (an internal set-aside of resources that allows KDI to offer catalytic design and planning services at no cost to clients). The district liked the idea and saw it as an opportunity to address the shortcomings of the first park and cultivate more community ownership over the next. Second, we helped the department develop an alternative financing strategy that raised additional philanthropic and government funding that augmented the budget for the North Shore park to one comparable to a park in the west valley.

Designing an amenity- and program-rich park through a robust community-engagement process and increasing the level of investment through creative financing strategies allowed us to deliver the high-quality, culturally reflective park the residents had envisioned and were excited to use. Despite the many challenges too often proffered to justify public space inequity—budget, bureaucracy, and political will—we, together with the community, designed, financed, and built a park that has bolstered the public-health, economic, and civic landscape of a low-income community.

The park has been open since August 2019 (figure 9.3), and much of that time has been under the fog of COVID-19. Nevertheless, within months of the park's opening, a survey of residents showed that the average number of community members' "visits to a park" has more than doubled, and perceptions of community trust and connection have increased significantly.

CONCLUSION: THE TRIPLE WIN FOR PUBLIC SPACE

The three case studies help us articulate three principles, which we follow and use as benchmarks in our work at KDI, partnering with low-income communities around the world.

First, for public spaces to be truly public, we must reconsider who designs them. For far too long, urban spaces in the US have been designed by white, upwardly mobile, able-bodied men. So, it should come as no surprise that these spaces are geared for those end-users whom the

9.3 Nuestro Lugar Park, North Shore, California (Eastern Coachella Valley). Planned and designed in full partnership with the local community, this new park provides public space in a region that had long lacked such space. *Source*: Kounkuey Design Initiative.

designers most closely understood: white, middle-class men. To design public spaces that work for everyone, we must ensure that the diversity of people sitting around the design table reflects the diversity of the communities that public spaces are meant to serve.

Second, for public spaces to be easily accessed in every neighborhood, we need to redefine what they look like and where they can be situated within existing urban landscapes. For too long, land-use decision making has been treated as a top-down process, creating a geography of low-income neighborhoods of color without parks and public space. To introduce new public spaces in neighborhoods that need them the most and in locations where they can best serve the community, we need to think creatively about how to make space public when it is in short supply and to engage the community in decisions about where to position it.

Third, for public spaces to be safe, effective, and functional, they must have a high-quality design, programming, and maintenance. To do this, we need to expand the way they are designed and financed, rethinking municipal budgets to capture public spaces as the essential civic services they are and tapping into creative funding strategies to augment budgets when necessary.

In conclusion, public spaces are essential for just, inclusive, and resilient communities—just as they are essential for the future of environmental equity, public health equity, and an equitable right to the city. To establish truly equitable and inclusive public space networks, built environment professionals need to consider anew the design and planning processes, site selection parameters, standards of quality, and funding mechanisms, and redesign them when necessary. In doing so, they are sure to encounter considerable constraints. But these constraints can also serve as drivers of innovation and impact. Across different political, geographic, and economic contexts, the urban design profession is being pushed to find alternative modes of delivery that bolster equity, resilience, justice, and inclusive economic opportunity on a timeline that meets the immediacy of the need. For all the sharp divisions and glaring inequities of 2020, this period of global adversity has highlighted, yet again, those things we share in common: our cities, our environments, our wellbeing, and our health. The future of public space must reflect these commonalities, creating just and equitable environments for all.

REFERENCES

Advocates for Public Spaces. (2015). *Informal Places for Active Recreation and Children's Play in Kampala Slums, Uganda*. Kampala, Uganda: Advocates for Public Spaces. https://healthbridge.ca/images/uploads/library/informal-open-spaces-report_final_2.pdf.

Braubach, M., Egorov, A., Mudu, P., Wolf, T., Ward Thompson, C., and Martuzzi, M. (2017). "Neighborhood Characteristics Favorable to Outdoor Physical Activity: Disparities by Socioeconomic and Racial/Ethnic Composition." In Kabisch, N., Korn, H., Stadler, J., and Bonn, A. (eds.). *Nature-Based Solutions to Climate Change Adaptation in Urban Areas*. Cham: Springer. doi:10.1016/j.healthplace.2009.10.009.

Closson, T. (2020). "Amy Cooper Falsely Accused Black Bird-Watcher in 2nd 911 Conversation." *New York Times*, October 14, 2020. https://www.nytimes.com/2020/10/14/nyregion/amy-cooper-false-report-charge.html.

Dahmann, N., Wolch, J., Joassart-Marcelli, P., Reynolds, K., and Jerrett, M. (2010). "The Active 662 City? Disparities in Provision of Urban Public Recreation Resources." *Health and Place* 16 (3): 431–445.

European Union Agency for Fundamental Rights. (2014). *EU LGBT: Survey European Union Lesbian, Gay, Bisexual and Transgender Survey*. Luxembourg: Publications Office of the European Union.

Glaeser, E. L., Resseger, M., and Tobio, K. (2009). "Inequality in Cities." *Journal of Regional Science* 49 (4): 617–646.

Gondon, S., Lieber, M., and Maillochon, F. (2007). "Feeling Unsafe in Public Places: Understanding Women's Fears." *Revue Française de Sociologie* 48 (May): 101–128.

Klinenberg, E. (2018). *Palaces for the People*. New York: Crown.

National Recreation and Park Association. (2017). *Homelessness in Parks: A Summary of Results from an NRPA Membership Survey*. Ashburn, VA: National Recreation and Park Association.

Placeworks. (2016). *Countywide Parks and Recreation Needs Assessment*. Los Angeles: Los Angeles County Department of Parks & Recreation. https://lacountyparkneeds.org/wp-content/uploads/2016/06/FinalReport.pdf.

Ranade, S. (2007). "The Way She Moves: Mapping the Everyday Production of Gender-Space." *Economic and Political Weekly* 42 (17) (April): 1519–1526.

Rothstein, R. (2017). *The Color of Law: A Forgotten History of How Our Government Segregated America*. New York: Liveright Publishing.

UNESCO. (2017). *Inclusion Through Access to Public Space*. Paris: UNESCO. http://www.unesco.org/new/en/social-and-human-sciences/themes/urban-development/migrants-inclusion-in-cities/good-practices/inclusion-through-access-to-public-space/.

Wen, M., Zhang, X., Harris, C. D., Holt, J. B., and Croft, J. B. (2013). "Spatial Disparities in the Distribution of Parks and Green Spaces in the USA." *Annals of Behavioral Medicine* 45 (1): S18–S27.

Woolf, N., and Wong, C. J. (2016). "San Francisco Retracts Program to Pay to Reserve Park's Lawn Areas amid Outrage." *Guardian*, May 24, 2016. https://www.theguardian.com/us-news/2016/may/24/san-francisco-dolores-park-reservation-policy-retracted.

World Health Organization Regional Office for Europe. (2017). *Urban Green Space Interventions and Health*. Copenhagen: WHO.

10

WHOSE CITY?
INVITATIONS AND IMAGINARIES AND THE NEHEMIAH INITIATIVE'S EXAMPLE FOR SEATTLE

Rachel Berney

A public city is one in which communities not only participate in public life but also make decisions about how their built environments evolve. Just urban design supports all communities in their use and enjoyment of everyday spaces. Thus, moving urban design toward a justice framework also supports the creation of the public city. This chapter explores the concepts of "just design" and "public city" through the lenses of two other concepts that directly relate to urban design practice: *invitation* (design approaches and interventions that invite a larger public to participate in the life of the city) and *imaginaries* (the types of spaces and publics that urban designers envision). I demonstrate these concepts through a case study detailing the efforts of the Nehemiah Initiative in Seattle, a collaboration of local Black churches that works to counteract forces of gentrification. The initiative exemplifies a move toward just design and the public city and contributes to changes in invitations and imaginaries.

Seattle has seen tremendous growth and change in the last few decades. Many local communities have felt the pressure of gentrification and the pain of displacement. None have felt this more strongly than Seattle's Central District, historically host to the city's African American community. The district's historic building stock, walkable neighborhoods, and adjacency to downtown have made it especially vulnerable to redevelopment and gentrification. Over 70 percent Black in the 1970s, the Central

District is now a predominantly white community with less than 16 percent Black residents in 2018 (Balk 2015; US Census Bureau 2018).

The financial and social pressures that have created this dramatic change are intense. However, a coalition of local Black churches and their leaders formed the Nehemiah Initiative (the initiative) in the fall of 2018 to address gentrification and displacement in Seattle's Central District. Local church leaders recognize that their congregations are changing. While the churches may not be cash-rich, they hold significant real estate assets in some of the city's most desirable areas. Church leaders believe these assets can be put to good use to retain, attract, and possibly return new and former residents and businesses. They intend to do this by redeveloping church properties to sustain the churches' economic needs and provide housing and commercial opportunities.

The Nehemiah Initiative counters the idea of the city as a crucible of market-based development, gentrification, and displacement. It leverages its impact by seeking grant funding from the city of Seattle and partnering with the University of Washington's College of Built Environments. This combined effort supports redistributive justice, better design and development outcomes for a historically significant but vulnerable community, and for the training of future urban design professionals.

In the chapter that follows, I outline how urban designers can contribute to just design and public cities. I describe invitations and imaginaries and their significance to just design efforts as interpreted through the Nehemiah Initiative. The chapter closes with a discussion about how a focus on redistributive justice can improve design and development outcomes.

MOVING TOWARD JUST DESIGN IN THE PUBLIC CITY

Justice discourses and critiques in planning have multiplied and deepened since the mid-twentieth century. One focus centers on "critical-spatial" justice, which examines how collective resources and services are spatially distributed among city residents (Dadashpoor and Alvandipour 2020, 1 and 6). Intersecting with a call for the equitable redistribution of resources and services across the city fabric is the idea of "just cities," where equality, democracy, and diversity flourish (Fainstein 2010).

Because some social groups have historically borne the brunt of injustice and oppression, calls for a just city recognize a "politics of difference" and the need to correct inequities (Young 1990). To do this, it is vital that urban designers create new "guiding, normative images" that allow us to disrupt our current unjust realities (Friedmann 2000). Disruption counters systemic racism and injustice concretized in our built environments.

In the context of the public city and just design, this chapter focuses on who exercises control over built environment decisions that shape the distribution of resources and services, who are invited to use spaces, and who are envisioned to occupy the spaces that we design. Public space is a collective resource that people share; it is also the primary domain in which urban design conducts its work. Taken together, the following definitions of *just*, *urban*, and *design* suggest shaping the appearance and function of public spaces and the neighborhoods that surround them in a morally right and fair manner.

just: (*adj.*) based on what is morally right and fair (dictionary.com n.d.a)

urban: (*adj.*) in, relating to, or characteristic of a town or city (dictionary.com n.d.b)

design: (*n.*) a plan or drawing produced to show the look and function or workings of a place before it is built or made

design: (*v.*) decide upon the look and functioning of (a place), by making a detailed drawing of it (dictionary.com n.d.c)

I interpret this combined definition as a call to pursue urban design through the lens of justice. Adding *justice* to *urban design* means committing to an ideal and broad change. In the context of the public city, just urban design supports the quality of being public and the ability of each person to be safe, happy, and free in public space. Just urban design and the public city encourage and support participation, access, and inclusion, including the right to appear and assemble (Butler 2015). The public city is a just city.

THE PUBLIC CITY

By envisioning the public city, it is possible to see a city where all people, independent of their individual characteristics, feel safe and welcome;

where multiple publics are recognized and celebrated; where people can individually and collectively engage in the right to the city; where public space and other collective resources are ample, accessible, and available to all; where urban amenities and disamenities are equitably distributed throughout neighborhoods, and where zip codes do not determine how long a person will live. A public city is one where people have options to stay in place when confronted by gentrification and displacement.

The public city allows people to express and engage their right to the city through such actions as the right to appear, assemble, or stay in place. Velásquez Carrillo (2004) defines the right to the city as full participation and belonging, equipped with the capacity to construct one's own life and participate in the equitable development of the city. David Harvey (2009) explains the right to the city as an evolving relationship. The right is a "means" rather than an "end"—an expanding effort through human collaboration, contestation, and negotiation. Harvey (2008) underscores the importance of the right to the city by naming it a human right. Human rights are fundamental rights; they are directly connected to issues of justice in urban design through first-generation rights (such as those connected to free speech) and second-generation rights (such as those affecting socioeconomic status) (Attoh 2011). Such rights can be selectively proffered and withheld in planning and design efforts (Berney 2012). Harvey (2009) also tells us that a right to the city means we can change ourselves by changing the city. And here is where urban design can come in. What better way to bend the arc of justice in the city positively than through a just urban design?

INVITATIONS AND IMAGINARIES IN URBAN DESIGN

Broadly speaking, urban design is the discipline that tends to the arrangement, appearance, and function of the built environment over time. This role contains tremendous political, social, cultural, and economic implications. Urban design as a profession produces formal and designed space, both material and as ideas about space.

Urban designers have a unique role and potential in shaping public space and the public city. This is because they can shape the *invitations* to use space and the *imagined* publics meant to be there. The focus on invitation and imaginary calls attention to the reality that urban design does not do a great job of encouraging multiple publics in public spaces. The loss of public life or "publicness" occurs when certain publics are excluded; it results in a lack of presence, comfort, and safety for many people. In urban design practice, *places* and *people* are frequently "othered," unintentionally or not. The public city is not attainable without inclusion and belonging woven throughout urban design. So, an important question is: How can urban design invite in communities that have been excluded, made to feel threatened, unsafe, or invisible?

INVITATIONS

Urban designer Jan Gehl has repeatedly said that people interact with their built environments based on the invitations their environments extend to them (McCay 2016). Invitations to participate in the city are a large part of what urban design should encourage. They signal opportunities for the public to come in, stay, and recreate in public space. Examples include soft edges, games to play, interactive features, desirable vistas, and comfortable spaces with shade and seating.

Invitations can encourage different types of activities and feelings: *physical* (encouraging activity), *social* and *cultural* (encouraging socializing, seeing friends, people-watching, cultural events), *symbolic belonging* and *feelings of ownership* (being part of creating a space, seeing other people like you, assembling, and protesting). Invitations can also be positive (inviting people), negative (excluding people), or neutral (having no positive or negative effect).

Invitations to participate in public life need to be inclusive and extended to all. But how to broaden the invitation? Half-hearted infrastructure is not enough to persuade people that the invitations extend to them. A city installing bike lanes when a community wants bus service is not an invitation, nor is making plans but not making good on them. When cities support community design and development efforts, rules and processes to gain project funding should be supportive and transparent.

An invitation to participate in public life needs to be inclusive and extended to all publics. We should rethink how we extend invitation through urban design norms and human expectations. Supporting communities to shape spaces and extend the invitation themselves is a positive step. Ensuring that invitation works in both directions through community and designer participation and engagement is another positive step.

One challenge in extending an invitation is breaking down the imaginary—the imagined publics that we think belong in public spaces. In a panel discussion on the art of Black urbanism at the University of Washington in 2019, Seattle artist and creative director Jessica Rycheal (2019) discussed her very presence as a disruptor in public space:

When Black, to show up anywhere is an act of heroism. . . .

Whenever/however a Black person shows up, claims that space, they aren't responsible for others. . . .

Presence as a disruptor . . . world is forced to move around you . . . can be awkward, frustrating, liberating, cathartic.

Jhamel Robinson, organizer of the yearly event BBQ'ing While Black, flips the everyday racism that many people of color experience regularly with a different type of invitation. Responding to the infamous "BBQ Becky," a woman who had called the police on a group of Black people barbequing at a firepit in the park surrounding Lake Merritt, Oakland, he stages an event that invites people to the same park and into a space of inclusion, fun, and food (figure 10.1).

When people have to put themselves out there as a form of self-invitation, they exercise "the right to appear, a bodily demand for a more livable set of lives" (Butler 2015, 24–25). The aforementioned examples show how people create invitations for themselves and help counter existing imaginaries. How can just design hold space open for and directly address a broader range of publicness and presence in public space?

IMAGINARIES

An imaginary represents who we design for—consciously or not. It is who urban designers imagine in a space—the presumed public(s) meant to be there. When we design, we draw from our histories, experiences, and sensibilities. And the imaginary we use is a shorthand for the values, practices, meanings, institutions, laws, and symbols common to us. Without deliberate growth and change, the dominant social group's imaginary, and no one else's, is likely to reflect itself closely in the built environment.

10.1   "A Tribe Called Oakland." Jhamel Robinson, organizer of the BBQ'ing While Black event. *Source*: Michael Short, *San Francisco Chronicle*.

Historically, much of urban design has depended upon a white, male, middle- to upper-class, able-bodied, cis-gendered, progrowth imaginary. As Dianne Harris (2007, 2) argues while discussing other closely related built-environment disciplines: "Plainly stated, architecture and landscape architecture (and the history of both fields) are overwhelming white disciplines/ professions in which the techniques of study and practice—and the questions they leave unasked—frequently render the operations of racism, privilege, and exclusion opaque, or reinforce their invisibility."

Differences can be smoothed over, disappear, or be erased in spaces because we see what we expect—what we usually see. "Issues about race and space can be particularly hard to see because they are completely naturalized within the space we daily inhabit" (Harris 2007, 4). If difference disappears, the dominant imaginary remains one that includes the minimization of difference and fails to help designers and others develop intercultural competency (Hammer 2012). Without difference, we fail to form inclusive understandings of the world around us. And yet, as Harris suggests: "Insofar as the built environment constitutes a primary structure for the performance of everyday life, it must be examined as an active agent in the formation of ideas about race, identity, belonging, exclusion, and minoritization" (Harris 2007, 4).

Ishmael Nuñez (2019) writes that lack of participation and presence, the policing of bodies of color, displacement, and erasure of the histories or place attachments are ubiquitous for people of color in the built environment. He expresses the dissonance between the ideal of democratic public space and the experience of being Black in public space; in his view, current urban design practices erase Black belonging (for more discussion on this topic, see also chapter 14). These experiences occur partly because invitations and imaginaries fail them.

We need multiple imaginaries in urban design to embolden just design and public cities. If we could design for other people's imaginaries, and not only our own, perhaps we could create spaces that work well for everyone. Without new imaginaries, conscious or unconscious ignorance of others' needs, lived experiences, and desires will continue to exacerbate disconnection and lack of belonging.

The sense of place for many people of color is erased by dominant culture discourses on race and space. Yet, considering these "seemingly unavailable worldviews enables the urban designer to engage in truly equitable placemaking for the broader public realm" (McKittrick and Woods 2007, 7). Additionally, George Lipsitz (2007) urges us to privilege a spatial imaginary that prioritizes use value over exchange value, sociability over selfishness, and inclusion over exclusion. These aims are reflected in the efforts of the Nehemiah Initiative in Seattle.

SEATTLE'S NEHEMIAH INITIATIVE

The Nehemiah Initiative creates opportunities for Seattle's Black churches, community, and partners to stimulate redistributive justice in the built environment. The initiative calls for the addition of resources where they are needed and helps retain the ability of people to stay in place and not be displaced from their neighborhoods.

Seattle's Central District is an area that lacks affordable housing and commercial spaces. Nevertheless, it is a highly desirable and walkable urban neighborhood with historic houses, good transit access, and proximity to downtown. While a home for many different communities over time, it is best and most recently known as the hub of the city's African American community, with a thriving culture of Black-owned businesses. But it is also a district shaped by racist policies and exclusion (Born et al. 2021).

While over 70 percent Black in the 1970s (Balk 2015), by the 1990s, the Black population had started leaving the Central District and dispersing south. With policies against housing discrimination gaining a foothold, Black families were no longer confined to one neighborhood, and many departed to pursue other opportunities. As the neighborhood became more integrated, however, property values began to rise, and services directed toward the Black community began to shift south with the population. In 1994, the Central District was one of the first neighborhoods designated as an urban village in Seattle's Comprehensive Plan, which signaled that the city was prepared to invest in the area to support additional density, development, and infrastructure, paving the way toward further gentrification (Born et al. 2021).

While the interplay between gentrification and increased density continues to be debated, especially regarding the benefits for people in need of affordable housing (Manville, Lens, and Monkkonen 2020; Rodriguez-Pose and Storper 2020), it is clear that infrastructure investments increase land values in surrounding areas (Zuk et al. 2018; Chapple and Loukaitou-Sideris 2019; Clute 2019). Reinvestment draws people interested in living and working near new amenities and services.

From 47 percent in 1990 to 16 percent in 2018, Black residents' concentration in the Central District has continued to decline (US Census Bureau 1990; 2018). As the number of high-paying jobs in the tech and other industries has continued to increase in Seattle, housing prices have risen dramatically across the city, including in the Central District, where residential values increased from around $200 per square foot in 2010 to over $400 per square foot in 2018 (Born et al. 2021). Increasing high-income newcomers and development pressure have made it difficult for Black families to retain their hold on aging single-family homes in the neighborhood. Many members of the Black community who left the neighborhood cannot afford to return to live near relatives and friends who remain in the area.

When many Black residents left, local Black churches saw their congregations and tithing shrink. The churches are now under increasing economic pressure to sell their high-value inner-city land, and several have already made the difficult decision to sell and either move south along with their congregations or close their doors permanently. Of the twenty-five Black churches in Seattle, twelve have closed or moved as congregants left or were displaced, pastors retired, and the economics of staying in an increasingly expensive city did not work out.

The Nehemiah Initiative began in 2018 as a conversation between a group of church members, community members, and long-standing community organizers led by Goodwill Missionary Baptist Church's Bishop Garry L. Tyson. They recognized the importance of Black-owned spaces and the potential collective power of the Black-owned churches' landholdings in the neighborhood. The fact that historic Black churches in Seattle and elsewhere may own their properties is a significant opportunity in the struggle for community well-being. The landholdings of some of the largest churches in the area—what the initiative leaders refer to as the "big eight"—include over five hundred thousand square feet in the Central District that, under current zoning, could be developed to provide over seven hundred new housing units (Born et al. 2021). The land collectively is valued at $150 million at the time of this writing.

The initiative focuses on collaborative efforts among the churches to stay in place by leveraging their significant real estate assets for long-term financial security and building a range of housing types and commercial space (Born et al. 2021). Through the initiative's formation, the churches are taking on the role of community designer and developer. In the white-dominated built environment professions, to be an organization focused on preserving, protecting, and building Black space is notable. The initiative is confronting and countering decades of institutionalized racism, including restrictive covenants and redlining in the city's historic African American community. It is doing so by leveraging two forces. The first is an oppositional force—against market dominance and professionals not concerned with the survival of the community. The second is a coopting force—harnessing the power of land ownership, the concerned built-environment professionals, the training of young professionals and laypeople, and the institutional power of the University of Washington (UW). The skills and efforts of diverse professionals and faculty bridge these forces.

In summer 2019, the initiative began a collaboration with the UW's College of Built Environments (CBE), which included a series of studios to map the district, foster community engagement, and develop design and real estate proposals on behalf of the churches. Much of this work has been interdisciplinary, including students from architecture, construction management, landscape architecture, real estate, and urban design and planning, and is supported by several faculty, intercultural communication training, and leadership from the dean's office. These studios also provide a medium to train and support students of color.

The initiative brings to the fore the promise of collective action and transformative design. It supports populations vulnerable to displacement in the Central District by asserting their right to make spatial and political claims and develop according to their vision. This is what Jeff Hou calls placemaking as emancipatory practice (Hou 2020), through which the initiative is building space, expertise, and relationships.

The CBE-initiative interdisciplinary studios that I co-instruct and coordinate have worked with seven institutions across six sites in the last two years. These studios are complemented by others in the College. In the studios, interdisciplinary student teams focus on delivering design, planning, and real estate solutions for Black churches and institutions. One project team worked with the pastor of Ebenezer AME Zion Church, the executive director of Meredith Mathews East Madison Y, and their networks to design a single building that allowed the two entities to pool their resources and make better use of their adjacent lots (figure 10.2).

10.2 Existing Ebenezer AME Zion Church and the Meredith Mathews East Madison Y seen from Twenty-Third Ave. S. *Source*: McKinley Futures Nehemiah Studio Book 2019, 60.

Welcoming people was a high priority in the new building (figure 10.3). Inviting entrances and glass created visual connections between inside and out and enhanced peoples' comfort and visual engagement with the site and the building design. The project sits on a prominent corner along a key avenue in the Central District (figure 10.4). Not only is the design welcoming, but its invitation is also highly visible. Everyone

10.3 Proposed building to house both Ebenezer AME Zion Church and Meredith Mathews East Madison Y. *Source*: McKinley Futures Nehemiah Studio Book 2019, 64.

10.4 Entry plaza on a prominent southwest corner invites street-level activity and gathering. *Source*: McKinley Futures Nehemiah Studio Book 2019, 70.

involved in the process learned from the experience. Clients and community members increased their knowledge about zoning, design, and development proposals. Students learned how to work in service to their clients on complex real-world projects.

This university-community collaboration creates proposals for beautiful, welcoming spaces and encourages a diverse range of people to come in and enjoy them. The collaboration increases student and community knowledge, potentially disrupting the imaginaries of who can become a developer, designer, or planner or who has a grounding in that experience to better engage with a future development team. Working with the initiative and the CBE will allow the community to extend invitations to use its spaces and shape the imagined publics that are meant to be there. Just design, as practiced by the initiative through its partnership with CBE, expands the invitation to the city and shifts the imaginary of who the city is for.

REDISTRIBUTIVE JUSTICE: BETTER DESIGN
AND DEVELOPMENT OUTCOMES

As the example of the Nehemiah Initiative indicates, urban design needs to move forward boldly and develop new collaborations and new practices to "remap the terrain, identify hegemonic and subaltern sites of relationships and, in the process, develop a new and critical cartography of social practices" (Laguerre 1999, 5). These practices must include the design and planning professions in collaboration with community groups and their institutions previously absent from design processes. According to Harris (2007, 2), "If we want to design for diversity, we have to design for opportunity and for increased life chances for everyone."

This is not to say that there are no challenges in advancing such a justice-oriented agenda in urban design. But the time is right—it is actually long overdue. This is true in light of two particular and pressing challenges that have led national headlines in 2020: the advent of COVID-19 and its disproportionate impacts on vulnerable populations and the resurgent activism against police brutality and systemic racism.

Cities have coped with a lack of sufficient and accessible public space for safely distanced recreation during the pandemic. The more successful design interventions toward this end take place in temporary spaces, in locations validated by community engagement, and where the imaginaries of people envisioned as using those spaces are inclusive, and the invitations are clear. In Seattle, the Stay Healthy Streets and Keep Moving Streets programs have created temporary public spaces with clear invitations and guidelines for safe use. According to Seattle Department of Transportation spokesperson Ethan Bergerson, "This health crisis has shown that we must collectively and proactively take steps to create the healthier, safer, happier and more equitable communities that advocates and leaders collectively say we want" (Tolmé 2020).

As the nation's attention focused in 2020 on systemic racism and police brutality, we witnessed protests in person and on computer and TV screens. The rights to appear and peacefully assemble and protest are enshrined in our conception of public space. But public space remains dangerous for any population that is othered. These challenges underscore the importance and need to recognize the struggle for the public city as a difficult but evolving process, one where all people should have the same right to the city.

A just design approach is needed to help shift the invitations and imaginaries that are currently present in urban design and planning practice. Just design supports publicness and spaces that are just and welcoming for all. Innovative collaborations like the one between the initiative and the CBE offer a model for new practices.

The collaboration offers solutions to the challenges based on the combination of church land ownership, community participation, professional skills, and vision in a rapidly growing region and local government and university support toward the goal of providing and preserving housing opportunities for all residents (Born et al. 2021). The initiative plays a significant role in shifting Black churches to addressing gentrification directly. This university-community partnership also supports sharing expertise and training students. Community partners can offer greater efficiency and legitimacy to the development process.

By developing and exploring a broader range of invitations and imaginaries in what they design, urban designers not only can help make peoples' lives better but will also make the public city and its design better. Indeed, to engage in just design is to welcome new theories of change and action into urban designers' work, as exemplified by the collaboration between the Nehemiah Initiative and the UW College of Built Environments.

A focus on expanding invitations and imaginaries supports just design and the public city. By working with and in-service to communities on redistributive justice, urban designers help enhance efficiency, equity, and legitimacy in urban design. They can do so by observing the following principles:

- *Dismantle political and social structures that segregate, seclude, or marginalize.*
- *Focus on public-interest rather than private-interest design.* Through community engagement, public leaders and designers can make *sure* that public expenditures and designs match community needs.
- *Build an urgentiste agenda* (Aquilano 2011). Support design leadership and service that engages with communities as an ally or cocreator; bridge design and activism in local, state, and national politics.
- *Cocreate design work and capacity-building with communities.* Write and draw the underrepresented into plans (Lipsitz 2007). Engage participation and engagement with a critical lens.
- *Allow communities to set the agenda, create the questions, and determine the solutions.*
- *Create better ways of listening and understanding.* Engage in deeper listening, storytelling, and sharing of lived experiences, remembering that invitation needs to work in both directions. Think about place support and place-keeping rather than place-making.
- *Promote local control of land and opportunities to build wealth in communities.* Give communities the power to decide what improvements to prioritize and guide those improvements to create value.
- *Transform the spatial imaginary.* Privilege spatial imaginaries that prioritize use value over exchange value, sociability over selfishness, and inclusion over exclusion (Lipsitz 2007). Use your understanding of the spatial imaginary of othered communities to benefit the community-design process and urban design as a whole (Nuñez 2019).
- *Protect and improve public spaces.* Create opportunities to bring people together to do something communally. Set the stage for chance encounters.

- *Champion diversification of the field by nurturing the careers of underrepresented students and professionals.* The design disciplines are disproportionately white and male. Training more students of color and other underrepresented students will allow communities to work with professionals that better reflect them.
- *Develop evidence-based design work.* It is important to show how we can design in more just ways, especially if advocating for and using public funds.

In conclusion, urban design must grow to meet today's challenges and help provide answers moving forward. The challenges are many and include the COVID-19 pandemic, precarity, rapid change and growth of sociophysical contexts, displacement, informality, and lack of inclusion and justice. Urban design can start addressing the challenges by reimagining and expanding the concepts of invitation and imaginary into developing a just design approach and building public cities.

ACKNOWLEDGMENT

I want to acknowledge the vital work of the Nehemiah Initiative Seattle, led by Donald King, Bishop Garry L. Tyson, and Aaron Fairchild. Their work is available at www.nehemiahinitiativeseattle.org. I also want to acknowledge my colleagues at the University of Washington College of Built Environments working on the NI-CBE collaboration, especially Dean Renée Cheng and Associate Professor Branden Born.

REFERENCES

Aquilino, M. J. (ed.) (2011). *Beyond Shelter: Architecture and Human Dignity.* New York: Metropolis.

Attoh, K. A. (2011). "What Kind of Right is the Right to the City?" *Progress in Human Geography* 35: 669–685.

Balk, G. (2015). "Historically Black Central District Could Be Less than 10% Black in a Decade." *Seattle Times*, May 26, 2015. www.seattletimes.com/seattle-news/data/historically-black-central-district-could-be-less-than-10-black-in-a-decade.

Berney, R. (2012). "Public Space versus Tableau: The Contradiction between the Right to the City and Neoliberal Capital in Bogotá, Colombia." In Samara Roshan, T. R., He, S., and Chen G., *Right to the City in the Global South: Transnational Urban Governance and Socio-Spatial Transformations.* New York: Routledge, 152–170.

Born, B., Berney, R., Baker, O., Jones, M., King, D., and Marcus, D. (2021). "Pushing Back on Displacement: Community-Based Redevelopment through Historically Black Churches." *Societies* 11 (1): 10; https://doi.org/10.3390/soc11010010.

Butler, J. (2015). *Notes toward a Performative Theory of Assembly*. Cambridge, MA: Harvard University Press.

Chapple, K., and Loukaitou-Sideris, A. (2019). *Transit-Oriented Displacement or Community Dividends? Understanding the Effects of Smarter Growth on Communities*. Cambridge, MA: MIT Press.

Clute, E. (2019). "Does Rail Transit Induce Displacement? A Longitudinal Study of 24 US Metro Areas from 2000–2017." MA thesis, University of Washington, Seattle.

Dadashpoor, H., and Alvandipour, N. (2020). "A Genealogy of the Five Schools of Justice in Planning Thought." *Habitat International* 101: 1–15. doi:10.1016/j.habitatint.2020.102189.

Dictionary.com. (n.d.a). s.v. "just (*adj.*)." Accessed December 11, 2020. https://www.dictionary.com/browse/just.

Dictionary.com. (n.d.b). s.v. "urban (*adj.*)." Accessed December 11, 2020. https://www.dictionary.com/browse/urban.

Dictionary.com. (n.d.c). s.v. "design (*n.* and *v.*)." Accessed December 11, 2020. https://www.dictionary.com/browse/design.

Fainstein, S. (2010). *The Just City*. Ithaca, NY: Cornell University Press.

Friedmann, J. (2000). "The Good City: In Defense of Utopian Thinking." *International Journal of Urban and Regional Research* 24 (2): 460–472.

Harris, D. (2007). "Race, Space, and the Destabilization of Practice." *Landscape Journal* 26 (1): 1–7.

Harvey, D. (2008). "The Right to the City." *New Left Review* 2 (53): 23–40.

Harvey, D. (2009). *Social Justice and the City*. Rev. ed. Athens: Georgia University Press.

Hammer, M. R. (2012). "The Intercultural Development Inventory: A New Frontier in Assessment and Development of Intercultural Competence." In Vande Berg, M., Paige, R. M., Lou, K. H. (eds.). *Student Learning Abroad: What Our Students Are Learning, What They're Not, and What We Can Do about It*, Sterling, VA: Stylus Publishing, 115–136.

Hou, J. (2020). "Placemaking as Emancipatory Practice in Asia?" In Karssenberg, H. and Veelders, S. (eds.). *The City at Eye Level Asia*. Amsterdam: STIPO Publishing, 320–325.

Laguerre, M. (1999). *Minoritized Space: An Inquiry into the Spatial Order of Things*. University of California, Berkeley: Institute of Governmental Studies Press.

Lipsitz, G. (2007). "The Racialization of Space and the Spatialization of Race: Theorizing the Hidden Architecture of Landscape." *Landscape Journal* 26 (1):10–23.

Manville, M., Lens, M., and Monkkonen, P. (2020). "Zoning and Affordability: A Reply to Rodríguez-Pose and Storper." *Urban Studies 59* (1): 36–58, doi:10.1177/0042098020910330.

McCay, L. (2016). "How Can Cities Invite Us to a Better 'Public Life'?" Centre for Urban Design and Mental Health," June 22, 2016. https://www.urbandesignmentalhealth .com/blog/how-can-cities-invite-us-to-a-better-public-life.

McKinley Futures Nehemiah Studio (2019). *Building Beloved Community: Envisioning Thriving Futures for Black Churches in Seattle's Central District.* Seattle: University of Washington, College of Built Environments.

McKittrick, K., and Woods, C. (2007). "No One Knows the Mysteries at the Bottom of the Ocean." In McKittrick, K., and Woods, C. (eds.). *Black Geographies and the Politics of Place.* Boston: South End Press, 1–13.

Nuñez Pedraza, I. (2019). "The Black Spatial Imaginary in Urban Design Practice: Lessons for Creating Black-Affirming Public Spaces." MA thesis, University of Washington, Seattle.

Rodríguez-Pose, A. and Storper, M. (2020). "Housing, Urban Growth and Inequalities: The Limits to Deregulation and Upzoning in Reducing Economic and Spatial Inequality." *Urban Studies* 57 (2): 223–248.

Rycheal, J. (2019). "The Art of Black Urbanism." Panel discussion at the University of Washington, February 6, 2019.

Tolmé, P. (2020). "Seattle Expands 'Stay Healthy Streets' Network as Cities Nationwide Create 'Pop-Up' Open Streets Programs." Cascade Bicycle Club, May 6, 2020. https:// cascade.org/blog/2020/05/seattle-expands-%E2%80%9Cstay-healthy-streets%E2%80%9D -network-cities-nationwide-create-%E2%80%9Cpop-%E2%80%9D-open.

US Census Bureau (1990). "Census of Population and Housing: Summary File, 1990." Washington State Geospatial Data Archive. http://wagda.lib.washington.edu /data/type/census/geodb/download.html#stf1census.

US Census Bureau (2018). "ACS 5-Year Estimates Data Profiles—ACS Demographic and Housing Estimates, 2018. American Community Survey." www.census.gov/acs /www/data/data-tables-and-tools/data-profiles.

Velasquez Carrillo, F. (ed.). (2004). *Ciudad e Inclusión. Por el Derecho a la Ciudad.* Bogotá: Fundación Foro Nacional por Colombia.

Young, I. M. (1990). *Justice and the Politics of Difference.* Princeton, NJ: Princeton University Press.

Zuk, M., Bierbaum, A., Chapple, K., Gorska, K., and Loukaitou-Sideris, A. (2018). "Gentrification, Displacement, and the Role of Public Investment." *Journal of Planning Literature* 33 (1): 31–44.

11

DESIGNING JUST RESILIENCE?
INNOVATION AND DISCONTENT IN POST–HURRICANE SANDY NEW YORK

Kian Goh

Design competitions have emerged as a way to envision more resilient cities and regions in the face of climate change. While they often promise tantalizing, idealized visions of safe and prosperous urban futures, their ability to deliver more just and sustainable cities has yet to be established, especially for marginalized communities on the ground in contested sites. This chapter probes the possibilities and constraints posed by the Rebuild by Design initiative in New York City after Hurricane Sandy. Using a theoretical framework of climate justice tuned to the spatial politics of urban design, it asks: To what extent have the post-Sandy resiliency design activities in New York City resulted in more just urban design processes and potentially more just outcomes? It looks at the Rebuild by Design initiative more generally, exploring the specific organization of the initiative and its model of an urban design competition linking private philanthropy and federal funding. It also investigates more closely the events and politics around a particular neighborhood, the Lower East Side in Manhattan, including the individuals, organizations, and designs involved. This mixed-methods study combines semistructured interviews with key informants (including those from Rebuild by Design, community groups, and city and federal government agencies) with analyses of design documents.[1]

This chapter concerns itself not so much on whether Rebuild by Design has delivered on its promises—the answer is mixed depending on how you look at it—but how the innovative organizational processes of the initiative boosted or hindered ongoing struggles for recognition and justice in the city, and the extent to which concepts and concerns of design, a key precept of the initiative, aided such processes. In other words, how does the politics of design contribute to just resilience? This chapter explains how design is part of the contested production of urban climate futures.

HURRICANE SANDY AND REBUILD BY DESIGN

Hurricane Sandy hit the New York region on October 29, 2012. The storm caused at least forty-three deaths and resulted in $19 billion in damages in the city. It was one of the worst disasters in the city's history—the catastrophe bringing into recognition the vulnerability of the metropolitan region to climate change–fueled extreme weather threats and precipitating actions in response. In the wake of Sandy's destruction, several initiatives were launched by city, state, and federal governments and nongovernmental organizations to help the region rebuild and plan for future disasters. One prominent initiative for recovery and rebuilding was Rebuild by Design, a design competition tasked with finding solutions to extreme weather events, sea-level rise, and flooding for the coastal urban region. Launched in June 2013, the competition garnered proposals from ten designer-led multidisciplinary teams. A year later, six winning proposals were announced, each awarded between $20 million and $335 million in federal funds for implementation.

Rebuild by Design involved a fairly unique organizational structure. Launched by the Presidential Hurricane Sandy Rebuilding Task Force, established by President Barack Obama one month after the storm, it was administered by the US Department of Housing and Urban Development (HUD). Support for the initiative involved the Institute for Public Knowledge at New York University, the Municipal Art Society, the Regional Plan Association, and the Van Alen Institute. The Rockefeller Foundation, a private foundation, was the primary funder of the competition phase of the initiative as well as the funder of the organizational entity of Rebuild by Design. Implementation of the winning proposals was secured through the allocation of $930 million in federal Community Development Block Grants—Disaster Recovery (CDBG-DR) funds. Rebuild by Design was also international in scope—with Henk Ovink, former director of Dutch spatial planning and water affairs, as its principal and featuring prominent international design expertise among competing teams—a characteristic of emerging, globally constituted urban environmental planning and design efforts (see Goh 2020a).

Rebuild by Design was hailed for its innovation, combining private philanthropy, public agencies, research and design, global and local partnerships, and a stakeholder-oriented participatory process in a climate change response initiative with federal government oversight. This model of a competition for resilience has since been replicated for the National Disaster Resilience Competition, launched by HUD in 2014, and the Resilient by Design Bay Area Challenge, conducted in 2017. While each of these took cues from the original initiative, none of the other examples have involved, together, the design competition, promise of federal implementation funds, and multilevel management structure behind Rebuild by Design.

DESIGNING (JUST) RESILIENCE

Rebuild by Design is part of emerging initiatives around urban resilience, often understood as the ability of cities to recover from and adapt to the environmental and socioeconomic impacts of climate change. Themes and concepts of resilience have increasingly dominated discussions on climate change preparedness and disaster risk reduction, especially since the adoption of the Hyogo Framework for Action at the UN World Conference on Disaster Reduction in 2005 and the roll-out of initiatives such as the Asian Cities Climate Change Resilience Network (ACCCRN), launched by the Rockefeller Foundation in 2008. The concept now appears across initiatives in global economic development and disaster management, including by organizations such as the US Federal Emergency Management Agency (FEMA), the US Agency for International Development (USAID), the United Kingdom's Department for International Development (DFID), and ICLEI—Local Governments for Sustainability. The 100 Resilient Cities initiative, enacted by the Rockefeller Foundation from

2013 to 2019, helped establish programs on resilience in municipal governments around the world.

But resilience is a contested concept. On the one hand, urban resilience is celebrated as a positive characteristic of people and places to "bounce back" from shocks and stresses. This notion is exemplified in former Rockefeller Foundation president Judith Rodin's book *The Resilience Dividend* (2014). Researchers of urban ecology, urban geography, environmental sciences, planning, design, and engineering (alongside city managers and built environment professionals) share a broad adherence to this idea, even if they may not agree about the specifics of the concept (see Meerow, Newell, and Stults 2016; also Cutter et al. 2013). But the concept of resilience has been increasingly challenged precisely for its vagueness and excessive malleability (Vale 2015) and because it can be used to promote and protect unjust status quo socioeconomic systems (MacKinnon and Derickson 2013; Fainstein 2015; Davoudi et al. 2019; Ranganathan and Bratman 2019). In effect, the concept's vagueness and malleability lend itself to cooptation by those in power and complicity with existing, unjust modes of urban development.

This is a concern when disparate power relationships are not explicitly challenged. Scholars and activists have long brought attention to environmental injustice, how marginalized groups—in the US, largely poor people of color—have suffered disproportionately from environmental harms because of systemic oppressions of race and class (Mohai et al. 2009). Now, in the face of climate change impacts, plans and policies ostensibly for resilience can often result in "green gentrification" or "climate gentrification," when actions taken to improve environmental conditions in vulnerable places lead to the displacement of poorer residents who live there (Checker 2011; Gould and Lewis 2017; Anguelovski et al. 2019).

Among its noteworthy aspects, Rebuild by Design centered *design* in conversations of resilience. *Design* itself is a vague term. Generally considered to be the act of envisioning or creating change based on an objective or plan, the specifics of design vary depending on the field or practice. Researchers and practitioners of urban ecology and the urban built environment have asserted that design plays a role in urban resilience (see, for example, Pickett, Cadenasso, and McGrath 2013). But it remains less well established how, precisely, design processes and practices are related to particular articulations of resilience. Or how, in practice, such designed efforts transcend the noted criticisms of vagueness, cooptation, or complicity that resilience as a concept has invited.

In the years since its launch and the conclusion of the competition stage, critiques of Rebuild by Design have focused on the slowness of the process after the conclusion of the competition phase, the prioritizing and phasing of projects, and the development-oriented nature of the proposals (see, for example, Iskander 2018; DuPuis and Greenberg 2019; Fleming 2019). Yet, it remains a much discussed and modeled initiative for urban interventions around climate change. Can such a model of design for urban resilience be just?

In this chapter, I build on theoretical frameworks developed in my previous writings to inquire specifically about the possibility of designing just resilience. The first framework relates to urban change and climate justice. Climate justice, as a socioecological concept and political rallying cry, coalesced in the decade leading up to the global climate strike in September 2019. In my view, looking at urban change through the lens of climate justice—in particular, its spatial and temporal organization—brings into focus, in simultaneous ways, views of class-based, globalized capital-oriented struggles with those of identity, community-oriented and place-based, and embodied ones (see Goh 2020b). The second framework is on urban design and justice. Looking at the relationship of urban design and urban political-economic processes, as well as ideas about the social production of space and the theoretical object of urban design and planning as public, civil society, I consider just urban design to be characterized as processes, practices, and outcomes that are explicitly public and collective, a "right" to change our urban social relationships and our urban spaces (Goh 2019).

In this chapter, I bring these two frameworks together—climate justice tuned to the spatial politics of urban design.

VIEWPOINTS OF DESIGN AND RESILIENCE

A cursory overview of sentiments around New York resilience initiatives after Hurricane Sandy reveals multifaceted notions of urban design and urban resilience:

- Henk Ovink, principal of Rebuild by Design, holds a view that epitomizes conceptual and practical design thinking. Design, in his view, is an expansive and enveloping process, a way to "step out of your preconceived ideas of how you deal with these things."[2] For him, Rebuild by Design offered such a process in temporal and physical ways.

- Damaris Reyes, a longtime community organizer and participant during the Rebuild by Design community engagement meetings, holds a notion of design that is arguably in line with the prevailing, popular idea. For her, design is primarily about practices around the physical and aesthetic outcomes. "The design itself, people like. What they don't like is what's getting done during what phase," she says, explaining some distinctions in how community participants viewed the implementation plans.[3]

- Amy Chester, manager of Rebuild by Design, takes up a reflexive view of design. She affirms the idea of "design as something that is beautiful . . . bringing aesthetics into the conversation." But, when speaking with some hindsight about the Rebuild by Design effort, she also notes, "Design can be policy . . . the design of policy. . . . Design is the answer to whatever the challenge is."[4]

Such multivalent and still overlapping views of design resonate with the meaning and role of urban design in society: on the one hand, as a professionalized undertaking with lineages of thought and practice as well as an academic field of study; on the other hand, the broad public sentiment about the meaning and value of design in the world and in peoples' lives. These disparate, if not contradictory, notions of design among those with clear stakes in the Rebuild by Design initiative raise the necessity for analytical frameworks that are suitably multiperspectival.

Here, three levels, or spheres, of phenomena make up the context of the problem framing or, in other words, the "sites" of investigation and analysis. The first is *organizational*, regarding the formation and organization of the entity of Rebuild by Design and the competition, the related agencies and institutions, and the implementation protocols. The second is *design-community interactional*, concerning the dynamics of the relationship among competition organizers, design teams, and community groups on the ground. The third is *urban socioecological*, consisting of the interrelated and historically dependent social and ecological relationships characterizing sites like the Lower East Side of Manhattan. The analyses of these three spheres drive the following sections on innovation and discontent.

INNOVATION

In New York, the Lower East Side neighborhood of Manhattan emerged as a focal point of post-Sandy design initiatives and political mobilization. Lower Manhattan was in the news from the start. In the days after Sandy, photographs of the southern tip of Manhattan enveloped in darkness emblazoned the covers of magazines and newspapers, the result of a blackout caused by an explosion during the storm at the Con Edison power plant on 14th Street in Manhattan. The sight of an epicenter of global urban flows in darkness spurred awe and imagination and reinforced the notion of the vulnerability of the city to climate change–fueled disasters.

Not surprisingly, given such focus, the proposal for Lower Manhattan by the team led by Danish architecture firm BIG drew its fair share of attention during the Rebuild by Design competition phase. The design team's proposal artfully hybridized Robert Moses and Jane Jacobs, the devil and angel of New York urban mythology, big infrastructure melded with notions of community (figure 11.1). The designers' visualization of the "BIG U" shows a bright green ribbon of various widths and intensities, depicting landscape and building elements, looping around the tip of a black-and-white photograph of the tip of the island (figure 11.2). The team's proposal envisioned infrastructural walls and landscaped berms, as well as new buildings and recreational spaces to protect against rising seas and storm surges. While the BIG team's initial concept involved a giant "U" along the entire bottom third of Manhattan, their final competition proposal focused on three areas from East 23rd Street along the East River down to the Battery, at the southern tip of the island, comprising neighborhoods including the East Village, the Lower East Side, Chinatown, and the Financial District.

Urban designers are often criticized for not taking into account local community positions and interests. Rebuild by Design, in contrast,

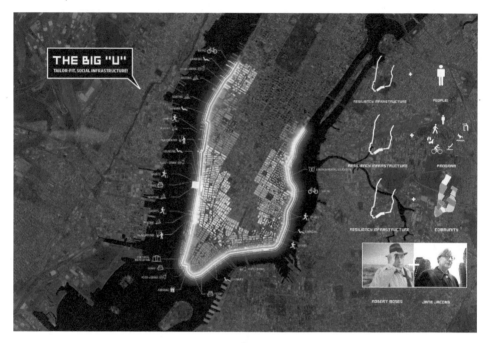

11.1 Plan diagram of the BIG U proposal by the BIG team, merging Robert Moses and Jane Jacobs. *Source*: Rebuild by Design.

11.2 Rendering of the "BIG U" proposal by the BIG team for the south tip of Manhattan. *Source*: Rebuild by Design.

required community engagement among the design teams. Teams had to prove that they had support for their projects from stakeholders to win the award. According to Amy Chester, manager of Rebuild by Design, the primary funders desired it, and so did the managing team. In meetings with groups on the ground during the competition phase, Chester emphasized to the attendees that the design teams would have to demonstrate that their feedback was taken into consideration.[5] The teams internalized this message. Chester notes that every team brought members of the local communities, including mayors, stakeholders, and advocates, to the final presentation meetings. The organizational structure and the stipulations of the competition organizers resulted in more community engagement than one necessarily expects among urban design teams.

These efforts were not in vain. In the Lower East Side, community stakeholders, such as those representing LES Ready!, a coalition of housing rights, community education and health, and legal aid and advocacy organizations, settlement houses, neighborhood councils, and individuals formed in the wake of Hurricane Sandy, by and large, were convinced by the engagement and responsiveness of the BIG team. Damaris Reyes of Good Old Lower East Side (GOLES), a longtime organizer around housing rights for public housing residents, who was appointed as cochair of LES Ready!, recounts how she and other community members were initially skeptical. Two issues, especially, were concerning to her. "We have a history of seeing beautification further exacerbate gentrification," she states. While recognizing that the BIG U project was not necessarily a beautification project, it seemed clear to her that it would increase property values in the area and threaten her community's displacement. Further, it was not immediately evident that anything would get done. She notes, "You know, this is not new anymore, the planning workshops. People have a little bit of planning fatigue. But more than that, you have all these kinds of processes that happen, and they don't always result in anything concrete. So we were, like, why you want my opinion? For what?"[6]

But Reyes and others in the neighborhood were appeased over subsequent meetings. Reyes explains: "I would say they made a commitment to me. I told them I hate that I have to be in this position, but I am going to work with you because it's important, right, for us as a community. But you have to understand that you need to work with me to make sure that nothing that you do there further exacerbates the speculation that the real estate community has in terms of our property. And they said that they would work with me in any way that they could to preserve that integrity. And I believed them." When the team returned with their new designs, it appeared to Reyes that they had indeed heard the residents and incorporated their ideas.[7] The designs featured improved access to the waterfront, wider berms providing open, green space, and low-cost or free recreational infrastructure, reflecting the participants' conveyed preferences. The design team also included a "toolkit" of strategies for maintaining and locating affordable housing and community centers, although these were not developed to the same level of detail as the primary protective infrastructure and park designs (see BIG Team 2014).

Jeremy Siegel, a designer and project leader with the BIG team, for his part has noted how the team approached community engagement as if it were an iterative design process (Ovink and Boeijenga 2018, 221). So by most accounts among the organizers of the competition, the designers, and the community activists, Rebuild by Design conducted a successful, community-engaged design process by the end of the competition phase in mid-2014.

DISCONTENT

The innovative organization behind Rebuild by Design ensured that private philanthropic funds could be used for a design competition for climate change, while federally backed block grant funds, meant primarily for low- and moderate-income communities, could be allocated for implementing the designed proposals. It linked an international competition structure to an existing appropriations structure.

But such an organization also necessitated that the postcompetition implementation work had to be separated from the competition process. CDBG-DR funds are allocated to localities and states. Each of the localities that were part of the winning proposals and awarded funds would then have to initiate their own public review and procurement processes for the projects. Already, shortly following the conclusion of the competition, in the fall of 2014, there was conflict emerging. Community members in the Lower East Side, who had been hit hardest by the storm (and were part of the community engagement meetings with the design team), asserted that they were not being prioritized in the phasing plan for implementation.[8]

The "BIG U," in the implementation phase, was divided into two main parts: (1) the East Side Coastal Resiliency (ESCR) project, from East 23rd Street along the East River down to Montgomery Street, comprising mainly the East River Park and Stuyvesant Cove Park. The ESCR project retains key members of the BIG U design team; and (2) the Lower Manhattan Coastal Resiliency (LMCR) project, from Montgomery Street, just north of the Manhattan Bridge, down around the southern tip of the island to Battery Park City. The LMCR project is further divided into four sections.

In early 2019, another conflict between the project team and community members developed when the ESCR design and planning team changed parts of the physical design and the phasing of the plan. While the previous design, communicated through competition phase engagement and developed in the following years, involved sets of berms along the western side of the East River Park, selectively allowing some flooding in the park during storms, the new design involves raising a reconstructed East River Park on landfill to the desired storm surge protection height (figure 11.3). This change was done ostensibly to minimize disruption to the adjacent FDR Drive and improve flood protection. According to some community members, the changes were done without further engagement on their part and will destroy existing riverfront ecology and disrupt park use for years to come (Hanania 2019). "Don't bury our park," read signs carried by protestors outside a New York City Council hearing in January 2019. This contestation around the park design, construction, and phasing has continued through mid-2021 (figure 11.4) (see also Araos 2021).

These conflicts bring up twin challenges of designing resilience, even when ostensibly successful participatory processes have been undertaken. First, how do we negotiate the possible tensions and contradictions between typical modes and practices of community engagement and the detailed planning, engineering, and building of large-scale, urban infrastructure, and, second, how do we keep the emphasis on the oft-stated desire for more ecological, selective, or fine-scaled approaches to climate change adaptation when confronted with a more expedient and nominally effective way to construct such infrastructure.

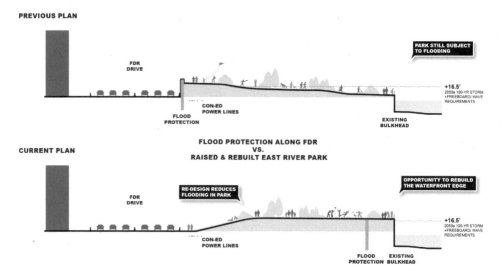

11.3 Section diagram of the proposed East River Park from the "Hearing on East Side Coastal Resiliency" presentation showing the initially designed plan and the current revised plan, January 23, 2019. *Source*: NYC Council, 2019.

CURRENT SITUATION

As of mid-2021, almost nine years after the storm and seven years after the conclusion of the competition phase, not many of the Rebuild by Design projects have specific timetables and scopes of work in tune with the ambitions of their competition proposals. One winning project, the part of the BIG U proposal now refashioned as the ESCR project, broke ground in the spring of 2021, and another, the SCAPE team's Living Break-waters project, in the summer of 2021. Smaller components of the OMA team's Hoboken–Weehawken–Jersey City project and the Interboro team's "Living with the Bay" project in Nassau County, Long Island, both now with different design teams, have also begun construction. The other projects are in various holding patterns or still in public review or consultant review processes.

Chester herself expresses some frustration about how the various projects were faring in mid-2018, stating, "We're not having the conversation about how to protect the entire city any longer, because we are focused on how to get this project built or that project built. . . . How do you keep both conversations at the same time? . . . What Rebuild was able

LESReady
@LESReadyNYC

"Closing the park for this long will have a devastating impact for residents." Read our statement on the revised #ESCR plan on our website --> ow.ly /Glkq30ns1mG #EastRiverPark

7:20 AM · Jan 25, 2019 · Hootsuite Inc.

11.4 LES Ready!'s Twitter post on January 25, 2019, decrying the decision to change the park design without community consultation. *Source*: Twitter, https://twitter.com/LESReadyNYC /status/1088818845542961152.

to do in the research stage was have this regional conversation that then ended when it became project based."[9] While noting some disappointment about the ongoing challenges, Chester is still convinced by the community engagement efforts of the initiative. She opines that Rebuild by Design was able to wedge open the system, just a bit, to foster some creative encounters between designers and community members and to give communities like Reyes's a voice and vision. I think that Chester is correct about that. But to what end, if the outcome appears to retread old patterns?

INNOVATION PRODUCES DISCONTENT?

By many measures, Rebuild by Design was innovative. It presented a new organizational structure for US urban climate change responses. It centered design in the conversation on urban resilience. It broached new conversations around urban climate initiatives in popular media. It focused urban design responses around a manner of community engagement. And yet, its constraints and shortcomings are becoming increasingly evident.

There have been numerous critiques of the BIG team's BIG U proposal. Natasha Iskander (2018) notes that projects like this reinforce the political-economic status quo: a big, expensive wall to maintain the exclusionary urban development processes already changing much of Manhattan. Billy Fleming (2019) echoes this sentiment, noting especially the discordance between the promises and fanfare of the competition alongside its vaunted community engagement processes, and what is turning out to be more the reality. He points to the weakened design ambitions of this and other Rebuild by Design proposals after the competition, and questions whether the outcomes would have been any different without the high-profile initiative. DuPuis and Greenberg (2019) note the fractious nature of the postcompetition planning process, foreclosing of community input and interests, and ongoing delays of the project compared to the more rapid development of luxury housing in the neighborhood.

I agree with many of the critiques. But I also think that there are further shades to this story that remain unexplained, and they might offer productive ways forward. It is not about one project per se or one specific design firm. Rebuild by Design's efforts around the Lower East Side raise fundamental questions about design processes around urban resilience. It is a particularly good case to probe this issue because it is one of two prominent, awarded projects that recently broke ground, for which significant team members and project scope were retained through the competition, procurement, and implementation stages. Here, we can see a probable outcome for what might be considered a critical case.

The key proposition and question are this: The innovation of Rebuild by Design changed expectations in the city. It did offer a new space for a different engagement, a different encounter. But did it change the terms of social relationships and political economy where it matters? I think not.

Understood through the spatial politics of the BIG U project, Rebuild by Design's noted innovation is entwined with the discontent it has and likely will continue to produce. The "private philanthropy plus CDBG-DR" funding model enabled innovative organization and, arguably, more positive modes of design-community engagement. But it also dictated a break and institutional reorganization between the competition and the implementation phases, leading to contestation and the dissolution of the collaborative vision. One might argue that this would happen in any circumstance where local, municipal review and procurement processes are separated, in institutional and governance terms, from participatory visioning. That's true. However, on another level, and in my view more important, it is also the case that this will happen as long as important urban climate change resilience projects are tied to dominant modes of urban development, and those dominant modes of development are held in constant conflict with the social and economic plight of marginalized communities. There are structural impediments to designing just resilience baked into city development and governance.

The design and organizational shifts brought innovation; the entrenched systems of urban development reverted the process back to political opposition. What can be done? First, we might take the lessons of innovation offered by this case to heart. New organizations among community groups, designers and planners, engineers, and research institutions can at least momentarily incite new relationships and invigorated thinking around urban problems. Maintaining and developing further new ways to provoke and nurture such relationships is important. Design visioning, in particular efforts that build engagement into core design processes, proves useful in bridging barriers among entities with historically different positions and privileges and helps build trust.

Second, we must make it so that such new and creative relationships have the chance to foster sustained change in the way cities are envisioned and made. We might work to disentangle specific parts of this problem. If cities, regions, and states consider large-scale resilience infrastructure to be of particular importance for public wellbeing and security, beyond the protection of centers of capital accumulation, their implementation should be detached from particular market mechanisms that now serve as the primary mode of urban development in US cities. But a tricky and possibly problematic parallel may also be stated: if those same levels of government consider such infrastructure to be important to protect vulnerable people and places in cities, their implementation should be detached from the unpredictable dynamics of how community engagement between designers and community stakeholders is typically conceptualized.

In the case explored here, most accounts, including those of GOLES and LES Ready!'s, are laudatory about the community engagement process in the immediate aftermath of Hurricane Sandy (see also Collier, Cox, and Grove 2014). Indeed, Reyes's explications of GOLES' work during this time stands as an example of a "just resilience," a resilience that does not simply appeal to "bouncing back" to prevailing conditions but one that epitomizes how marginalized communities, facing shared struggles, pose a positional and grounded response to social and environmental challenges.[10]

As urban researchers and planners, we can look to strong community organizers, but we cannot count on their presence and their wherewithal, especially in isolated, one-off circumstances, to guide resilience projects in more just directions in every instance. The challenge of urban responses to the urgencies of climate change and the injustices of marginalized communities is to address both together. Large-scale climate-responsive infrastructure needs to be accorded a different position in urban governance. Possibly, in parallel with how critical communications networks are generally prioritized, or, more fittingly, how public housing, in its best iterations, has been conceptualized (and, arguably, should be again)—as state responsibilities for the broader public good and for the rights of those most vulnerable and historically most oppressed. Considering infrastructures for climate resilience in this manner requires a different organization of planning and implementation and a practice of ongoing, everyday—not remarkable, not exemplary—deliberations with organizers and stakeholders across various communities in cities.

CONCLUSION

Resilience design competitions such as Rebuild by Design offer alluring glimpses of better ways to imagine more sustainable urban futures. But they also highlight the intractability of particular structures of urban governance and the continual injustices of dominant modes of urban development. We need a new kind of urban development, a more radical urban adaptation. This should be not only in response to the specific, projected impacts of climate change but also in expectation of the necessary changes in society that engender climate stability and dismantle unjust social hierarchies. This is a big ask, and one not likely to be achieved within the ten to thirty years cited by the recent Intergovernmental Panel on Climate Change's 1.5° global warming report as critical to act to prevent the most catastrophic consequences (IPCC 2018).

Activists, planners and urban designers, and progressive legislators will continue the fight for such far-reaching systemic transformation. We, the planners and designers in these efforts, might also insist on something more concretely actionable right now—to envision large-scale, state-led, and regionally coordinated urban climate development initiatives that *default* to a "marginalized-first" protection scheme from the start, one that systemically prioritizes historically vulnerable people and places on questions about who, where, and how to implement plans. Such action, done right, would break historically oppositional encounters and build and maintain trust in new urban climate infrastructural development when we need it most—the very near future.

NOTES

1. This chapter is part of my larger study on the spatial politics of urban climate change responses across sites in New York City, Jakarta, Indonesia, and Rotterdam, the Netherlands, involving field visits, participant observation, approximately fifty-five semistructured interviews, and review of thirty-five planning and design documents, conducted between 2013 and 2019 (Goh 2021).

2. Interview, November 24, 2014.

3. Interview, New York, NY, December 18, 2014.

4. Interviews, New York, NY, June 19, 2014, and July 18, 2018.

5. Interview, New York, NY, June 19, 2014.

6. Interview, New York, NY, December 18, 2014.

7. Interview, New York, NY, December 18, 2014.

8. Interview, New York, NY, December 18, 2014. See also Malesevic (2014).

9. Interview by the author, New York, NY, July 18, 2018.

10. I have elaborated on this in my book (see Goh 2021).

REFERENCES

Anguelovski, I., Connolly, J. J., Pearsall, H., Shokry, G., Checker, M., Maantay, J., Gould, K., Lewis, T., Maroko, A., & Roberts, J. T. (2019). "Opinion: Why Green

'Climate Gentrification' Threatens Poor and Vulnerable Populations." *Proceedings of the National Academy of Sciences* 116 (52): 26139–26143.

Araos, M. (2021). "Democracy Underwater: Public Participation, Technical Expertise, and Climate Infrastructure Planning in New York City." *Theory and Society*, 1–34. doi:10.1007/s11186-021-09459-9.

BIG Team. (2014). "The BIG 'U.'" Rebuild by Design. http://www.rebuildbydesign .org/project/big-team-final-proposal/.

Checker, M. (2011). "Wiped Out by the 'Greenwave': Environmental Gentrification and the Paradoxical Politics of Urban Sustainability." *City & Society* 23 (2): 210–229.

Collier, S. J., Cox, S., and Grove, K. (2016). "Rebuilding by Design in Post-Sandy New York." *Limn*, July 21, 2016. https://limn.it/articles/rebuilding-by-design-in-post -sandy-new-york/.

Cutter, S. L., Ahearn, J. A., Amadei, B., Crawford, P., Eide, E. A., Galloway, G. E., Goodchild, M. F., Kunreuther, H. C., Li-Vollmer, M., and Schoch-Spana, M. (2013). "Disaster Resilience: A National Imperative." *Environment: Science and Policy for Sustainable Development* 55 (2): 25–29.

Davoudi, S., Lawrence, J., and Bohland, J. (2019). "Anatomy of the Resilience Machine." In Bohland, J., Davoudi, S., and Lawrence, J. (eds.). *The Resilience Machine*. Abingdon: Routledge, 12–28.

DuPuis, E. M., and Greenberg, M. (2019). "The Right to the Resilient City: Progressive Politics and the Green Growth Machine in New York City." *Journal of Environmental Studies and Sciences* 9 (3): 352–363.

Fainstein, S. (2015). "Resilience and Justice." *International Journal of Urban and Regional Research* 39 (1): 157–167.

Fleming, B. (2019). "Design and the Green New Deal." *Places Journal*, April.

Goh, K. (2019). "Toward Transformative Urban Spatial Change: Views from Jakarta." In Banerjee, T., and Loukaitou-Sideris, A. *The New Companion to Urban Design*, Abingdon: Routledge, 519–532.

Goh, K. (2020a). "Flows in Formation: The Global-Urban Networks of Climate Change Adaptation." *Urban Studies* 57 (11), 2222–2240.

Goh, K. (2020b). "Urbanising Climate Justice: Constructing Scales and Politicising Difference." *Cambridge Journal of Regions, Economy and Society* 13 (3): 559–574.

Goh, K. (2021). *Form and Flow: The Spatial Politics of Urban Resilience and Climate Justice*. Cambridge, MA: The MIT Press.

Gould, K. A., and Lewis, T. L. (2017). *Green Gentrification: Urban Sustainability and the Struggle for Environmental Justice*. London: Routledge.

Hanania, J. (2019). "To Save East River Park, the City Intends to Bury It." *New York Times*, January 18, 2019.

Intergovernmental Panel on Climate Change. (2018). "Global Warming of 1.5°C." https://www.ipcc.ch/sr15/.

Iskander, N. (2018). "Design Thinking Is Fundamentally Conservative and Preserves the Status Quo." *Harvard Business Review*, September 5, 2018.

MacKinnon, D., and Driscoll Derickson, K. (2013). "From Resilience to Resourcefulness: A Critique of Resilience Policy and Activism." *Progress in Human Geography* 37 (2): 253–270.

Malesevic, Dusica S. (2014). "2 Years after Sandy, Who Will Get Shelter from the Storm? Only Some Downtown." *Downtown Express*, October 29, 2014.

Meerow, S., Newell, J. P., and Stults, M. (2016). "Defining Urban Resilience: A Review." *Landscape and Urban Planning* 147: 38–49.

Mohai, P., Pellow, D., and Roberts, J. T. (2009). "Environmental Justice." *Annual Review of Environment and Resources* 34: 405–430.

New York City Council on Parks and Recreation and Environmental Protection (NYC Council) (2019). "Hearing on East Side Coastal Resiliency." Presented at the New York City Council, January 23, 2019, https://www1.nyc.gov/assets/escr/downloads/pdf/190123-ESCR-NYC-Council-Hearing.pdf.

Ovink, H., and Boeijenga, J. (2018). *Too Big: Rebuild by Design: A Transformative Approach to Climate Change*. Rotterdam: nai010 publishers.

Pickett, S. T., Cadenasso, M. L., and McGrath, B. (eds.) (2013). *Resilience in Ecology and Urban Design: Linking Theory and Practice for Sustainable Cities*. Dordrecht; New York: Springer.

Ranganathan, M. and Bratman, E. (2019). "From Urban Resilience to Abolitionist Climate Justice in Washington, DC." *Antipode*, June 28, 2019. doi:10.1111/anti.12555.

Rodin, J. (2014). *The Resilience Dividend: Being Strong in a World Where Things Go Wrong*. New York: Public Affairs.

Vale, L. J. (2015). "Resilient Cities: Clarifying Concept or Catch-All Cliché?" In LeGates, R. T., and Stout, F. (eds.). *The City Reader*. London: Routledge, 618–628.

IV

DESIGN FOR DIFFERENCE

12

URBAN RIGHTS
TOP DOWN/BOTTOM UP

Teddy Cruz and Fonna Forman

HUMAN RIGHTS: AN URGENT PRELUDE FOR URBANISTS

At this moment, migrant populations are in jeopardy across the world. Human rights norms are being trampled as the world watches. Old habits of nationalism, isolationism, racism, anti-intellectualism, obsession with law-and-order, and disdain for a free press are being reinvigorated, even though these impulses had been largely kept in check for decades by a global community that no longer tolerated them.[1]

We live and work at the US-Mexico border, in the largest binational urban region and the busiest land-crossing in the western hemisphere: the metropolis of San Diego-Tijuana. The global political climate today strikes an urgent chord in our region, where thousands of Central American migrants wait for US asylum at the border wall in Tijuana. On the US side of the wall, the Immigration and Customs Enforcement (ICE) agency of the Department of Homeland Security is formally constrained by law and protocol, but there are countless stories of egregious human rights violations, mass sweeps, seizures without a warrant, and detention of minors in adult facilities. Immigrant men and women who have lived, worked, and contributed in countless ways to their communities in the US over decades are enduring waves of public hatred and are terrorized by threats of the proverbial "knock at the door." Fear of political oppression and deportation has produced unprecedented anxiety in the immigrant communities of San Diego county.

This is an essay on urban rights. We focus on informal urban processes as emancipatory energies in the city. Our focus is on the ingenuity and resilience of the bottom up. But we begin by asserting clearly the imperative for a top-down, coordinated commitment to human rights at all scales of governance, particularly the right of asylum for those escaping cruelty, persecution, poverty, and the impacts of climate change. We advocate a return to the modern foundations of international human rights law and our duty to the "stranger in distress" articulated by the seventeenth-century Dutch jurist Hugo Grotius ([1603] 1964). As architects and urbanists, we believe this translates today into a commitment to intervene into the first site of contact between the nation and "the other": the host city. Hospitality is the first gesture, but *inclusivity* means integrating the immigrant and her children into the social, economic, and political realities of the city, creating spaces for meaningful participation in the civic life of the community, opportunities for education, and psychological and spiritual health. Real inclusion is more than a charitable embrace; it is a process through which we ourselves transform alongside the other.

Although this is not the subject of our chapter, we could not begin a discussion about rights in the city (urban rights) without citing, first, the accelerating migration crisis. Cities across the US and the world are currently swept up in a nativist panic. Urbanists and urban designers committed to designing for equity and justice must confront this social and political challenge head-on. It is reassuring that many cities have declared themselves as "sanctuaries" for immigrants and fortresses of resistance against the violation of human rights and dignity of the most vulnerable people on our planet. While the racist rhetoric ratchets up, we are also witnessing an unprecedented commitment among local jurisdictions to defy federal mandates that criminalize immigrants.[2]

URBAN RIGHTS FROM THE TOP DOWN: A CULTURAL AGENDA

The idea of "urban rights" is closely aligned with Henri Lefebvre's (1968) celebrated idea of the "right to the city." On its face, the formulation can seem strange, for its linguistic alignment with an individualist language of rights. But Lefebvre was eager to take the concept of rights back for a distinctively public and emancipatory agenda. Urban rights reflect a social and collective idea of the city, animated by the agency of those who inhabit and build it. Urban rights are grounded in a tradition of rights and practices of rights-claiming, but they are extricated from an individualistic lineage oriented around private property and autonomy, where the public good is too often reduced to the dehumanizing language of charity or top-down beneficence. Urban rights are grounded in the agency of the marginalized and dispossessed and their collective entitlement to share and coproduce a more just and equitable city (Lefebvre 1968; Kohn 2016).[3] Redistribution of urban amenities and resources is then not a response to an individual's moral failure but a just egalitarian response to structural conditions of poverty and inequality. Urban rights, then, are understood as a practice of collective rights-claiming and resistance to unjust power structures in the city—urban norms, policies, procedures, and spaces. Urban justice is understood as the fulfillment, or meaningful momentum toward the fulfillment, of these rights. It will necessarily entail confrontation with the institutions, policies, and practices that formally govern urban development from the top down. In most cases today, these urban power structures are tightly aligned with neoliberal agendas of privatization and dispossession in the city. But there are also exceptions when municipalities have resisted the forces of neoliberalism and advanced more deliberate egalitarian, public strategies. These are the cases that have most inspired us (Cruz and Forman 2016).

We contextualize our conceptual framework with an exemplar of urban rights. When philosopher Antanas Mockus became mayor of Bogotá, Colombia, in 1995, the city was in a free-fall of urban violence, poverty, and infrastructural failure. People referred to Bogotá at that time as the most dangerous city on the planet. Rejecting the conventional law-and-order response to urban violence, Mockus came up with some very different ideas. From the start, he committed his administration to a concept of justice rooted in social equity and the redistribution of wealth. As he described his mandate: "Those who have come to the world at a disadvantage, those who live in extreme poverty and lack the means to have access to health services, or to adequate nutrition and education, have an inalienable right to a minimum standard of living. These minimum conditions must be sufficient for each to be able to begin building their own life as they imagine and desire it" (Mockus n.d.).

But his strategies went beyond providing social services and public infrastructure from the top down. While public provision was essential to reducing poverty and restoring human dignity in the urban periphery, Mockus argued that the production of a more just and equitable city must simultaneously engage public culture. Urban transformation, he believed, is as much about changing patterns of public trust and social cooperation as it is about changing urban policy and infrastructure (Mockus 2012). His provocation for urbanists is that before transforming the city physically, we must first transform social norms—intervene in the belief systems that perpetuate an acceptance of dramatic inequality, violence, and corruption in the city. He targeted not only those with resources and power but, more essentially, the marginalized and the poor, who, through decades of neglect, had come to accept their condition as natural and were resistant to structural change. Drawing on the emancipatory pedagogic theories of the Brazilian educator Paulo Freire (1970) designed to reclaim the humanity of the colonized, Mockus believed that restoring urban dignity, a sense of possibility, a right to the neighborhood, and a belief in collective agency are all essential to a just and equitable urban agenda.

Political leadership was a critical part of the story. Mockus emphatically declared the norms that should regulate social relations in the city— that human life is sacred, that radical inequality is unjust, that adequate education and health are human rights, that gender violence is unacceptable. He reoriented public policy to nurture a new "citizenship culture" in Bogotá grounded in a shared commitment to human dignity—that all human beings, regardless of formal legal citizenship or race, deserve respect and basic quality of life.

But Mockus also understood that these human rights norms could only take root and thrive in a participatory civic culture. As he put it, "The foundation here is the respect for life itself, as common ground. But this needs specific cultural strategies of intervention" (Mockus 2012, 145). To achieve this, he designed an urban pedagogy of sometimes outrageous performative interventions that have inspired generations of civic actors, urbanists, and artists across Latin America to think more creatively about transforming urban norms and behavior (Forman 2018). One of his very first acts in office was the distribution of "citizen cards"—depicting a big thumb that could be used performatively to communicate approval or disapproval. Hundreds of thousands of these placards were distributed to the residents of Bogotá, who were encouraged to use them as they moved through the city. A positive social act would earn a thumbs-up; an act that violated one's sense of civic decency, a thumbs-down. Through this performative gesture, people began to look at one another again and recognize the reciprocal impact of urban behaviors—that one's behavior has an impact on others and vice-versa. Without realizing it, they were deciding together what kind of city they wanted to inhabit; what kind of city they wanted to be in. From the bottom up, they began to construct a new citizenship culture based on the shared expectations they had of one another and their collective responsibilities to the city.

The impact on the quality of life on Bogotá during Mockus's first administration was truly remarkable: murders were reduced by 70 percent, traffic fatalities by 50 percent, tax collection nearly doubled, and water consumption decreased by 40 percent, even as water and sewer services were extended to nearly all households. (Tognato 2018).

It is from cities like Bogotá that we can learn the most about urban pedagogy, about designing civic processes and cultural interventions in the city to yield more just and equitable outcomes (Scruggs 2015).

URBAN RIGHTS FROM THE BOTTOM UP: INFORMAL PRAXIS

Elsewhere, privatization has turned cities into sites of consumption and display. Local culture is instrumentalized as a tool. Private developers and cities glamorize local neighborhoods with tactics of beautification, appealing to the "creative class," and promoting the arts, food, and café culture as the hip cultural language of gentrification. As Michael Henry Adams (2016) puts it, "Every new building, every historic renovation, every boutique clothing shop—indeed, every tree and every flower in every park improvement—is not a life-enhancing benefit, but a harbinger of a local community's own displacement." Yet, at the margins, a very different and more inclusive politics of urban growth is being shaped from the bottom up.

The performativity of the informal also expands notions of the political and provokes an alternative, more practical conception of urban rights. We have come to understand urban rights less as a set of mandates designed from above (the conventional way of thinking about rights) and more as a set of performative urban actions from below (Cruz and Forman 2017a). This bottom-up action can take the shape of emergent, everyday lived practices among marginalized communities or more deliberate strategies of urban intervention designed to counter exclusionary political and economic power. We have argued that these bottom-up social and economic exchanges, spatial flows, and actions are the building blocks for a more just and equitable city (Cruz and Forman 2022; 2023). Contrasting the neoliberal hegemony that organizes the global city through logics of consumption, privatization, and display, these informal urbanizations at the margins sustain themselves with their own resources through logics of local productivity, negotiating time, space, boundaries, and resources in conditions of scarcity and emergency. In these peripheral communities, we find economic configurations that emerge and thrive through tactical adaptation and retrofit that transgress discriminatory zoning and exclusionary economic development.

URBAN RIGHTS: TOP DOWN/BOTTOM UP

We have been inspired by a twentieth-century lineage of participatory urbanization in parts of Latin America, where these strategies of coproduction improved the quality of life for the most marginalized populations in some cities (Cruz and Forman 2016). From Porto Alegre to Curitiba, from Bogotá to Medellín, from Quito to Mexico City, we have been documenting these cases over the last years in close collaboration and dialogue with the key political and civic actors who led them: the mayors and their staff, the business leaders and urban designers, the civic leaders and academic researchers, the grassroots organizers and the cultural producers. We have recognized some common patterns and consistencies across the many municipalities we studied. Across the board, these cities committed to simultaneous cultural, institutional, and spatial reform: working with neighborhood agencies to stimulate civic engagement among the marginalized; transforming municipal bureaucracy into a more efficient, transparent, and accountable system; and advancing public works projects and educational infrastructure in the poorest and most neglected zones of the city.

An exemplary case is Medellín, Colombia, once a battleground of drug lords, paramilitaries, and left-wing guerillas, a site of violence, severe unemployment, and poverty. Today, Medellín has become legendary among urbanists, architects, and planners across the world as a model of equitable urban transformation. Here again, political leadership was essential. When mathematician Sergio Fajardo became mayor in 2005, he declared: "We will not build down here [in the wealthy center], but up there [in the periphery, where the necessities are]" (Romero 2007). Public infrastructure became the physical manifestation of civic commitment to a just city, spatializing Antanas Mockus's idea of citizenship culture and Freire's critical pedagogy. Fajardo committed to transforming Medellín into "the most educated" city in Colombia, insisting that social justice depended not only on the redistribution of resources but also on the redistribution of knowledge. This manifested most clearly in Fajardo's famous Library Parks projects that moved the discussion of public space from a neutral urban commodity animated by beauty, leisure, and random encounters to a deliberate democratization of public space in the city's less affluent neighborhoods on the periphery. Fajardo committed to designing each public space in tandem with pedagogical support systems facilitated by cross-sector coalitions to activate civic activity, educational programming, urban pedagogy, vocational training, cultural production, and small-scale economic development.

Most accounts of Medellín's successes in the last decade have focused on its public transportation infrastructure and world-class public architecture inserted strategically into the city's most vulnerable zones. And as models go, there is always an urge to emulate. What struck us, however, is that so few people were asking *how* Medellín was able to accomplish so much (Cruz and Forman 2018). How can a city activate projects of the scale that Medellín did, and so rapidly? Medellín is remarkable not only for its public architecture and infrastructural interventions but for the egalitarian vision that inspired them and the innovative political and civic processes that enabled them. To appreciate how Medellín might become a political and civic model that might be translated and adapted to other contexts, it is essential to understand just *how* the city managed to reorient resources on such a massive scale toward sites of greatest need. What did the city do? How did its governance need to transform? What kinds of institutional intersections were necessary? What was the role of the bottom up in enabling these interventions to succeed and be sustained over time? These are the questions we wanted to pursue. These are the processes we wanted to translate so that Medellín might become intelligible not only as a set of buildings, structures, and spaces but also primarily as an imaginative set of political and civic processes.

In 2011, we joined forces with Fajardo and Alejandro Echeverri (former "urban curator" of Medellín, responsible for many of the city's most iconic urban interventions) on a multiyear research project to visualize the political and civic processes that enabled Medellín's rapid transformation (figure 12.1) (Cruz et al. n.d.). We wanted to design a diagram useful to the citizens of Medellín as a reservoir of institutional memory to guide future interventions and to municipalities elsewhere eager to emulate Medellín's achievements. Ultimately, it is not by emulating buildings and transport systems that cities across the globe can approximate the inclusive urbanization that transformed Medellín over the last two decades. We began by conducting interviews with dozens of key political and civic actors since what happened there was a complex process of negotiation and collaboration across institutions and publics. We interviewed the mayors and their staffs, the business leaders and urban designers, the civic leaders and academic researchers, the grassroots organizers and the cultural producers. We translated and stitched together stories and anecdotes, identified connections, mapped the way ideas and actions evolved across time to visualize their complexity. What emerged was a visual tool called Medellín Diagram, designed to advance public knowledge and challenge the perception that Medellín's transformation was only about architecture and infrastructure (Cruz et al. n.d.).

Bogotá and Medellín are part of a long lineage of "social urbanism" across the continent, led by mayors who committed their administrations to reducing poverty, cultivating civic participation, and stewarding cross-sector investment in public wellbeing. In both cases, these municipalities became think tanks, problem-solving laboratories, facilitated by urban curators who mediated the interface among academics, the private

PRIORITIES · PROCESSES · INTERVENTIONS

PRIORITIES	PROCESSES	INTERVENTIONS
1. Confronting inequality — Constructing a new political agenda	**2. Designing Governance** — Transforming municipal bureaucracy	**3. Spatializing Citizenship** — Building performative infrastructures of inclusion

1. Confronting inequality

1.A Committing to fight segregation	1.B Mediating urban conflict	1.C Cultivating a new civic imagination
1.A.1 Declaring that violence is rooted in poverty	1.B.1 Pursuing social order not through police repression but through community processes	1.C.5 Summoning artists to resuscitate urban memory
1.A.2 Re-imagining the city from its periphery	1.B.2 Embracing empathy as a pathway to inclusive urbanization	1.C.6 Cultivating respect for human dignity
1.A.3 Identifying sites of urgency, and investing in the poorest zones of the city	1.B.3 Creating spaces for mediation and conflict resolution	1.C.7 Facilitating community forums to discuss the future of the city
1.A.4 Building immediate public trust with small-scale neighborhood interventions while planning a long-term urban vision	1.B.4 Mediating divergent perspectives and challenging polarization with constructive dialogue and debate	1.C.8 Designing new platforms for public communication

2. Designing Governance

2.A Assembling transparent and inclusive public management	2.B Integrating and redistributing knowledges and resources	2.C Bringing design intelligence into public policy
2.A.1 Urban equity demanding a transformation of government bureaucracy	2.B.1 Mediating interfaces between top-down institutions and bottom-up agency	2.C.1 Engaging local universities to rethink urban policy
2.A.2 Tackling institutional corruption	2.B.2 Summoning and redistributing cross-sector priorities, knowledges and resources	2.C.2 Co-producing the city with communities
2.A.3 Prioritizing bureaucratic efficiency and agility	2.B.3 Re-directing public resources toward socially responsible development	
2.A.4 Designing municipal structures and procedures for participatory governance		
2.A.5 Repairing public trust across institutions		
2.A.6 Embracing progressive taxation as the foundation for equitable urbanization		
2.A.7 Creating new public institutions tasked with social and economic inclusion		

3. Spatializing Citizenship

3.A Transgressing urban borders	3.B Creating public spaces that educate	3.C Designing sustainable civic management strategies
3.A.1 Identifying poverty zones for integrated urban design intervention	3.B.1 Advancing the rights to the city through a new public space agenda	3.C.1 Designing spaces, programs and protocols simultaneously
3.A.2 Penetrating into segregated communities with public works	3.B.2 Viewing public infrastructure as the armature of progressive governance	
3.A.3 Shrinking distance between wealthy and poor zones to increase accessibility	3.B.3 Intervening into public space to re-organize social norms	
3.A.4 Orchestrating diverse social encounters in urban space	3.B.4 Elevating urban pedagogy and education to democratize the city	
3.A.5 Conceptualizing natural systems as a framework for integrating the city	3.B.5 Elevating art as a tool for publics to comprehend urban complexity	
	3.B.6 Connecting citizenship to a visual awareness of the territory	

12.1 The Medellin Diagram, showing the priorities for confronting inequality, the governance processes, and interventions for strengthening spatial citizenship, from left to right. *Source:* Teddy Cruz + Fonna Forman with Alejandro Echeverri and Matthias Görlich, 2014.

sector, grassroots organizations, and cultural producers to transform urban norms and design new strategies of civic engagement, public management, and infrastructural renewal. Both Bogotá and Medellín invested massively in public infrastructure and transportation projects, especially to shrink distance and stimulate movement and flow. Both cities concentrated investment in their most marginalized zones, building schools, libraries, and parks infused with cultural amenities and social services and extending water and sewerage services to nearly all residents. But equally important to both cities was the creation of new bonds of trust across sectors and a sense of urban dignity and collective ownership of the city. This tradition still thrives in cities across the continent, from La Paz to Quito to Mexico City.

As we think about urban strategies for San Diego-Tijuana, we have been inspired by Medellín's commitment to mobilizing citizenship through cultural action in public space. At this moment, escalating conflict at the border wall has attracted artists and cultural producers from across the world to engage in acts of performative protest. While these gestures by visitors are often creative and provocative, we have been largely critical of this recent uptick in ephemeral acts of resistance and short-term artistic and cultural interventions that dip in and out of the conflict—the energy that produces them quickly dissipates, and they tend to be short-lived in their impact.

We have been advocating for a longer view of resistance and more strategic thinking about cultural, institutional, and spatial transformation in the border region. To enable this, we have been developing an infrastructure for crossborder cooperation spatialized through a network of public spaces located in neighborhoods on both sides of the wall. The University of California, San Diego (UCSD) Community Stations (figure 12.2) are public spaces where university researchers and community residents converge to share resources and knowledge (Cruz and Forman 2019; Forman forthcoming). Each station is a robust partnership between the UCSD campus and an embedded grassroots organization designed, funded, built, programmed, and maintained collaboratively. The community stations are sites for cultural production, collaborative research, youth mentorship, and urban pedagogy.[4] They are platforms of knowledge exchange for codeveloping long-term urban projects, increasing community capacity for political and environmental action, and communicating urban

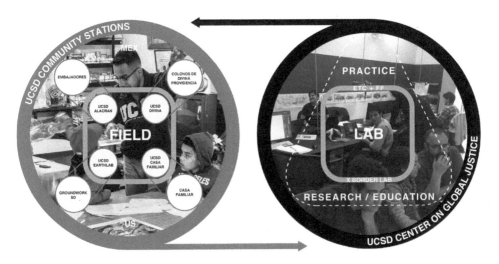

12.2 The UCSD Community Stations network, diagram. *Source*: Estudio Teddy Cruz+ Fonna Forman, 2019.

knowledge to the diverse sectors in the city that govern urban development and manage resources.

Seeing universities and communities as codevelopers of a more just city and a more just border region requires a fundamental cultural shift in the way universities typically understand their relation to marginalized communities. Too often, the university sees itself as the bearer of all knowledge and resources and sees communities as passive recipients, empty receptacles waiting to be filled, mere subjects of data, or laboratories for testing university inventions. Communities are typically perceived by universities as tools of research rather than participants with agency. University scholarship is infused with assumptions that we know more—that only we are the "experts" and only we can convey complex ideas and practices or have the analytical tools to make sense of and "fix" the chaotic tangle of life. An engagement with worlds of practice reveals, however, that these assumptions are flawed and ultimately unethical. We do not know everything we think we know, and we have possibly more to learn from the world than it does from us.

Through the community stations platform (figure 12.3), we seek to tip the relation between universities and communities from a vertical plane to a horizontal one. University researchers need to cultivate practices of

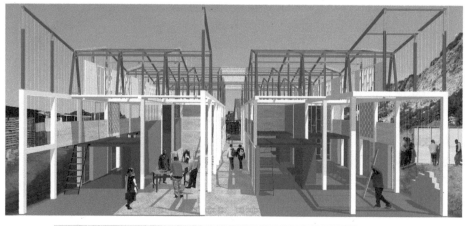

12.3 The UCSD community stations model: lab and field, diagram. *Source*: Estudio Teddy Cruz + Fonna Forman, 2019.

epistemic humility when they enter the field and recognize the resources, knowledge, and capacities that communities contribute, and which are essential to producing new knowledge about the city. This is a very different kind of activity than service, charity, or applied research, which are all vertical gestures. Community-engaged urban research and practice are horizontal and collaborative—a model of *partnership* in which university and community together coproduce new knowledge and codevelop urban projects (figure 12.4).

PRACTICING URBAN RIGHTS: INFORMAL PUBLIC DEMANDS

Urban rights should be understood as a collective practice of resistance to unjust power structures in the city, namely the urban norms, policies, procedures, and spaces that perpetuate increasingly uneven patterns of urban development. Designing more just and equitable cities must begin as a social and cultural project from the bottom up, changing hearts and minds. Urban activism should focus on increasing public knowledge;

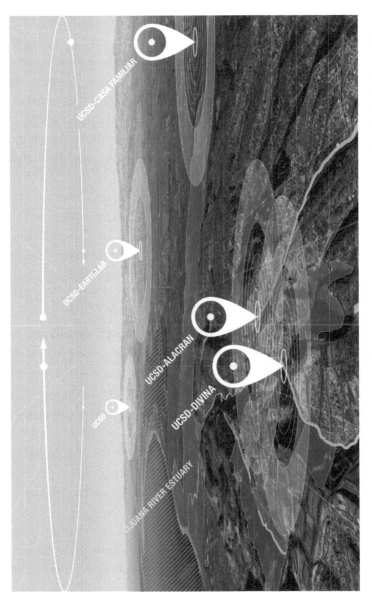

12.4 The UCSD-Alacrán Community Station, Tijuana, rendering and diagram. *Source:* Estudio Teddy Cruz+Fonna Forman, 2019.

rejecting hierarchical social norms that validate neglect, exploitation, and dispossession in the city; igniting civic dignity; repairing public trust; and restoring a belief in community agency at the neighborhood scale. Only then can top-down governance and spatial intervention produce meaningful change. In this light, municipalities must rethink conventional advocacy planning protocols, which are too often box-ticking exercises that engage the same voices over and over again. These protocols are typically not inclusive and reproduce false perceptions that residents in neglected urban neighborhoods are disinterested, not knowledgeable, or incapable of collective agency and need to be taken care of by others. Cities should find ways to drill deeper into the community, deeper into demographics that have peeled away, having been marginalized for decades from the city's scope of moral concern. Municipalities need to restore public trust by earning it—even if it takes time, even if it slows projects down. They need to stop coming in and simply rearranging the furniture.

As such, practicing urban rights begins with a set of normative demands and cultural processes, followed by demands for more democratic and collaborative forms of governance, culminating in a set of policy demands focused on the equitable spatial transformation of the city (Cruz and Forman 2022; 2023). We conclude our chapter by declaring these demands as a mandate for urban designers, planners, policymakers, and community activists.

- Transform cultural practices of social exclusion and the corresponding denigration of public goods by cultivating new urban norms of human dignity and equality.
- Advance a language of "rights to the city" to stimulate a new sense of possibility in communities long marginalized by city planning agendas.
- Close the gap between large-scale abstract planning logic and the realities of everyday practices.
- Design mediating agencies that curate the interface between top-down institutional support (government, universities, foundations, cultural institutions) and creative bottom-up intelligence and sweat equity of communities and activists.
- Enable more inclusive and meaningful systems of political representation and civic engagement at the neighborhood scale, tactically balancing individual and collective interests.

- Produce new forms of local governance along with social protection systems that provide guarantees for marginalized communities and protect their right to control their own modes of production and share in the profits of urbanization.
- Challenge existing models of property with a more inclusive idea of ownership that redefines affordability and the value of social participation, augments the role of communities in coproducing housing and public infrastructure, and prevents gentrification.
- Mobilize and support social networks to develop new spatial and economic infrastructures that benefit local communities in the long term, beyond the short-term problem-solving logics of private developers or philanthropic institutions.
- Question exclusionary logics of land use. See zoning not only as a punitive technical tool that prevents socialization but also as a generative tool that organizes and anticipates social and economic activity in neighborhoods.
- Politicize density by no longer measuring it as an abstract number of objects per acre but rather as the concentration of socio-economic exchanges per acre.
- Retrofit the large with the small so that the microsocial and economic contingencies of informal uses transform the homogeneous largeness of formal urbanization, creating more sustainable, plural, and complex environments.
- Abandon conventional government protocols that privilege abstract administrative boundaries over more informal social and environmental boundaries that construct communities.
- Challenge the idea of public space as a manicured site of beauty and leisure, and reclaim it as a site of civic activity, urban pedagogy, and cultural production.

If pursued and realized, the aforementioned mandate will bring about a just urban design.

NOTES

1. An earlier version of this paper appeared in French in Contal and Revedin (2018). Our great thanks to Vinit Mukhija, Anastasia Loukaitou-Sideris, and Kian Goh for

inviting our participation, and to Antanas Mockus, Sergio Fajardo, and Alejandro Echeverri, as always, for their inspiration.

2. For more discussion on the current crisis at the border between San Diego and Tijuana and cultural strategies for transgressing national policy, see Cruz and Forman (2017b) and Forman (forthcoming).

3. Margaret Kohn's idea of the "urban commonwealth" is a fusion of Lefebvre's "right to the city" and the nineteenth-century French Republican tradition of "solidarism."

4. Many of the cultural strategies, programs, and activities of the community stations are inspired by the critical pedagogy of Freire, for whom education is political. For Freire, democracy materializes through the habits of everyday practice.

REFERENCES

Adams, M. H. (2016). "The End of Black Harlem." *New York Times*, May 29, 2016. https://www.nytimes.com/2016/05/29/opinion/sunday/the-end-of-black-harlem .html.

Contal, M-H., and Revedin, J. (eds.). (2018). *Invisible Resources / Ressources Invisibles*. Paris: Gallimard.

Cruz, T., and Forman, F. (2016). "Latin America and a New Political Leadership: Experimental Acts of Co-Existence." In Burton, J., Jackson, S., and Willsdon, D. (eds.). *Public Servants: Art and the Crisis of the Common Good*. Cambridge, MA: MIT Press, 71–90.

Cruz, T., and Forman, F. (2017a). "The Cross-Border Public." In Urbonas, G., Lui, A., and Freeman, L. (eds.). *Public Space? Lost and Found*. Cambridge, MA: MIT Press, 189–215.

Cruz, T., and Forman, F. (2017b). "Unwalling Citizenship." In Graham, J. (ed.). *Avery Review: Critical Essays on Architecture*. New York: Columbia University Publications, 21: 98–109.

Cruz, T., and Forman, F. (2018). "Global Justice at the Municipal Scale: The Case of Medellín Colombia." In Cabrera, L. (ed.). *Institutional Cosmopolitanism*. New York: Oxford University Press, 189–215.

Cruz, T., and Forman, F. (2019) "Critical Proximities at the Border: Redistributing Knowledges Across Walls." In Dodd, M. (ed.). *Spatial Practices: Modes of Action and Engagement in the City*. London: Routledge, 189–202.

Cruz, T., and Forman, F. (2022). *Spatializing Justice: Building Blocks*. Cambridge, MA: MIT Press.

Cruz, T., and Forman, F. (forthcoming in 2023). *Socializing Architecture: Top-Down/ Bottom-Up*. Cambridge, MA: MIT Press.

Cruz, T., Forman, F., Echeverri, Al, and Görlich, M. (n.d.). "*Medellín Diagram*." UCSD Center on Global Justice, accessed December 11, 2021. http://gjustice.ucsd.edu /medellin-diagram/.

Forman, F. (Forthcoming). "Unwalling Citizenship." In Tully, J., Cherry, K., Forman, F., et al. (eds.). *Democratic Multiplicities: Perceiving, Enacting and Integrating Democratic Diversity*. New York: Cambridge University Press.

Forman, F. (2018). "Social Norms and the Cross-Border Citizen: From Adam Smith to Antanas Mockus." In Tognato, C. (ed.). *Cultural Agents Reloaded: The Legacy of Antanas Mockus*. Cambridge, MA: Harvard University Press, 333–356.

Freire, P. (1970). *Pedagogy of the Oppressed*. New York: Continuum.

Grotius, H. [1603] (1964). *Commentary on the Law of Prize and Booty*. Translation by Williams. G. L., and Zeydel, W. H. New York: Oceana Publishing.

Kohn, M. (2016). *The Death and Life of the Urban Commonwealth*. New York: Oxford University Press.

Lefebvre, H. (1968). *Le Droit à la Ville*. Paris: Editions Athropos Paris.

Mockus, A. (n.d.). "Bogotá's Capacity for Self-Transformation and Citizenship Building." Bogotá: unpublished paper, 6–7.

Mockus, A. (2012). "Building 'Citizenhip Culture' in Bogotá." *Journal of International Affairs* 65 (2): 143–146.

Romero, S. (2007). "Mayor of Medellín Brings Architecture to the People." *New York Times*, July 15, 2007. https://www.nytimes.com/2007/07/15/world/americas/15iht-colombia.1.6660612.html.

Scruggs, G. (2015). *"New San Diego-Tijuana Survey Holds Mirror Up to Border Cities."* Next City, February 26, 2015, accessed January, 2022. https://nextcity.org/urbanist-news/binational-survey-san-diego-tijuana-border-antanas-mockus.

Tognato, C. (ed.) (2018). *Cultural Agents Reloaded: The Legacy of Antanas Mockus*. Cambridge, MA: Harvard University Press, 2018.

13

EMPOWERING DIFFERENCE
JUST URBAN DESIGN FOR THE IMMIGRANT STREET VENDORS OF ROME

Francesca Piazzoni and Anastasia Loukaitou-Sideris

Street vendors are a common sight in public spaces across the globe. Regardless of whether they comply with regulations or eke out a living informally, policymakers often treat vendors as a sign of disorder, a symbol of backwardness that collides with dominant images of world-class landscapes. Evictions, exclusionary regulations, and selective law enforcement are employed to push vendors away. Urban design is also frequently used to banish sellers—built environments are produced and maintained to neglect vendors' needs while conveying dominant ideas of "appropriate" uses that make sellers stand out as "undesirables."

Vendors, however, are not passive victims of exclusion. They resist coercive municipal ordinances and regulations through insurgent practices that change the ways cities look and function. At times, vendors confront authorities by organizing grassroots movements and advocating for their rights. Scholars have investigated how vendors also challenge exclusion more implicitly by defying dominant *strategies* of control through ordinary yet equally political spatial *tactics* (Certeau 1984; Kamel 2014). Indeed, a city's urban form—the ways it discourages or accommodates difference—can help intensify the oppression of vendors or facilitate their insurgent practices.

While significant literature has examined street vending (Bromley 2000; Cross and Morales 2007; Graaf and Ha 2015; Mörtenböeck et al.

2015), scholars have given little attention to how urban designers can draw from and respond to the vendors' practices in order to advance social justice. This chapter highlights placemaking strategies that can help empower and accommodate street vendors. Like other authors in this book, we align with scholarship that interprets urban design as an always political, open-ended process that can produce more equitable spatial arrangements (Loukaitou-Sideris 2012; Tonkiss 2017). Against neoliberal dynamics that make cities increasingly hostile to marginalized groups, we suggest that a just urban design should enable oppressed subjects to claim a *right to difference*, or the "right to presence, to occupy public space, and to participate as equals in public affairs," regardless of one's gender, sexuality, class, race/ethnicity, or health (Sandercock 2003, 103). We argue for a just and empowering placemaking approach that meets the needs of vendors while enabling them to occupy, use, and alter space.

We demonstrate our argument for an urban design of empowerment by analyzing street vending in Rome. Prior to February 2020, when the COVID-19 pandemic emptied the city's public spaces, roughly two thousand immigrants occupied Rome's iconic tourist sites, selling trinkets without licenses. Most vendors were men from Bangladesh who often lacked a regular immigration status. After presenting a brief overview of the street vending literature, we detail how growing xenophobia, ambiguous regulations, and discretional law enforcement expose Rome's immigrant vendors to the risks of fines, detention, and deportation. We then draw from observations, mapping, and interviews to analyze the tactics that help Bangladeshi vendors navigate everyday challenges. We find that vendors enact three kinds of spatial tactics to defy exclusion. First, they seize economic opportunities by strategically positioning themselves within the built environment. Second, they satisfy their basic needs by inhabiting networks of hiding places. And third, they emplace their belonging by occupying public spaces outside of working hours to relax, pray, or videochat with their families in Bangladesh.

The vendors' practices result in tactical urbanism that challenges dominant ideas of "the appropriate" (as in chapter 2, tactical urbanism emerges from the practices of cultural and political resistance that marginalized subjects enact in the spaces of everyday life). We suggest that urban designers should learn from this tactical urbanism in order to help empower vendors to assert a right to difference. Drawing from our findings, we offer three design strategies that respectively enhance opportunities, accommodate needs, and make visible the vendors' geographies of belonging. Inscribing a right to difference into the built environment, these strategies can empower vendors to appropriate spaces while expanding ideas of who belongs to the city.

STREET VENDING: AN OVERVIEW

Ideally open and accessible to all, public spaces provide excellent opportunities to meet people and engage in commercial transactions. And indeed, streets across the world have served as marketplaces since antiquity, making cities like Athens, Mexico City, Rome, or Yangzhou known for their vibrant public life (Çelik, Favro, and Ingersoll 1994; Hartnett 2017; Calaresu and Heuvel 2018). Starting in the late nineteenth century, but accelerating in the twentieth century, modernizing imperatives prompted policymakers to regulate street activities while criminalizing uses (and users) that appeared to them as compromising order in public space. A variety of municipal ordinances and regulations helped marginalize sellers, who continued to operate at the shifting edges of formalized production and consumption networks (Loukaitou-Sideris and Ehrenfeucht 2009; Blomley 2011).

While early studies associated street commerce with the Global South and its "informal" economies (Hart 1973), researchers since the 1990s have highlighted how vending represents an equally crucial resource for historically excluded groups in cities across Europe and North America (Austin 1994; Reyneri 1998; Duneier 1999). In the 2000s, intensified migration flows, privatization of public assets, cuts in welfare provisions, and regulations of public spaces led scholars to acknowledge that formal and informal domains overlap and intersect beyond the conventional north/south divides (Morales 2010; Mukhija and Loukaitou-Sideris 2014).

As widening inequalities make cities increasingly hostile to the underprivileged, street vending continues to be an accessible activity for poor urbanites worldwide (WIEGO 2020), and in particular for immigrants in cities of the Global North (Devlin 2018; Alford, Kothari, and Pottinger 2019). Yet, policymakers continue to see street vendors as a disturbance to be banished. Ordinances and regulations especially target vendors in prime spaces, where their presence compromises dominant narratives of who is entitled to be visible in the city (Cross and Carides 2007; Yatmo 2008; Crossa 2016). Social and spatial constructions of race play a key role in this process. Law enforcers across the south-north divide spatialize "whitening" logics by targeting and removing vendors of color more than others (Munoz 2018; Tucker and Devlin 2019). While often it is the visibility of vendors as "undesirables" that motivates hostile regulations, policymakers seek to banish them on the basis of familiar tropes: casting sellers as tax dodgers, unfair competitors to formal shop-owners, or sellers of counterfeit and unsafe products. In other cases, vendors are accused of compromising health and sanitation by littering streets or hindering pedestrian and vehicular flows (Cross and Morales 2007; Skinner and Reed 2020).

To be sure, authorities do not always see street vending as a symptom of disorder and backwardness. In cities of Europe and North America, policymakers promote "pop-up" and "gourmet" markets or "designer" taco trucks that appeal to tourists and white-collar professionals while displacing less privileged groups (Agyeman, Matthews, and Sobel 2017). Planners and designers are complicit in these operations. Engaging in the production of "vibrant" places without critically assessing the sociopolitical effects of their work, designers often promote "vending urbanisms" (Loukaitou-Sideris and Mukhija 2019) that boost tourism and increase property values while excluding marginalized groups further (Bostic, Kim, and Valenzuela 2016).

In most cases, however, authorities target underprivileged vendors through exclusionary urban policies that banish them from historic downtowns and their "congested" streets (Huang, Xue, and Li 2014; Roever and Skinner 2016). The removal of vendors also occurs through more implicit but equally oppressive methods. Urban regulations are often designed to outlaw people who stand rather than walk along sidewalks, de facto criminalizing vendors who occupy public spaces (Loukaitou-Sideris and Ehrenfeucht 2009; Blomley 2011). Vending and permitting policies are generally ambiguous, rapidly changing, and hardly accessible, making it difficult for vendors to comply with the law (Kettles 2014; Batreau and Bonnet 2016). Finally, and crucially to the argument of this chapter, the ways that spaces are designed and maintained also tend to make streets hostile to vendors by preventing them access, making it difficult to move around, or creating environments where it is uncomfortable to stay for prolonged times (Kamalipour and Peimani 2019; Carr, 2020).

Street vendors do not endure exclusion passively but rather engage in practices of resistance. This occurs, for example, when vendors mobilize and confront authorities to negotiate their rights. In India, vendors' protests led to the 2014 Street Vending Act, which prompted local governments to accommodate their demands, albeit more formally than substantially (Cannon et al. 2019). In New York, the Street Vendor Project is a grassroots advocacy group with the mission to correct injustices faced by vendors and often represents vendors in courts. In Los Angeles, after years of advocacy, the city council countered the Trump administration's anti-immigration policies by legalizing street vending (Crisman and Kim 2019). Despite these examples, street vendors often do not have the time, organizational power, or will to explicitly confront authorities. Bayat (2000) has argued that in most cases, it is the "quiet encroachments" through which vendors and other marginalized groups occupy public spaces that constitute political assertions of difference in the city. Focusing on tactical forms of resistance, scholars have studied the ways by which diverse vendors ordinarily negotiate spaces to sell (Vargas and Valencia 2019), work out relationships with law enforcement (Lata, Walters, and Roitman 2019), equip and transform public spaces to make them better vending locations (Rios 2014; Kim 2015), and hide during police raids (Crossa 2009).

Scholars have thus acknowledged that space plays a crucial role in furthering the exclusion of vulnerable vendors and, occasionally, in enabling them to resist such exclusion. Little systematic attention, however, has been given to how built environments affect these dynamics and how placemaking approaches can facilitate vendors' resistance. With this purpose in mind, we turn to analyze how Rome's public spaces foster the marginalization of immigrant vendors while also enabling them to emplace their geographies of resistance and belonging.

VENDING REGULATIONS AND SPATIAL CLEANSING IN ROME

Institutional attempts to sanitize prime spaces are apparent in Rome, a city where ambiguous vending regulations, increased xenophobia, and selective law enforcement continue to oppress immigrants. Vendors who sell informally in the streets of Rome are exposed to multiple risks: a fine of 5,162 euros and confiscation of merchandise (for vending without a license), possible incarceration from six months to four years and a fine of up to 35,000 euros (if they sell counterfeit merchandise), and incarceration and deportation (in case of irregular immigration status). These risks reflect wider trends that have progressively "beautified" historic Rome as a pristine site inhabited by white people. Since the 1970s, a booming tourist economy has prompted city authorities to displace low-income residents and privatize public spaces (Agnew 1995). Neoliberal processes have accelerated these trends by furthering the homogenization of commercial landscapes, the spread of hotels and motels, and the closure of public hospitals and schools in the historic center (Lelo, Monni, and Tomassi 2019).

Sanitization and privatization processes render the lives of immigrant vendors more and more precarious. Obtaining vending permits to sell itinerantly is relatively straightforward according to Italian laws: one must pay 60 euros to the city, register for VAT (value-added tax), and join the chamber of commerce. These seemingly smooth steps, however, are hard for people who lack connections and especially for immigrants. Lamenting the presence of too many vendors, city officials stopped giving licenses in the late 1990s and formalized this practice in the early 2000s. Very few people can afford to buy licenses from retiring vendors, which today costs 40,000–60,000 euros. Most vendors have no choice other than to sell informally. Imposed by city authorities, this informal vending regime facilitates clientelism and discretionary law enforcement. Among the vendors not possessing a license, some old-timers—generally Italian natives—can count on strong social ties to participate in the networks of power that regulate everyday street life. Other, mostly immigrant vendors, lack connections and remain exposed to the ostracism of policemen.

Rampant xenophobia aggravates the struggles of these less privileged vendors. Selling on the street provided immigrants with an accessible, albeit precarious, source of income since the 1900s (Reyneri 1998). The tourist industry of Rome quickly attracted Bangladeshis who, when not hired in hotels and restaurants in the center, took advantage of their familiarity with English by selling roses and gadgets to tourists (King and Knights 1994). The presence of immigrant vendors in Rome prompted xenophobic reactions from residents and policymakers. In 2009, Rome's mayor Gianni Alemanno issued an ordinance outlawing individuals who entered the city center with "big bags," a rule that was part of a larger "zero tolerance" policy targeting "inappropriate" behavior and people (Comune di Roma 2011).

These oppressive conditions have worsened over the past few years. Riding the wave of racism enhanced by the "immigration crisis," in 2017, the Italian government approved the Urgent Measures in Defense of Urban Safety and Decorum law that allows mayors to banish individuals who "disturb" the "free use" of public spaces from historic centers. People who sell merchandise without licenses are listed among such disturbing individuals. In June 2019, Rome's mayor Virginia Raggi incorporated the Urban Safety and Decorum measures in the so-called urban police rules, confirming that individuals who behave "improperly" would be fined and banished from the historic center for a period between forty-eight hours and six months. Hostility toward immigrant vendors has continued to rise as recent immigration flows brought new people into vending, lowering the average income of each vendor from about 40 to 20 euros a day. While increased competition has exacerbated frictions among sellers, police tend to ignore native, white vendors and almost exclusively chase immigrants.

RESISTANCE AND BELONGING AT THE CENTER OF ROME

It is in this hostile environment that immigrant vendors eke out a living every day, risking fines, detention, and deportation. But the center of Rome is not only a space of exclusion and oppression. It is also an arena where vendors place their own geographies of resistance and belonging by occupying, appropriating, and marking spaces with their bodies and merchandise. To understand these dynamics, we studied thirty vending locations and interviewed twenty-eight vendors along with police officers, workers, residents, and tourists in the pedestrian-only historic center of Rome, an area that extends over 1.5 square miles (figure 13.1). We focused on Bangladeshis, who compose the greatest number of vendors in Rome (IDOS 2020). We collected data between November 2017 and August 2018. Through observations, maps, and interviews, we investigated how they use and perceive spaces as well as their relationships with

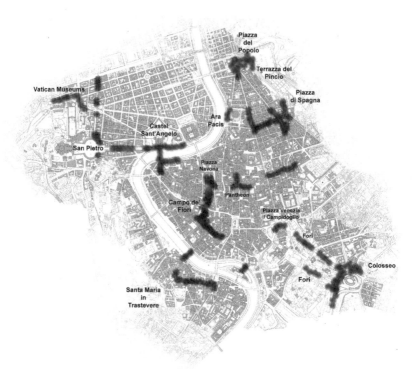

13.1 Concentrations of vendors in the historic center of Rome. *Source*: Francesca Piazzoni.

other vendors. Interviews lasted forty-five to ninety minutes, were carried outside of selling hours, and took place in locations chosen by the interviewees (usually in cafés or on streets near vending areas). As detailed elsewhere (Piazzoni 2020; 2022), recruitment and interviewing methods evolved through time, as relationships of trust emerged between respondents and the first author of this chapter, who undertook the fieldwork.

Vendors compose a very diverse group of men whose immigration status and seniority on the street determine hierarchies of power within the vending community. Most vendors prefer to live as close as possible to their vending location in order to minimize commuting time and avoid traveling through peripheral districts. For 150 euros a month, vendors live in overcrowded basements or building attics that are just a few blocks away from key tourist sites. Rented by one or two compatriots with regular immigration status, these units host up to eleven men per room, forcing up to twenty-five people to share a bathroom. Lack of space and privacy push vendors to occupy public spaces, not only to seize economic opportunities but also to satisfy personal needs that would remain otherwise unmet and to carry out effective and spiritual practices.

SEIZING OPPORTUNITIES

Vendors start selling around 10:00 a.m. and continue for eight to fourteen hours depending on police controls, weather conditions, and tourists' presence. We identified four types of vending locations across the historic center: streets connecting tourist sites (figure 13.2), streets leading to a landmark (figure 13.3), piazzas (figure 13.4), and panoramic terraces (figure 13.5). Vendors position themselves differently within each of these space typologies. They seek to approach as many tourists as possible while remaining near escape routes in order to run if the police show up. Vendors tend to align next to each other along the sides of a street while waiting for people to pass by. If a landmark at the end of the street distracts tourists, vendors prefer to walk toward the passersby showcasing their items for sale. Similarly, vendors' tactics vary between piazzas, where they occupy central positions near fountains or statues, and terraces, where they position themselves at the edges.

13.2 Via delle Muratte, a popular vending location that connects the Trevi Fountain to the Pantheon. *Source*: Francesca Piazzoni.

13.3 The Sant Angelo bridge connecting Piazza Navona to the Saint Peter Basilica ends in a landmark. *Source*: Francesca Piazzoni.

13.4 Vendors in front of the "Four River" fountain in Piazza Navona. *Source*: Francesca Piazzoni.

13.5 The panoramic terrace in front of the Colosseum provides vendors with a strategic location to wait for tourists. *Source*: Francesca Piazzoni.

Diverse vendors choose to occupy a place for different reasons, such as the presence of friends, commuting time, frequency of police raids, proximity to escape routes, or familiarity with monuments that vendors might have seen in pictures before moving to Italy. Vendor Rahul, for instance, continued selling in Piazza del Popolo after he moved to a new house close to the Colosseum. Rather than going to the nearest vending location, Rahul preferred walking an extra thirty minutes to work where he felt "not at home, but almost at home." Some features of the built environment, such as lighting, street width, presence of shops, or even pavement type and quality (which may prevent or facilitate escape and display of merchandise), determine which selling spots are the best within each vending location.

SATISFYING NEEDS

Vendors develop and inhabit networks of safe places in order to hide from police and satisfy needs that would remain otherwise unmet. The porousness of Rome's urban fabric provides plenty of tunnels, lanes, churches, and courtyards that they can use to disappear quickly during police raids. Hiding merchandise is crucial, not only when police are close but also at night when some vendors prefer leaving goods in public spaces rather than bringing them home where space is minimal. Ordinary city elements such as electrical boxes, sewer covers, or bushes become precious "closets" to leave merchandise and food. Around noon, for example, a Bangladeshi cook leaves packaged meals in an electric box for vendors to gather during their break. Police officers avoid interrupting this informal lunch-delivery system, which most patrollers reported seeing as an innocuous activity unrelated to vending infractions.

Vendors take advantage of the ordinary disorder of the city to hide objects in plain sight. Some leave merchandise near uncollected garbage, counting on the fact that no one will pick it up, while others leave their goods within fenced areas that are inconvenient to reach, knowing that the police will not bother going there. The complexity and permeability of the built environment also accommodate vendors wishing to take a break. Vendors use bushes and trees to create a toilet area and beds to rest between 2 and 4 p.m., during the afternoon break when police controls are more frequent. At times, the solidarity of others, such as restaurant employees, may help vendors satisfy needs like using a restroom or charging their phones.

EMPLACING BELONGING

Vendors use iconic sites not only to work but also to carry out personal activities. Green areas become gathering spaces where they go to chat, relax, and play cricket. Most vendors stay in the city center after work to video-chat with their distant wives and children. Chain restaurants such as McDonald's or Burger King are comfortable environments for vendors to remain unnoticed among the crowds. Restaurant employees at times buy vendors coffee so that they can stay indoors during cold days. Bustling public spaces also provide vendors with the privacy they want. Some like to call relatives standing in front of iconic landmarks. A vendor who does not want to disclose his precarious housing conditions to his wife, for example, calls her from Piazza Navona, a "beautiful" site which he believes conveys the image of his "European success."

Reciting Muslim prayers is another activity that vendors cannot carry out in the open, and for which they need to find the appropriate infrastructure—running water for ablutions and a clean space to stand, bow, and kneel facing toward the Kaaba. Some vendors in small groups occupy quiet areas such as neglected green spaces or tranquil alleys. Others reach out to informal prayer halls at the backs of shops or mezzanines of Bangladeshi-run convenient shops that have sprung around the historic center. Still, other vendors pray in front of monuments, prime areas that are cleaner than other spaces and where they feel protected by the presence of tourists. Such historic settings satisfy needs that their designers had never envisioned, such as when vendors use staircases of churches to bow, the window bars of monuments to hide prayer rugs, or the water of nineteenth-century fountains to wash before praying.

AN URBAN DESIGN OF EMPOWERMENT

Immigrant street vendors thus place their own geographies of resistance and belonging by occupying, appropriating, and transforming the center of Rome. Their ordinary practices configure tactical urbanism that disrupts dominant constructions of who has the right to inhabit the city. Rather than simply acknowledging these kinds of tactical urbanism, we argue that just urban design should actively empower deprived subjects to occupy, use, and transform spaces according to their needs. We call for empowering placemaking strategies that inscribe a right to difference in the built form. Acknowledging the political implications of urban design, scholars have suggested that urban spaces should better respond to the ways that marginalized publics appropriate cities (Loukaitou-Sideris and Mukhija 2016; 2019). Street vending and other informal uses of public space typify the kinds of activities that urban designers have long ignored, if not purposely tried to eliminate. We suggest that designers should engage with these dynamics by enabling marginalized groups to assert their right to difference. More concretely, we draw from the vendors' tactics and propose three kinds of empowering spatial interventions that exemplify just urban design practices for street vendors.

ENHANCING OPPORTUNITIES

The ways that vendors appropriate and use spaces suggest opportunities for creating more hospitable places to sell. For one, urban design should acknowledge the importance of public space maintenance. Our fieldwork showed how seemingly banal interventions, such as filling up holes in street pavements, regulating traffic lights to ensure regular pedestrian flows, or fixing broken balustrades, can affect the ways vendors appropriate spaces and interact with tourists. Ongoing maintenance should seek to repair the built environments that marginalized groups occupy to survive. A second strategy requires designers to create new selling infrastructures while acknowledging the overlapping temporalities of vending and other activities. Streets that are used by vendors during certain hours of the day would benefit from provisional infrastructure (removable stalls, shades, trashcans, lighting, and storage spaces). Finally, it is essential to provide vendors with spaces where they can meet, socialize, and organize. Creating such spaces would improve the chances for vendors to designate representatives and advocate for their rights.

ACCOMMODATING NEEDS

Designers should create environments that accommodate the vendors' neglected needs comfortably. Conflict and othering frequently occur because vendors are forced to occupy settings used for other activities. Public restrooms and showers are a case in point. While some shops in the center of Rome let vendors use their toilets, many vendors have no choice but to urinate and defecate in public spaces. Furnishing the center of Rome with accessible public restrooms would ensure the dignity of vendors while also providing a much-needed service to other groups. Public showers are equally needed, especially given the precarious living conditions of the vendors who lack space and privacy at home, and refrain from using showers at night to avoid drawing the attention of wealthier building residents. Similarly, installing public facilities to charge electric appliances would considerably improve the everyday lives of vendors and other groups. Other elements that could make the vendors' long hours on the pavement more comfortable but would also be beneficial for other groups include trees for shade and benches for seating.

MAKING BELONGING VISIBLE

Designers should put their expertise at the service of marginalized groups, helping shape landscapes that convey those groups' ideas of belonging.

Taking advantage of their privileged position, designers should assist deprived people in voicing their needs and making their practices visible, disrupting normative aesthetics of who belongs to the city. Providing vendors (and Muslim publics more broadly) with designated areas to pray in the center of Rome would not only prevent people from overcrowding unequipped and unsafe spaces but would also challenge popular understandings of Rome as an exclusively Catholic city. Equipping public parks with cricket fields would accommodate the ways by which Bangladeshis already use green areas and defy the notion of soccer as the sole sport representative of Italy. Finally, designers could develop signage for tourists that would acknowledge the hidden histories of other groups in the city—laborers, ethnic groups, religious minorities, and immigrants—who have also shaped the landscapes of Rome but whose histories remain neglected by the dominant construction of "historic Rome." By making difference visible in iconic landscapes, these spaces would disrupt dominant perceptions of "the appropriate," inscribe the recognition of difference into the built environment, and facilitate microgeographies of cosmopolitanism among diverse groups.

CONCLUSION

As neoliberal trends push underprivileged groups out of prime spaces worldwide, just urban design should promote placemaking strategies that enhance, accommodate, and make visible opportunities for such groups to live in the city. In the center of Rome, xenophobia, vending regulations, and discretional law enforcement marginalize immigrant vendors. While structural injustices and precarious living conditions have so far prevented Rome's immigrant vendors from organizing into advocacy movements, the vendors implicitly claim a *right to difference* (Sandercock 2003) through their everyday appropriations of space. Seemingly mundane spatial features bear crucial political implications as they facilitate or prevent these appropriations. The vendors' encroachments materialize tactical urbanism that satisfies their otherwise neglected needs and disrupts hegemonic constructions of "historic" Rome. We suggest that urban designers should learn from and respond to this tactical urbanism.

Drawing from the quotidian practices of Rome's vendors, we propose
three empowering placemaking strategies. First, as vendors seize economic
opportunities by appropriating spaces, designers should enhance these
opportunities. This would imply upkeeping the built environment (critically assessing what elements to fix, integrate, or remove and acknowledging the political implications of care and repair) so that vendors can
continue to sell, create new vending infrastructures, and have spaces to
socialize and organize. Second, as vendors satisfy their needs by finding
provisional refuge in the urban fabric, designers should create more permanent spaces to accommodate them, such as public restrooms, showers,
and electric charging and Wi-Fi stations. Finally, as vendors emplace their
sense of belonging by carrying out personal activities, designers should
create and make visible spaces for these activities. Prayer rooms, facilities
to play sports, and multicultural tourist signs would emplace the right
to difference of vendors and other minority groups who inhabit Rome's
center every day.

The way by which public spaces are designed and maintained concretely impacts the abilities of marginalized groups to make a living, feel
safe, and negotiate a sense of belonging in cities across the globe. Empowering placemaking strategies acknowledges these dynamics and advance
justice by welcoming rather than excluding marginalized people. By spatializing and making visible *a right to difference* in the built form, just
urban design can defy dominant definitions of "the proper" and let all
urban dwellers make a city their home.

AFTERWORD

The fieldwork for this chapter was carried out before the COVID-19 pandemic emptied Rome's streets in February 2020. As rumors of an immi-
nent lockdown spread, a few vendors returned to Bangladesh or moved to
other European countries. Most, however, remained in Rome, jobless and
unable to seek assistance from service facilities that were closed or chari-
ties. When shops and restaurants started reopening in June 2020, vendors
returned to sell on the streets. But the presence of only a few tourists
made eking out a living even harder than before. Moreover, far-right narratives of immigrants as carriers of the COVID-19 virus further stigmatize

vendors. While post-COVID recovery measures approved by the Italian government include the regularization of immigrants, these regularizations only benefit people with specific service jobs such as caregivers and agricultural workers. In order to keep businesses open, city authorities have allowed cafés and restaurants in the city center to occupy more outdoor space, but no space was extended for street commerce. As we write, migrant vendors continue their struggle to survive on the streets of Rome, hoping for a better future.

REFERENCES

Agnew, J. (1995). *Rome*. Chichester, UK: John Wiley & Sons.

Agyeman, J., Matthews, C., and Sobel, H. (2017). *Food Trucks, Cultural Identity, and Social Justice. From Loncheras to Lobsta Love*. Cambridge, MA: MIT Press.

Alford, M., Kothari, U., and Pottinger, L. (2019). "Re-Articulating Labour in Global Production Networks: The Case of Street Traders in Barcelona." *Environment and Planning D* 37 (6): 1081–1099.

Austin, R. (1994). "An Honest Living": Street Vendors, Municipal Regulation and the Black Public Sphere." *Yale Law Journal* 103: 2120–2131.

Batreau, Q., and Bonnet, F. (2016). "Managed Informality: Regulating Street Vendors in Bangkok." *City and Community* 15 (1): 29–43.

Bayat, A. (2000). "From 'Dangerous Classes' to 'Quiet Rebels': Politics of the Urban Subaltern in the Global South." *International Sociology* 15 (3): 533–557.

Blomley, N. (2011). *Rights of Passage: Sidewalks and the Regulation of Public Flow*. New York: Routledge.

Bostic, R., Kim, A. M., and Valenzuela, A. (2016). "Contesting the Streets, Vending and Public Space in Global Cities." *Cityscape* 18: 3–10.

Bromley, R. D. (2000). "Street Vending and Public Policy: A Global Review." *International Journal of Sociology and Social Policy* 20 (1/2): 1–28.

Calaresu, M., and Heuvel, D. (2018). *Food Hawkers: Selling in the Streets from Antiquity to the Present*. London: Routledge.

Cannon, M., Thorpe, J., Emili, S., and Lintelo, D. (2019). *National Street Vendor Association: Lobbying for a National Urban Street Vendor Policy in India*. Brighton: IDS.

Carr, C. (2020). "For Street Vendors, Finding Water and Toilets Isn't Just A Nuisance, It's Cutting into Earnings." In WIEGO, *Street Vendors and Public Space*. WIEGO, 22–25.

Çelik, Z., Favro, D. G., and Ingersoll, R. (1994). *Streets: Critical Perspectives on Public Space*. Berkeley: University of California Press.

Certeau, M. D. (1984). *The Practice of Everyday Life.* Berkeley: University of California Press.

Comune di Roma (2011). "Decoro Urbano, Campidoglio al Lavoro Su Più Fronti." https://www.comune.roma.it/pcr/it/newsview.page?contentId=NEW151532.

Crisman, J. J., and Kim, A. (2019). "Property Outlaws in the Southland: The Potential and Limits of Guerrilla Urbanism in the Cases of Arts Gentrification in Boyle Heights and Street Vending Decriminalization in Los Angeles." *Urban Design International* 24 (3): 159–170.

Cross, J., and Karides, M. (2007). "Capitalism, Modernity, and the 'Appropriate' Use of Space." In Cross, J., and Morales, A. (eds.). *Street Enterpreneurs.* New York: Routledge, 19–35.

Cross, J. C., and Morales, A. (2007). "Introduction. Locating Street Markets in the Modern/Postmodern World." In Cross, J., and Morales, A. (eds.). *Street Entrepreneurs: People, Place and Politics in Local and Global Perspective.* London: Routledge, 1–14.

Crossa, V. (2009). "Resisting the Entrepreneurial City: Street Vendors' Struggle in Mexico City's Historic Center." *International Journal of Urban and Regional Research* 33 (1): 43–63.

Crossa, V. (2016). "Reading for Difference on the Street: De-Homogenising Street Vending in Mexico City." *Urban Studies* 53 (2): 287–301.

Devlin, R. (2018). "Global Best Practice or Regulating Fiction? Zero Tolerance and Conflicts over Public Space in New York, 1980–2000." *International Journal of Urban and Regional Research* 42 (3): 517–532.

Duneier, M. (1999). *Sidewalk.* New York: Farrar, Straus and Giroux.

Graaf, K., and Ha, N. (2015). *Street Vending in the Neoliberal City: A Global Perspective on the Practices and Policies of a Marginalized Economy.* New York: Berghahn.

Hart, K. (1973). "Informal Income Opportunities and Urban Employment in Ghana." *Journal of Modern African Studies* 11 (1): 61-89.

Hartnett, J. (2017). *The Roman Street: Urban Life and Society in Pompeii, Herculaneum, and Rome.* Cambridge, UK: Cambridge University Press.

Huang, G., Xue, D., and Li, Z. (2014). "From Revanchism to Ambivalence: The Changing Politics of Street Vending in Guangzhou." *Antipode* 46 (1): 170–179.

IDOS. (2020). *Osservatorio Romano sulle Migrazioni.* Roma: Centro Studi e Ricerche IDOS.

Kamalipour, H., and Peimani, N. (2019). "Negotiating Space and Visibility: Forms of Informality in Public Space." *Sustainability* 11: 1–19.

Kamel, N. (2014). "Learning from the Margin: Placemaking Tactics." In Mukhija, V., and Loukaitou-Sideris, A. (eds.). *The Informal American City: Beyond Taco Trucks and Day Labor.* Cambridge, MA: MIT Press, 119–136.

Kettles, G. (2014). "Crystals, Mud, and Space: Street Vending and Informality." In Mukhija, V., and Loukaitou-Sideris, A. *The Informal American City*. Cambridge, MA: MIT Press, 227–242.

Kim, A. (2015). *Sidewalk City: Remapping Public Space in Ho Chi Minch City*. Chicago: University of Chicago Press.

King, R., and Knights, M. (1994). "Bangladeshis in Rome: A Case of Migratory Opportunism." In Gould, W., and Findlay, A. M. (eds.). *Population Migration and the Changing World Order*. Chichester, UK: Wiley.

Lata, L., Walters, P., and Roitman, S. (2019). "A Marriage of Convenience: Street Vendors' Everyday Accommodation of Power in Dhaka, Bangladesh." *Cities* 84: 143–150.

Lelo, K., Monni, S., and Tomassi, F. (2019). "Socio-Spatial Inequalities and Urban Transformation: The Case of Rome Districts." *Socio-Economic Planning Sciences* (March): 1–11.

Loukaitou-Sideris, A. (2012). "Addressing the Challenges of Urban Landscapes: Normative Goals for Urban Design." *Journal of Urban Design* 17 (4): 467–484.

Loukaitou-Sideris, A., and Ehrenfeucht, R. (2009). *Sidewalks: Conflict and Negotiation over Public Space*. Cambridge, MA: MIT Press.

Loukaitou-Sideris, A., and Mukhija, V. (2016). "Responding to Informality through Urban Design Studio Pedagogy." *Journal of Urban Design*: 577–595.

Loukaitou-Sideris, A., and Mukhija, V. (2019). "Informal Urbanism and the American City." In Arefi, M., and Kickert, C. (eds.). *The Palgrave Handbook of Bottom-Up Urbanism*. London: Palgrave Macmillan, 83–98.

Morales, A. (2010). "Planning and the Self-Organization of Marketplaces." *Journal of Planning Education and Research* 30 (2), 182–197.

Mörtenböeck, P., Mooshammer, H., Cruz, T., and Forman, F. (2015). *Informal Market Worlds—Reader. The Architecture of Economic Pressure*. Amsterdam: nai010.

Mukhija, V. and Loukaitou-Sideris, A. (2014). *The Informal American City: From Taco Trucks to Day Labor*. Cambridge, MA: MIT Press.

Munoz, L. (2018). " 'Recovering' Public Space and Race: Afro-Colombian Street Vendors in Bogota, Colombia." *Environment and Planning C* 36 (4): 573–588.

Piazzoni, F. (2020). "Visibility as Justice: Immigrant Street Vendors and the Right to Difference in Rome." *Journal of Planning Education and Research* (September 2020): doi:10.1177/0739456X20956387.

Piazzoni, F. (2022). "Material Agencies of Survival: Street Vending on a Roman Bridge." *Cities* (January 2022) doi: 10.1016/j.cities.2021.103412.

Reyneri, E. (1998). "The Role of the Underground Economy in Irregular Migration to Italy: Cause or Effect?" *Journal of Ethnic and Migration Studies* 24 (2): 313–331.

Rios, M. (2014). "Learning from Informal Practices: Implications for Urban Design." In Mukhija, V., and Loukaitou-Sideris, A. *The Informal American City*. Cambridge, MA: MIT Press, 173–191.

Roever, S., and Skinner, C. (2016). "Street Vendors and Cities." *Environment and Urbanization* 28 (2): 359–374.

Sandercock, L. (2003). *Cosmopolis II: Mongrel Cities in the 21st Century*. London: Continuum.

Skinner, C., and Reed, S. (2020). "Myths and Facts about Street Vendors." In WIEGO, *Street Vendors and Public Space*, 12–16.

Tonkiss, F. (2017). "Socialising Design? From Consumption to Production." *City* 21 (6): 872–882.

Tucker, J. L., and Devlin, R. T. (2019). "Uncertainty and the Governance of Street Vending: A Critical Comparison across the North/South Divide." *International Journal of Urban and Regional Research* 43 (3): 460–475.

Vargas, A. M., and Valencia, S. (2019). "Beyond State Regulation of Informality: Understanding Access to Public Space by Street Vendors in Bogotá." *International Development Planning Review* 41 (1): 85–105.

WIEGO. (2020). *Street Vendors and Public Space*. February 2020. https://www.wiego .org/resources/street-vendors-and-public-space-interactive-e-book.

Yatmo, Y. A. (2008). "Street Vendors as 'Out of Place' Urban Elements." *Journal of Urban Design* 13 (3): 387–402.

14

BUILDING A BLACK PUBLIC REALM AND PUBLIC CULTURE

LEARNING FROM LEIMERT PARK VILLAGE

Matthew Jordan-Miller Kenyatta

Few works in urban planning and design explore the geography of Black space with attention to how Black artists and entrepreneurs claim, make, and keep places. Even fewer make meaningful connections between cultural production and sustainability and Black economic geographies. Yet, there are several virtues to understanding the economic and cultural bases that a Black public realm can offer cities. In this chapter, I develop the idea of a public city by asking: *What if Blackness mattered to urban design's public function and forms?* To motivate this question theoretically, I reinterpret the concept of Blackness as publicness as the practice of developing freedom from society's margins through spatial agency and belongingness. Further, by using a Pan-Africanist place identity as a politically valuable cultural resource, my conceptualization of Blackness as publicness seeks to provide a counterweight that balances deficit-driven narratives about Black space. Using a case study of Black cultural entrepreneurs in the Leimert Park neighborhood in Los Angeles, I reveal ongoing opportunities to design and keep Black public spaces.

BLACKNESS AS PUBLICNESS: CREATING FREEDOMS, SPATIALIZING AGENCY, AND EMPLACING BELONGINGNESS

Urban designers have primarily proposed colorblind frameworks for publicness in the conventional practice of forging public space (Varna and

Tiesdell 2010; Carmona 2015). For example, the star model proposed by George Varna and Steve Tiesdell (2010) conceptualizes publicness in five meta dimensions—ownership, control, civility, physical configuration, and animation—but does not directly mention racial or ethnic diversity. While the authors cite accessibility and tolerance as background, they do not elevate diversity as a central component of publicness. Similarly, Matthew Carmona's (2015, 399) work on the development of "pragmatic principles" argues for a "new normative" retheorization of public space and attempts to defend against scholarly public space critiques. But while Carmona notes that his case study spaces in London have not suffered from contemporary neglect, he concludes with a problematic interpretation of "evolving (sometimes neglected)" public spaces. As he argues: "Although neglect can and should be criticised, it is also part of natural evolutionary processes that eventually (in many places) lead to renewal, either through regeneration or redevelopment." He concludes, "[Neglect] is part of a normal place-shaping continuum in which innovation and change is, and should be, a key feature."

Carmona's musings have dangerously unexamined implications for the racialized American context. Critical race theory provides a view of racism as "normalcy" itself, which, if gone unchallenged, as the aforementioned framework permits, spatial neglect due to anti-Blackness will be normalized as "pragmatic" to justify innovation. Indeed, by either skirting racial injustice questions or rationalizing the histories of urban neglect, urban design thought has either ignored or naturalized mechanisms of anti-Blackness. History tugs the tusk of an ever-present elephant in the room: *What can urban design mean for Black people excluded from the public realm through systemic, violent racism?* To relate racial equity to publicness within urban design, I turn to history and political philosophy to argue that a just urban design praxis must usher in the "unoppressive city" (Young 1990) by addressing the history of racial planning (Williams 2020). Publicness here means developing freedom by advancing specific "central capabilities" that give denizens agency to choose how they function (Sen 2001; Nussbaum 2011). However, these developmental capabilities must manifest in *spaces* and *places* that matter to marginalized people, freeing the agency within Black lives. In contrast, urban designers are largely employed to build exclusionary public spaces—corporate plazas, fortress malls, and gated communities—that keep the marginalized at bay in service of whiteness. Given how indifferent conventional definitions of publicness are toward anti-Blackness, dismantling exclusionary publicness requires race-aware frames of reference.

African American history frames this need for a spatial agency within the public realm as "the ability to be in, act on or exert control over a desired part of the built-and-natural environment" (Montgomery 2016, 777). Enmeshing urban design with Black history grounds publicness in actual lives—not abstract urban avatars. Following Paul Taylor (2016), I define Blackness as an Afrodiasporic, indigenous, earthbound worldview derived from the intimate life-worlds of people racially positioned as Black. While Black culture is regionally and temporally specific, nearly all formats derive from the rural Southern United States, the Global South, and racially segregated urban-suburban life. Blackness appears in all media: architecture, fashion, spirituality, music, visual art, food, dance, literature, education, politics, and increasingly science/technology (Dent 1992; Powell 2002; Moya and Markus 2010). From the Harlem Renaissance of the 1920s to the Black Arts Movement of the 1970s to the New Black Aesthetic of the 1990s, Black arts and culture have been historic ingredients in the cosmopolitan recipe of urbanism itself. By providing avenues for the creolization of world cultures (Taylor 2016) and the interaction of seemingly disparate diasporas in dense urban villages, people racially positioned as Black often wrestle with the problems of the colonial urban condition with nonwhite neighbors.

Urban disinvestment and racialized exploitation are inseparable scaffolds from which Black creativity has evolved. While the Black middle class saw returning to inner cities in the 1980s onward as a form of "racial uplift" (Boyd 2005), the white creative class saw returning as a cosmopolitan transaction: gentrifying and transmuting "grit into glamour" (Lloyd 2014). White creatives made urban economic downturns into their "competitive advantage" (Porter 1995). "Creativity" became a colorblind exercise fueling the neocolonization of inner-city neighborhoods, combining economic segregation with a "winner takes all" political society and fueling the "new urban crisis" (Florida 2017). Beginning in 2020, the COVID-19 pandemic began exposing these vulnerabilities. According to federal watchdog testimony by the US Government Accountability Office to Congress, the Trump administration botched Small Business

Administration loans funded by the CARES Act due to "fraud" and "lack of controls" (Shear 2020). By April 2020, over 41 percent of small Black-owned businesses (BOBs) had closed (Fairlie 2020). Meanwhile, the "Black summer" of racial protest due to police murders mainstreamed the Black Lives Matter movement. Corporate America has partly responded with some sympathy for BOBs: from the digital public realm of logistics apps like Uber waiving fees for BOBs to physical retailers painting "Black Lives Matter" on the pavement or ornamenting with virtue-signaling signage their boarded-up façades. Sympathy, however, is not equity.

BOBs offer political, social, and economic value to neighborhoods, and significant urban studies have attested to their anchoring effects (Bates 2006; Wang 2012). Yet, BOBs remain entirely invisible in urban design, with zero articles in design journals analyzing them. During the Obama administration years, BOBs employed on average one-fifth of the Black labor force and generated $150 billion annually (Association for Enterprise Opportunity 2017). Successful Black "mom & pop" shops are inversely related to high crime among youth (Parker 2015) and social activism (Gill 2010). Unlike the larger white creative class, whose presence in neighborhoods is associated with gentrification and income inequality, the Black creative class has "moderating effects" on economic segregation (Florida 2017).

Just urban design based on Blackness as publicness should conceptualize these freedom-enhancing realms and spaces by considering the spatial mechanics of belongingness. Belongingness can be understood as a binary set of dimensions of "place-belongingness" or the "politics of belongingness" (Antonsich 2010), with the former as the experience of being "at home," and the latter a more discursive means of resisting socio-spatial exclusion. Place-belongingness spans several domains and scales: relational, legal, economic, spatio-temporal, cultural, autobiographical. Because the notion of freedom is baked into its ongoing history of resistance to exclusion in the public realm (that is, school desegregation, diner sit-ins, transportation boycotts), Blackness is a breath away from place-belongingness. Thus, in the remainder of this chapter, I observe Black belongingness at work in a single place through a cultural and economic examination of place-belongingness.

OBSERVING LEIMERT PARK'S BLACK CULTURAL ENTREPRENEURS

Black artistic and cultural geographies do not have a prominent place in the urban design literature. Given the elusiveness of the spatial mechanisms by which Black cultural entrepreneurs fashion publicness in the admittedly "fuzzy" design practice of creative placemaking (Markusen 2013; Nicodemus 2013), I explore how they make, claim, and/or keep places for everyday Black culture. In earlier work, I documented that minority business clusters can be found throughout the state of California, but South Los Angeles has the highest concentrations of Black entrepreneurship (Miller 2018). Between 2016 and 2018, I collected data as a participant-observer in Leimert Park, a neighborhood that represents the creative hub of South Los Angeles. In my ethnographic work, I observed the inner and outer workings of nearly two dozen cultural entrepreneurs—retail merchants, service-based nonprofits, property managers—who shape both Leimert Park Village ("the village") and its commercial corridor, Crenshaw Boulevard. While I participated as a visitor and consumer, I also conducted semistructured interviews and actively collaborated with interested stakeholders. My collaborations included assisting in forming an area-based programming nonprofit, codesigning a community-driven film, assisting with documenting community planning and development needs, and facilitating a community discussion around perceived gentrification. During the COVID-19 pandemic, many formal community meetings took place online, while informal public gatherings still activated the village. To maintain the privacy of certain subjects, I have anonymized them through pseudonyms, minimizing exact quotes, and sparsely referencing interpersonal conflicts.

BUILDING AND KEEPING A BLACK PUBLIC CULTURE
IN LEIMERT PARK

Leimert Park has earned a reputation as a Black political, economic, and cultural mecca in Los Angeles (LA). Its neighborhood retail zone, Leimert Park Village, looms large in local media and pop culture as LA's contemporary Black historical and cultural heart (figure 14.1). The village's long-term tenants—cultural nonprofits and community businesses, such as The World Stage, Eso Won Books, Kaos Networks, and LA Commons, have contributed to the development of a Black culture locally and beyond.

14.1 African wax print–inspired mural on a vacant building across from Leimert Park Village, December 2019. *Source*: Matthew Jordan-Miller Kenyatta.

Educational events and music performances, such as seasonal jazz festivals, weekly African drumming, and underground hip-hop, serve as major cultural attractions (Isoardi 2006; Lee 2016). Black food, literature, film, and fine art are complementary cultural institutions. Artists emerging from or moving to the village include newer musicians Kamasi Washington and Terrace Martin, older artists Horace Tapscott and Barbara Morrison, as well as internationally renowned visual artist and native son of Leimert Park, Mark Bradford.

Similar to the adjacent residential area that is full of Spanish Revival–styled homes, the Leimert Park Village holds architectural significance because of its 1920s art deco–style buildings. Both the commercial and residential areas were originally designed by the landscape architecture firm Olmsted Brothers for the Leimert Corporation in anticipation of the Olympics of 1932. Like the brownstones and bodegas of New York City's historically Black enclaves of Harlem and Fort Greene, Leimert Park has attracted and retained middle-class and upper-middle-class Black gentry since at least the 1990s. The late Oscar-winning filmmaker and tenant businessman John Singleton bestowed the neighborhood with the moniker of "Black Greenwich Village." In 2018, the village's plaza and park were included among the landmarks of the City of Los Angeles directory of historical-cultural monuments.

Leimert Park's creative actors have amassed and preserved spaces that produce a contested yet steady baseline of Black economic and cultural belongingness. As I discuss below, Black businesses in Leimert Park have organized themselves in several institutions across generations to create and sustain the makings of their Black public culture by balancing the demands of economic viability and cultural identity through place-keeping (figure 14.2). Central to this balancing act is their place-based Pan-Africanist identity, developed across generations of Black residents and visitors, which honors the complexity of competing demands within the community of merchants, vendors, and landowners.

SUSTAINING BLACK BELONGINGNESS: BALANCING ECONOMIC VIABILITY AND CULTURAL PRODUCTION IN PLACE-KEEPING

Property owners in Leimert Park and the surrounding Crenshaw corridor have carefully selected their tenants to curate the village's cohesive identity as a Black creative center vibrating with cultural production and economic vitality. They balance these intentions through a commitment to steward the spaces around sociality, long-term management, and social justice: in short, Black place-keeping. Put differently, longstanding Black property owners and merchants operate commercially with capacious consideration for the "good of the house," as the self-titled "Old Guard" who meet in monthly stakeholder meetings. Their commitment

14.2   African sculptural and visual art displayed on Crenshaw Boulevard across the site of the incoming Leimert Park metro station, December 2019. *Source:* Matthew Jordan-Miller Kenyatta.

to Black place-keeping is evident at multiple scales in Crenshaw's Black public realm. Place-keeping is present in the imaginaries of the unhoused artists who congregate to create street jazz under the coral tree canopy of the village's Degnan Boulevard, which they have dubbed the "Tree of Life." Place-keeping is present within the aesthetics of the everyday street artists making African masks from the fallen fronds of palm trees on the sidewalk. Place-keeping is celebrated within the aesthetics of the spectacular art institution Art+Practice, founded by Leimert Park native Mark Bradford. He recycles "endpapers" from curling hair in his mother's former Leimert Park Village salon into his now-lucrative form of collaging, critically engaging with the visual economies of excess that pollute Crenshaw's landscape (that is, billboards advertising guns, flyers by speculative property sharks preying on foreclosed homes). Place-keeping is present in the legal briefings of Crenshaw activists, who are tenants in the village and have sued the Los Angeles Metropolitan Transportation Authority (Metro) to secure environmental protections from the incoming light-rail interrupting flows of community commerce.[1] This social attentiveness to the racial politics of play, power, and place acts as an authentic buffer to unfettered profit-making, which might otherwise displace Black memories from public realms.

The Old Guard—baby boomer property-owning merchants—have had the most spatial agency to demonstrate how each tenant can contribute to developing a regional Black cultural destination. The longest-standing Old Guard property owner, eighty-year-old Ward Robinson, applies business tactics acquired from a twenty-year career in furniture and interior design sales to assemble complementary Black retailers and nonprofits. First, he aims to see a business plan. This step eliminates prospective tenants who might not operate using standardized hours, products, or even accounting methods for paid employees. Second, he scans for how they would recruit and brand the area around Black culture. Third, he tries to gauge their social character in a type of match-making conversation to ensure the prospective merchant is a "good person" with no criminal proclivities and a commitment to conduct themselves professionally if conflicts arise. These tactics, Ward touts, have helped him assemble profitable tenants who have complementary goods, services, and hours of operation on his block.

These three tactics, however, take a backseat to his main economic and spatial goal—preventing vacancy. In the interest of neighborhood character and preventing perceptions of blight, Ward perceives commerce as a community safety tactic, especially during nighttime. Thus, Ward keeps the rent lower than the market rate to attract promising entrepreneurs who need support and time to succeed. Given the structural volatility in cultural industries, Ward's balancing act has not always lasted on this block—or among other village property owners with a similar commitment to avoid blight. Several cherished businesses have cycled in and out of his block due to a variety of factors: loss of grants, death, poor marketing from tenants. Over the past three decades, the longest-running business has been Ward's own—a rental venue hosting weekly evening parties, community meetings, and comedy shows. Unlike other merchants who orient their business to Crenshaw's Black upper-middle class, Ward caters to lower-middle-class and working-class consumers who can afford to splurge once a week to have an "uptown" experience. His Black place-keeping strategies inform other property owners' calculations of what is possible.

PRESERVING SANKOFA: A PAN-AFRICANIST PLACE IDENTITY

The village positions itself as a campus of cultural engagement by emphasizing precolonial African culture and a commitment to political agency through Afrodiasporic arts, often inspired by the Ghanaian portmanteau *Sankofa* (meaning "go back and get what you have forgotten"). Other than the property owners and tenants, village leaders employ collaborators and consultants who specialize in cultivating African cultural festivals. Annually, these include the Day of the Ancestors: Festival of the Masks, Martin Luther King Jr. "Freedom Day" festival, the Leimert Park book fair, and the Juneteenth festival. During my observation period, nearly twenty cultural festivals occurred in this square mile surrounding the village. On the other hand, the Old Guards have emplaced their spatial imaginary in a more everyday sense through an urban economic policy: the creation of a community-managed, property owner–run Business Improvement District (BID). Since 2005, the mostly African American property owners of the Greater Leimert Park Village—Crenshaw Corridor Business Improvement District (GLPVCC) have coordinated over two hundred tax-assessed parcels in three zones along Crenshaw Boulevard: the Baldwin Hills-Crenshaw Plaza mall (zone 1), Crenshaw corridor (zone 2), and Leimert Park Village (zone 3). The village is the zone where "an African flavor" is collectively emplaced and kept.

"The focus [is] on keeping it clean, and also creating a community character," BID director Nia Benet (interview 2018) remarks about the BID's budgetary priorities. With reauthorization every five years by the City and County, GLPVCC has sought to keep a clean environment for the merchants while building the Village's cultural identity. According to the BID's 2013–2018 budgets, the "Clean and Green Program" is its largest expense (Greater Leimert Park Village—Crenshaw Corridor Business Improvement District 2018, 17). Further, GLPVCC contracts with the street maintenance and landscaping social enterprise Chrysalis Works, staffed by formerly incarcerated, returning citizens, thus doubling down on its mission to invest in Crenshaw's disadvantaged community members.

In other contexts, BIDs have operated according to corporate logic and profit motives, which favor business over community interests (Madden 2010). But unlike most other BIDs engaged in exclusionary practices, which only attract the gentry, the GLPVCC is managed by a nonprofit—Community

Build Inc—which has worked since the 1992 civil unrest to address economic disinvestment in the community.

Three BID tactics reinforce the village's Pan-Africanist place identity while evincing a cultural commitment to Black place-keeping. First, the BID bejewels the community's urban forestry with symbols of Blackness by maintaining a fleet of 106 Adinkra symbol-stamped clay pots. "So . . . if you are here, you can tell you're in this business improvement district by the pots that you see," Benet notes about the Pan-African-colored, red-green-yellow accented pottery hosting low-maintenance desert plants that complement an already lush corridor of coral trees that define the village boundaries. Second, historic preservation informs the BID's cultural strategy. Dubbed Sankofa Passage in November 2007, the BID infused sixteen bronze plaques into Degnan Boulevard's sidewalk, dedicating the village's "Walk of Fame" to local legends in Crenshaw's creative economy. Third, the BID has marshaled mural arts to enliven vacant walls. Its longest-lasting project is the Niger River Mural, created in 2002, along an alleyway connecting African history with contemporary artists. This riparian theme is complemented by aquatic animalistic cosmologies—turtles, fish, and so on—also engraved alongside Sankofa Passage. Black businesses like Eso Won Books (meaning "water over rocks") echo this in their names, while others like Hot & Cool Café reflect it in their interior designs.

Meanwhile, younger artists and property owners, dubbed the "New Vanguard" by the Old Guards, have begun to exercise spatial agency over the village by engaging with technology and media arts via Afrofuturism as influenced by the Black Speculative Arts Movement (BSAM).[2] Members of the New Vanguard are collaborative and open-sourced with their approach. In the global shadow of Marvel's *Black Panther* touted by Hollywood, Afrofuturism became the dominant wing of the BSAM and prominent in Leimert Park's spatial imaginary (figure 14.3). The New Vanguard infuses Afrofuturism into the village's marketing language for cultural planning via community visioning sessions; some enthusiastic Old Guards even latch onto Wakanda to petition to rename the Leimert Park Village "Africatown."

Some contestation exists because the village is not a monolithic Black community. Beyond branding, longstanding divergences between pro-Africatown proponents and pro-Leimert Park defenders beleaguer the BID, which maintains the public realm, especially People's Street Plaza on

14.3 An image from a design fiction community workshop in Leimert Park Village for the 2018 film, *Sankofa City*. *Source*: Stephan Park and Raul-David Poblano.

Sundays. While street vendors imagine the village as an African-inspired open-air market, some brick-and-mortar merchants see it as a disorderly physical liability to their Black Main Street appeal. BID leaders often remind them of their shared merchant status to induce collaboration. Often, the only site of agreement is the existence of the drum circle—a decades-old institution honed by the World Stage musicians yet offered as a free outdoor attraction. Unlike the off-and-on merchants' association, individualistic street vendors have not organized to negotiate collectively. BID regulations entrust the property owners with the greatest responsibility for providing outdoor cleaning services. Yet, if services disproportionately go to the village over other tax-assessed zones, GLPVCC could be legally exposed. On multiple occasions, this has led both merchants and the BID to invite Black LAPD officers to stakeholder meetings or employ Black unarmed Nation of Islam–affiliated guards to encourage cleaning on Sundays.

As digital natives, the New Vanguard intervenes by introducing equipment, technology, and social resources to popularize and sustain place-keeping flows achieved by the Old Guards, who can become territorial. While a couple of New Vanguard entrepreneurs complained about the initial reluctance of Old Guard members in welcoming their involvement or renting them space, the latter has publicly and privately confessed the need for "young blood." Despite early growing pains, examples of intergenerational mentorship and collaboration now visibly exist. Quiava Rashad, a twenty-five-year-old cultural organizer at a public arts nonprofit, is universally touted by the Old Guards to external entities as a community leader. Bradley Johnson, a forty-year-old filmmaker and art consultant, has led most public arts programming and grant writing since he arrived in the summer of 2017. Both New Vanguard leaders share consistent relationships with Old Guard members and have similar socio-spatial goals for the village: (1) creating a refuge from institutionalized racism, (2) achieving cultural congregation, (3) repopulating abandoned spaces, and (4) preserving or creating their own legacy.

While many old-guard leaders acknowledge the role of technology as an avenue for Black spatial agency, the New Vanguard wields it through its "radical reimagining" of Leimert Park as an "Afrotech" hub. Film-making projects like *Sankofa City*, which aims to reimagine the village in 2050, evince this Afrofuturism. Yet, this New Vanguard energy has been anchored to Old Guard wisdom at every stage. In 2015, Lester Russoy, a Black visual artist and Old Guard property owner, spatialized his inter-est in Afrotech by converting deserted payphones into tools for "urban theater" by staging dramatic conversations about issues such as imprison-ment and food justice in the outdoor foyer of the Vision Theatre. Those payphones made cameos in the 2018 *Sankofa City* film and subsequent planning efforts (figure 14.3). Johnson has co-organized the Technology, Entertainment, Culture (TEC) Leimert conference in the village since 2017, which fortified Russoy's efforts.

The most extensive public effort to institutionalize an intergenerational Pan-African sense of place is the constellation of design projects promoted by Destination Crenshaw (DC). Launched publicly in 2017, DC is a coali-tion of artists and elected officials designing "unapologetically Black" pub-lic art on and near transit. DC emerged from a 2016 private workshop at a high school on Crenshaw Boulevard convened by New Vanguard coun-cilmember Marqueece Harris-Dawson, the late New Vanguard rapper and technology entrepreneur Ermias Asghedom ("Nipsey Hussle"), and Old

Guard architect Martin Abraham. According to Abraham, the teenagers conceived the title. With the help of the National Organization for Minority Architects (NOMA), DC recruited African American architects such as Gabrielle Bullock and Phil Freelon from the global firm Perkins+Will to help concretize their playbook. A wide-ruled twenty-page laminated prospectus outlines Crenshaw's identity around seven design themes (Perkins+Will, Studio MLA, Roland A. Wiley (RAW) Architects International 2017, 26–27):

1. Telling "A Black LA Story"
2. Showcasing South LA arts
3. Developing "A Green and Sustainable Crenshaw"
4. "Leverage Existing Assets"
5. "Transform Intersections" from Forty-Eighth to Sixtieth streets,
6. Better "Connect East and West,"
7. Engaging Metro infrastructure.

Since 2016, navy signs with a spiraling canary yellow "Destination Crenshaw" logo have perched on Crenshaw Boulevard's light poles, priming the public for future community plans. That future is nearly the present. In late 2019, the county board of supervisors allocated $15 million to DC's Sankofa Park near the Leimert Park MTA station, thanks to former Los Angeles City Council member and current Los Angeles County Supervisor Mark Ridley-Thomas. Sankofa Park broke ground in February 2020 and is now under construction, despite the COVID-19 pandemic. By focusing on "unapologetically Black" place-keeping and a Pan-Africanist identity, DC promises to ennoble Black public culture by emplacing it within Crenshaw's gentrifying public realm.

TOWARD A TWENTY-FIRST CENTURY UNAPOLOGETICALLY BLACK URBANISM

If Blackness mattered to urban design, urbanists would study how Black belongingness, freedom, and spatial agency show up in the public realm. Most urban studies scholars, however, narrate what has happened *to* Black Angelenos rather than *because* of them and *by* them. The Leimert Park case invokes key motifs missing from urban designers' planning imaginations and broader sociological conceptions of how Blackness could help real places: Pan-Africanism, Afrofuturism, Black place-keeping, Black urbanism. Building a public city through urban design requires that designers emplace Blackness as the basis for spatial practices that embody freedom, spatial agency, and belongingness.

This chapter explored a case where Blackness matters to justly design public spaces. Still, challenges abound internally and externally, as Black artists and property owners adapt privatized tools to match their public cultural intentions. The BID—though managed by a nonprofit social justice organization—is still a property-owner-led entity. In times of economic stress and political peril, as COVID-19 has provoked, it is predisposed to involve police forces in problem-solving. Regional approaches to planning and designing transportation systems are still skewed toward securing middle-class interests, particularly the introduction of light-rail in the district. While village activists have successfully resisted exclusion through pressuring their Black elected officials, few are rallying for investments in bus transit, the egregiously underfunded transportation system used by most low-income patrons of the village. Further, village leaders have not resisted how the City of LA (failingly) provides cleaning services for their popular destination, forcing merchants to foot a community bill. In a city-region seeped in white supremacist structures, the transformative power of Blackness as publicness has not been fully explored by any actor.

The hegemonic state of knowledge in urban design is partly to blame. At best, it has tokenized Blackness as an "alternative," which is a white supremacist stance. Singular architecture firms providing *pro bono* design playbooks to communities without an accompanying strategy that critiques dispossession and displacement—as Perkins + Will did for the village—better resemble charity institutions than equity partners. Both grass-tops Black institutions like NOMA and white-established institutions like Perkins + Will must commit intellectual resources for mainstreaming Black spatial imaginaries—and not just because they are currently popular. Professional organizations like the American Institute of Architects (AIA) and the American Planning Association (APA) need to play a role in institutionalizing designing for Blackness as publicness as a norm and as an approach for public engagement with Black communities. Proactively archiving and spotlighting Blackness may also reduce the unreasonable pressure on everyday Black communities to be twice as spectacular so as to be seen as somewhat valuable.

Because Blackness is already beautiful.

NOTES

1. Between 2009 and 2012, Damien Goodmon, a charismatic, media-savvy leader in Crenshaw, sustained a public pressure campaign against Metro's light-rail systems with a coalition called Fix the Expo. In online and print media, Goodmon, alongside a robust intergenerational set of stakeholders against gentrification in Crenshaw, complicated narratives about the purported benefits of regional transit investments for South LA. From 2013 onward, this advocacy evolved into the Crenshaw Subway Coalition, which managed to recruit environmental legal help to sue both the MTA and the Federal Department of Transportation for unjustly funding and "fast-tracking" at-grade rail projects, despite flaws that could endanger nearby vulnerable people.

2. The BSAM is known for Afrofuturism, but it also includes "Astro Blackness, Afro-Surrealism, Afro-Pessimism, Ethno Gothic, Black Digital Humanities, The Black Fantastic, Magical Realism, and The Esoteric" (Anderson 2016, 233).

REFERENCES

Anderson, R. (2016). "Afrofuturism 2.0 & the Black Speculative Arts Movement: Notes on a Manifesto." *Obsidian* 42 (1/2): 228–236.

Antonsich, M. (2010). "Searching for Belonging–An Analytical Framework." *Geography Compass* 4 (6): 644–659.

Association for Enterprise Opportunity. (2017). "The Tapestry of Black Business Ownership in America: Untapped Opportunities for Success." Washington, DC: The Association for Enterprise Opportunity, published online February 16, 2017. https://aeoworks.org/wp-content/uploads/2019/03/AEO_Black_Owned_Business _Report_02_16_17_FOR_WEB-1.pdf.

Bates, T. (2006). "The Urban Development Potential of Black-Owned Businesses." *Journal of the American Planning Association* 72 (2): 227–237.

Benet, Nia. (2018). Interview (in-person), Director Greater Leimert Park Village—Crenshaw Corridor Business Improvement District, City of Los Angeles, January 13, 2018.

Boyd, M. (2005). "The Downside of Racial Uplift: Meaning of Gentrification in an African American Neighborhood." *City & Society* 17 (2): 265–288.

Carmona, M. (2015). "Re-Theorising Contemporary Public Space: A New Narrative and a New Normative." *Journal of Urbanism* 8 (4): 373–405.

Dent, G. (ed.) (1992). *Black Popular Culture: A Project by Michele Wallace*. Seattle: Bay Press.

Fairlie, R. W. (2020). "The Impact of Covid-19 on Small Business Owners: Evidence of Early-Stage Losses from the April 2020 Current Population Survey." Working paper 27309, National Bureau of Economic Research. https://www.nber.org/system/files/working_papers/w27309/w27309.pdf.

Florida, R. (2017). *The New Urban Crisis: How Our Cities Are Increasing Inequality, Deepening Segregation, and Failing the Middle Class—And What We Can Do about It*. New York: Basic Books.

Gill, T. M. (2010). *Beauty Shop Politics: African American Women's Activism in the Beauty Industry*. Chicago: University of Illinois Press.

Greater Leimert Park Village—Crenshaw Corridor Business Improvement District. (2018). "Greater Leimert Park Village—Crenshaw Corridor Business Improvement District Management District Plan." Greater Leimert Park Village—Crenshaw Corridor Business Improvement District, April 2018.

Isoardi, S. (2006). *The Dark Tree: Jazz and the Community Arts in Los Angeles*. Berkeley: University of California Press.

Lee, J. (2016). *Blowin' Up: Rap Dreams in South Central*. Chicago: University of Chicago Press.

Lloyd, R. (2014). "Grit as Glamour." In Duneier, M., Murphy, A., and Kasinitz, P. (eds.). *The Urban Ethnography Reader*. Oxford: Oxford University Press, 123–134.

Madden, D. (2010). "Revisiting the End of Public Space: Assembling the Public in an Urban Park." *City and Community* 9 (2): 187–207.

Markusen, A. (2013). "Fuzzy Concepts, Proxy Data: Why Indicators Would Not Track Creative Placemaking Success." *International Journal of Urban Sciences* 17 (3): 291–303.

Miller, M. J. (2018). "The Geography of Black Commerce and Culture: Los Angeles, California, and Beyond." PhD dissertation, Los Angeles: University of Southern California.

Montgomery, A. (2016). "Reappearance of the Public: Placemaking, Minoritization and Resistance in Detroit." *International Journal of Urban and Regional Research* 40 (4): 776–799.

Moya, P. M. L., and Hazel, R. M. (2010). "Doing Race: An Introduction." *Doing Race: 21 Essays for the 21st Century*. New York: Norton & Horton, 1–101.

Nicodemus Gadwa, A. (2013). "Fuzzy Vibrancy: Creative Placemaking as Ascendant US Cultural Policy." *Cultural Trends* 22 (3–4): 213–222.

Nussbaum, M. C. (2011). *Creating Capabilities*. Cambridge, MA: Harvard University Press.

Parker, K. F. (2015). "The African-American Entrepreneur–Crime Drop Relationship: Growing African-American Business Ownership and Declining Youth Violence." *Urban Affairs Review* 51 (6): 751–780.

Perkins+Will, Studio MLA, Roland A. Wiley (RAW) Architects International. (2018). "Chapter 4. Outcomes—Section 4.1 Prevailing Design Themes." In *#DestinationCrenshaw*, 26–27.

Porter, M. E. (1995). "The Competitive Advantage of the Inner City." *Harvard Business Review* 73 (3): 55–71.

Powell, R. J. (2002). *Black Art: A Cultural History*. London: Thames & Hudson.

Sen, A. (2001). *Development as Freedom*. Oxford: Oxford Paperbacks.

Shear, W. B. (2020). "Small Business Administration COVID-19 Loans Lack Controls and Are Susceptible to Fraud, Testimony before the Subcommittee on Investigations, Oversight, and Regulations, Committee on Small Business, House of Representatives." Washington D.C: United States Government Accountability Office, October 1, 2020. https://www.gao.gov/assets/710/709912.pdf.

Taylor, P. C. (2016). *Black Is Beautiful: A Philosophy of Black Aesthetics*. Boston: John Wiley & Sons.

Varna, G., and Tiesdell, S. (2010). "Assessing the Publicness of Public Space: The Star Model of Publicness." *Journal of Urban Design* 15 (4): 575–598.

Wang, Q. (2012). "Ethnic Entrepreneurship Studies in Geography: A Review." *Geography Compass* 6 (4): 227–240.

Williams, R. A. (2020). "From Racial to Reparative Planning: Confronting the White Side of Planning." *Journal of Planning Education and Research*. doi:0739456X20946416.

Young, I. M. (1990). "City Life and Difference." In Low, S., Gieseking, J. J., Katz, C., Saegert, S., Mangold, W. (eds). *People, Place and Space Reader*. New York: Routledge, 247–251.

15

THE RIGHT TO WALK IN THE NEIGHBORHOOD
DESIGNING INCLUSIVE SIDEWALKS FOR OLDER ADULTS

Anastasia Loukaitou-Sideris

Sidewalks are the most public neighborhood spaces (Jacobs 1961; Loukaitou-Sideris and Ehrenfeucht 2009). Sidewalks enable walking, an essential activity for performing everyday chores and reaching neighborhood destinations. Walking in the neighborhood is particularly important for low-income, urban-living older adults, as many do not own a car or can no longer drive. For them, the ability to walk safely and without obstructions to the grocery store, bus stop, or neighborhood park enables independent living.

Henry Lefebvre has described the right to the city as "a demand for a transformed and renewed access to urban life" (Lefebvre quoted in Kofman and Lebas 1996, 158). The ability to walk in one's neighborhood should be considered such a right to the city. But urban-living, older adults can only enjoy this right if their neighborhood sidewalks are designed to be inclusive spaces for them. This chapter reports on a study of older adults living in Westlake, a typical inner-city neighborhood of Los Angeles, to detail the experiences and challenges they face walking in their neighborhood. Following a methodology first introduced by Kevin Lynch and Malcolm Rivkin (1959), we accompanied these older residents on a walk around the block where they live and let them explain in their own voices their walking experience. The objective was to uncover through their eyes the environmental, social, and traffic impediments that obstruct their walks and make inner-city sidewalks not inclusive public spaces and to consider design interventions that can make these inner-city sidewalks more inclusive.

These elders shared a deep concern for safety while walking on their neighborhood streets. Their walks encounter a dystopic landscape: broken and uneven sidewalks, graffiti and trash, fast-moving traffic, wide and difficult-to-cross intersections, and the ever-present signs of homelessness and drunkenness on the sidewalks. This environment denies many older adults the right to their neighborhood. While our walks took place before the COVID-19 pandemic, the situation became even worse after the global outbreak when, in addition to the aforementioned elements, the fear of the disease kept these elders confined at home (Low and Loukaitou-Sideris 2021). Can design respond to this plight of urban-living older adults? We deem that one responsibility of just urban design is the creation of age-friendly cities. One aspect of this involves understanding and responding to older adults' mobility needs and designing walkable neighborhoods and inclusive public spaces (World Health Organization 2007).

In this chapter, I first present an overview of the literature on the factors affecting walking by older adults, followed by a discussion of Lynch and Rivkin's "walk around the block" study. I then turn to the findings of the empirical study and discuss the experiences and impressions of eleven older adults during a walk around their neighborhood. Drawing from the everyday reality of these older adults, I conclude the chapter with a discussion of how just urban design can make sidewalks more inclusive for them.

OLDER ADULTS AND WALKING

Physical mobility creates opportunities to enjoy a better life for older adults. Being able to navigate their neighborhood on foot effectively and reach various destinations helps them acquire independence in their daily activities (Yen, Michael, and Perdue 2009; Rosenbloom and Herbel 2009; Kim 2011). Indeed, scholars find that walking is essential for the quality of life of older adults and the fulfillment of utilitarian, psychosocial (Musselwhite 2015), and health needs (Taylor and Tripodes 2001; Levy-Storms, Chen, and Loukaitou-Sideris 2018). In contrast, reduction in mobility may lead to decreased participation in out-of-home activities, which, in

turn, may result in depression, isolation, and ultimately institutionaliza-
tion (Marottoli 2009). For this reason, transportation constitutes one of
the domains of age-friendly cities (World Health Organization 2007).[1]

For older adults living in urban settings, walking represents the most
common form of mobility aside from vehicular travel (Satariano et al. 2012).
Declines in physical and cognitive functioning and increased difficulty with
driving eventually reduce older adults' mobility, making them more reliant
on services and amenities within their neighborhoods (Yen, Michael, and
Perdue 2009). As car driving declines with age, walking becomes a more
dominant mode of travel (Mattson 2011; Boschmann and Brady 2013) for
those who do not suffer from "mobility disability" (Clark et al. 1996).

Walking is also important because it is the most accessible form of
physical activity for older adults (Horner et al. 2015). The ability to walk,
however, is influenced by the characteristics of the built environment and
its public spaces—the proximity of destinations to older adults' residence,
and the comfort, cleanliness, and perceived safety of the neighborhood
and its walking infrastructure. Research has shown a positive association
between walkable neighborhoods with accessible design features and
higher levels of walking among residents (Cao, Handy, and Mokhtarian
2007; Clark et al. 2009; Yen, Michael, and Perdue 2009; Satariano et al.
2012; Boschmann and Brady 2013). Studies find that the presence of well-
maintained sidewalks and nearby neighborhood amenities contribute to
walking among older adults (Cao, Handy, and Mokhtarian 2007), while
the absence of a pedestrian-friendly infrastructure in the suburbs contributes to low levels of walking among US elders (Rosenbloom and Herbel
2009).

The provision of a safe walking infrastructure is of primary importance
for older pedestrians (Yen, Michael, and Perdue 2009). This includes
safety from traffic and also from tripping and falling, which is one of the
major causes of injury of older adults in public spaces (Naumann et al.
2011). Indeed, high curbs and uneven sidewalks represent significant cul-
prits in fall-related injuries. In contrast, obstruction-free and continuous
sidewalks, curb extensions near bus stops, pedestrian crossing features
such as curb ramps and refuge areas, and signage and lighting tend to
increase safety and help them to avoid traffic injuries and falls (Stollof
and Barlow 2008).

Fear of crime also acts as a deterrent to walking, and older adults are more likely to report safety as a major concern than younger individuals (Cao, Handy, and Mokhtarian 2007) and often have to alter their travel behavior to avoid dangerous public spaces (Clark et al. 1996). The negative effect of perceived lack of safety on walking is stronger among those who are poor, live in high-crime neighborhoods, and lack the resources to buffer the effects of neighborhood conditions (Clark et al. 2009).

Overall, few researchers directly interact with older adults to understand their specific needs and challenges when walking in their neighborhoods. Instead, the majority of studies on older adult mobility rely on aggregate data and statistical associations. But while secondary data from statewide or citywide household travel surveys can reveal aggregate travel patterns, they cannot convey the individuals' experiences while taking trips in their neighborhoods. Here Lynch's methodology comes in handy.

VIEWING URBAN FORM THROUGH PEOPLE'S EYES

Kevin Lynch has made many important contributions to the theory and practice of city design. One of his most lasting and valuable contributions relates to research methodologies for the study of cities. He pioneered methods for documenting, analyzing, and visualizing sociospatial relations in the city, which privilege the perspectives of city users. As Tridib Banerjee and Michael Southworth (1990, 4) write in their introduction to the collection of Lynch's work, *City Sense and City Design*, Lynch was "curious to know how the public, not the trained designer, saw and understood the everyday environment, what they valued in it, how it shaped their lives and activities, and how they in turn shaped urban form." In a period of top-down urban renewal practices, Lynch's studies conversely underscored that what makes urban design "good" is its public acceptance. Lynch was also interested in the "sensuous qualities" of places—their looks, feels, sounds, and smells—as people experienced them in their everyday lives. The experts for the design of these environments were not the designers or the planners but the people themselves. Therefore, Lynch's qualitative methodologies aspired to give urban design professionals valuable knowledge of the city as seen and experienced through the eyes of residents, thus making urban design de facto more inclusive and just.

In a 1959 study, Lynch and Rivkin took a few individuals around a city block in Boston and recorded and analyzed their comments on what they encountered along this walk. Their purpose was to identify "what does the ordinary individual perceive in his landscape?" and "what makes the strongest impression on him, and how does he react to it?" (Lynch and Rivkin, 1959, 24). While social scientists criticized Lynch's studies because of their small samples, Lynch reflected later that "the small group of informants produced an astonishing flood of perceptions. . . . Our conclusion . . . was that people had a relatively coherent and detailed mental image of their city, which had been created in an interaction between self and place, and this image was both essential to their actual function, and also important to their emotional wellbeing" (Banerjee and Southworth 1990, 248).

One can argue that these early qualitative methodologies, which developed further in the *Image of the City* (Lynch 1960), planted the seeds for contemporary discourses around critical cartography, critical spatial analysis (through Geographic Information Systems), and spatial ethnography. At the same time, "the walk around the block" evolved into "walkability audits" that have been used as a tool by researchers and public agencies wishing to gather information directly from individuals about their perceived safety, comfort, and legibility of urban environments. Unfortunately, these methods are not widely used. Even Lynch, in a self-reflection and evaluation of his work twenty-five years later, wrote: "What was not foreseen, however, was that this study whose principal aim was to urge on designers the necessity of consulting those who live in a place, had at first a diametrically opposite result. It seemed to many planners that here was a new technique—complete with the magical classifications of node, landmark, district, edge, and path" (Lynch 1985, in Banerjee and Southworth 1990, 251).

While Lynch and Rivkin used the "walk around the block" to understand what makes urban form imageable and legible for city dwellers, our study had a different goal. We wished to understand the perceived and encountered impediments faced by older inner-city living adults when walking in their neighborhood, how such impediments affect their mobility, and what planners and urban designers need to know to make sidewalks more inclusive for older adults.

TAKING INNER-CITY OLDER ADULTS FOR A WALK AROUND THE BLOCK

In October 2017, we conducted a walkabout with eleven low-income older (over sixty-five) adults who live at Union Tower, a two-hundred-unit affordable apartment building in Westlake, a neighborhood just west of downtown Los Angeles. This was part of a larger study that examined the mobility needs of older adults in inner-city neighborhoods (Loukaitou-Sideris, Wachs, and Pinski 2019). Westlake residents are overwhelmingly renters (92 percent), nonwhite (94.6 percent), and mostly low-income (39 percent under the poverty line). Ten percent of residents are over sixty-five. The neighborhood is predominantly Latino (58 percent) and has significant numbers of Asian Americans, mostly Koreans (29 percent).

Walkabouts or walkability audits involve walking with individuals along a predetermined part of the city and asking them to talk about their experiences along the route. The purpose is to understand the parts and aspects of the walk they enjoy and the elements and circumstances they find problematic. The researcher sits down with each participant at the end of the walk and asks some follow-up questions about their experience. By repeating the process with a number of individuals, researchers can collect a rich array of qualitative information and gain a good understanding of the subjects' experiences, fears, or aspirations while walking in a specific neighborhood.

Of the walkabout participants, seven were female and four male; eight were in their seventies, one in her sixties, and two in their eighties. Six were Korean, four Latino, and one Native American. The weather during all walks was sunny and warm (around 85 degrees). All walking trips started from Union Tower. For each trip, one researcher was matched with one older adult.

At the very beginning of each walk, we told the older adult what Lynch and Rivkin (1959, 24) had told their subjects: "We are about to take a short walk. Please don't look for anything in particular, but tell me about the things you see, hear, or smell; everything and anything you notice." We recorded our conversations with the older adults throughout the walking trip after receiving each participant's permission. Throughout the walk, we prompted participants with these questions:

Describe the street and sidewalk for me. How does it make you feel?
How do you go about crossing this street?
What about this walking environment do you enjoy?
What about this walking environment do you *not* enjoy?

After returning to the participants' residence at the end of the walkabout, we asked them the following:

What things, in particular, did you remember from the walk?
How comfortable did you feel during the walk?
What was your overall experience?
What stood out from the walk?
Do you usually take precautions to walk in your neighborhood?
What would you change if you could?

THE WALK AROUND THE BLOCK

The walkabout (figure 15.1) was along a typical stretch of the Los Angeles inner-city, sprinkled with apartment buildings and commercial facilities. The route's length was 0.4 miles, and the walk took about twenty to twenty-five minutes to complete. However, the walk duration varied among participants; one older adult took nearly forty minutes to complete it. The route started at the entrance of Union Tower and headed southwest toward West Sixth Street, a four-lane commercial street with a moderate amount of traffic. It passed the Dollar Mart store with its large parking lot, a clothing store, and a dental clinic. At the end of the block, the walking route crossed the street at a traffic signal and a marked crosswalk. On the south side of Sixth Street, the walk continued along a large parking lot, which serves customers of Home Depot, Food 4 Less, and a stretch of small retail stores. At the end of the block, the route crossed Sixth Street at a traffic signal with a visible crosswalk. The walk continued along the north side of Sixth Street, passing by small stores and a large restaurant; it crossed Union Ave. and proceeded back north, returning to Union Tower.

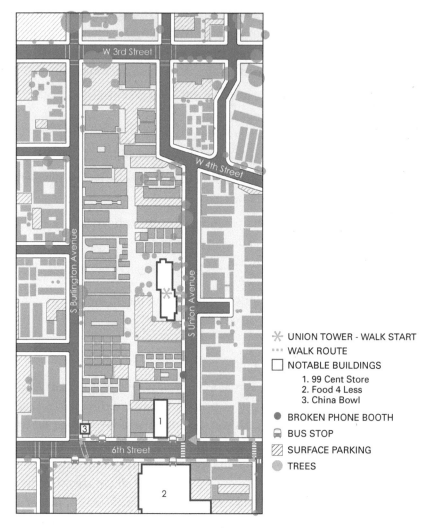

15.1 The route of the walk, Westlake neighborhood in Los Angeles. *Source*: Rayne Laborde.

CHALLENGES AND IMPEDIMENTS OF WALKING

Walking around the block was not pleasurable. At times, it was uncomfortable and even scary for all study participants. The eleven older adults who participated encountered three categories of impediments: environmental, social, and traffic-related. All participants referred to specific elements of the built environment that made them feel aggravated, uncomfortable, and even scared. Environmental impediments consisted of urban form features that can contribute to *setting aggravation* because of undesirable elements or *setting deprivation* because of the lack of desirable amenities (Banerjee and Baer 1984), both of which can generate negative feelings. Table 15.1 shows the frequency of different environmental impediments encountered by the participants.

Participants repeatedly mentioned the trash on the sidewalks (even the presence of a dead rat), as it was often obstructing their steps and offending their sense of well-being. In their own words:

Part of the street is almost never clean. There is so much trash all over the street and sidewalk.

Table 15.1 Environmental impediments encountered

Environmental impediment	Frequency of responses	Type of nuisance
Trash	10	Setting aggravation
Lack of shade/trees	9	Setting deprivation
Cracked, uneven, high-curb sidewalks	6	Setting aggravation
Barbed-wire fences	5	Setting aggravation
Lack of benches	5	Setting deprivation
Lack of trash cans	4	Setting deprivation
Paddle of dirty water	4	Setting aggravation
Bad smells	3	Setting aggravation
Ugly buildings	2	Setting aggravation
Broken public phone box	2	Setting aggravation
Graffiti	1	Setting aggravation
Shop signs blocking sidewalk	1	Setting aggravation
Overhead electrical wires	1	Setting aggravation
Lack of birds	1	Setting deprivation
Traffic noise	1	Setting aggravation
Dirty restaurants	1	Setting aggravation
Security bars on windows	1	Setting aggravation

The sidewalk is sticky with trash. It has even dog crap that people don't clean after.

Sometimes it is hard to make a step because of trash.

The street environment is full of trash and food waste. One time, I even witnessed a driver just dumping his trash on the street at the stop sign.

While some elders were critical of other residents dumping their trash in streets and sidewalks (figure 15.2), most blamed the city for not providing enough trashcans and cleaning up the debris:

The government should place more trashcans and fine people who throw trash on the street.

There should be more trashcans; maybe that way, people would throw their trash in them instead of on the ground.

The Westlake neighborhood has a dearth of street trees along its sidewalks. During the walkabouts, the hot weather combined with the lack of shade contributed to uncomfortable and sweaty walks. As a Latina woman explained:

15.2   Trash and a mattress dumped on the sidewalk. *Source:* Anastasia Loukaitou-Sideris.

There are no more trees! There used to be trees, but they've been removing them. A business owner can say that the tree is impacting his business and call the city to remove it.

Some referred to the holes left behind when trees are removed as a particular danger for tripping and falling, while others pointed to the cracked and uneven sidewalks (figure 15.3). In their own words:

There are now holes on the sidewalk where trees used to be, and they get filled up with trash.

The sidewalks here are deteriorated and very uneven. The cracks make it difficult for me to walk. . . . See, I am walking on this part of the sidewalk to avoid the big crack. Since I use a little shopping cart as my walker, my cart will get stuck on the crack. I have to go around it. I have to be always looking down and find a path that's even, so my cart doesn't get stuck.

The barbed wire and metal fences lining up parts of the sidewalk and the absence of street benches contributed to setting aggravation and pedestrian unfriendliness. They were noticed and commented upon by about half of the elders:

15.3 Uneven and cracked sidewalks in Westlake. *Source*: Anastasia Loukaitou-Sideris.

There is nothing nice to look at along the street—only barb-wired fences.

I want to take a rest break on this little wall. You see there is nowhere for me to sit and take a rest.

I often have to walk a shorter route because of lack of places to rest. Having some benches, would have been useful!

Walks were characterized by aggravating negative elements and a simultaneous absence of satisfying positive features. Some mentioned the presence of bad smells, ugly buildings, graffiti, overhead electrical wires, broken public phones (figure 15.4), and security bars on the windows as aggravating elements. One person lamented the lack of birds and the

15.4 Broken public phone with trash and graffiti. *Source:* Anastasia Loukaitou-Sideris.

domination of the soundscape by traffic noise, while a puddle of dirty water at the end of a crosswalk was particularly offensive to several older adults:

This dirty water is always here, and I don't want to push my walker through the dirty water, so I have to go around and up the driveway into the Food 4 Less parking lot to get back on the sidewalk.

I don't know where the water comes from, but it is always there. . . . I have to go around it. It smells bad.

But it was not only the physical landscape that was aggravating to older adults; social impediments were also blocking their walks and challenging their mobility. They talked about drunk people leaving empty beer bottles on the pavement, drug dealers hiding drugs in different nooks and corners, unhoused individuals blocking the sidewalks with makeshift tents, gangs cruising the street menacingly, and people urinating in public. Many felt that the behavior of particular groups or individuals encountered along the walk contributed to their general lack of safety while walking (table 15.2). Older adults were primarily concerned about not only victimization but also traffic danger and tripping and falling.

Drunkenness, homelessness, and drug dealing in this inner-city neighborhood make these older adults scared to walk. These social impediments also leave physical traces. Empty beer cans and liquor bottles littered the sidewalks, while the signs of homelessness (blankets, abandoned carts) were omnipresent on sidewalks. Almost every older adult had something to say about the social disorder of the streets. In their own voices:

There are lots of people drinking and doing drugs in the streets. Being here makes me nervous.

There are people lying on the ground near Food 4 Less.

I feel unsafe waiting for the bus with all these drunk people around.

The area may appear calm, but it's daytime. At night, things around here are different. I don't go out at night because I am scared.

People drinking alcohol are sitting on the ground. . . . These people around make you feel not good to walk.

Rowdy teenagers in gangs are always hanging out in front of houses. Teens are too loud especially on weekends.

Table 15.2 Social impediments encountered by frequency

Social Impediment	Frequency of responses
Drunk people	8
Homeless	6
Drug dealers	3
Rowdy teenagers	2
People peeing on sidewalk	2
Gangs	1

At Sixth and Burlington one day, I witnessed someone peeing on the street; it was disgusting.

Sometimes, I have to step over a man lying on the street, and I don't like people approaching me. . . . Local gangs are more active at night, and I'm worried about having a run-in.

Traffic safety concerns composed a third category of walking impediments (table 15.3). In a neighborhood that includes wide arterials and intersections, most older adults shared their fear that a car might hit them while crossing the street. During the follow-up interviews, many remembered the experience of crossing the street as the most stressful part of their walking trip. More than half of the respondents were also frustrated by the traffic lights that turned red before they had the chance to reach the sidewalk, while others talked about cars driving too fast and recklessly and drivers having no patience for crossing pedestrians. As argued:

I need to hustle across the street because there isn't enough time to cross before the light turns red. I don't feel safe crossing at either crosswalk.

I walk slowly and the light changes so quickly when I am in the middle of the street.

That car just whizzed by! People get scared crossing the street because the drivers don't respect the pedestrian or speeding laws. . . . The crosswalks are very dangerous because drivers are speeding.

Table 15.3 Traffic impediment

Traffic impediment	Frequency of responses
Wide streets/intersections	7
Short traffic signal "walk" cycle	6
Fast-moving traffic	5
Reckless drivers	3
Impatient drivers	2

PRECAUTIONS AND BEHAVIORAL ADAPTATIONS

Our interviews revealed that these older adults take precautions and often have to adapt their behaviors when walking in their neighborhood as a result of impediments. Most participants indicated that they only walk when absolutely necessary to go to the market, reach the bus stop, or a dental clinic, and they mostly avoid walking for pleasure or exercise. Some elders reported walking only within a very narrow spatial range. One Latina woman indicated that she tries to walk inside her apartment building along its corridors. An Asian American woman reported that she only walks when she visits her sister, who lives in an affluent neighborhood. Almost everyone avoided walking in the neighborhood after dark. Some also explained that they often have to change their routes to avoid passing in front of places and people they deem as dangerous. As many sidewalks are cracked and uneven, one older adult mentioned that she cannot take notice of the environment around her while walking because she feels compelled to "pay attention to the ground" so that she does not trip and fall. Another individual indicated that he avoids interacting with people on the street out of fear that they will bother him or take advantage of him.

Thus, the physical and social landscape of this inner-city neighborhood limits the mobility of its older adult residents, thus, taking away this important right to the city. The eleven older adults who participated in the walk around the block experienced an aggravating and stressful walking environment. Tellingly, no one described their walk as pleasurable, and only a few items emerged as positive elements of walking around the block. These included the community's mixed-use environment and presence of neighborhood retail stores, the few lonely street trees that appear here and there, and the presence of other people waiting at the bus stops or coming in and out of commercial establishments.

In general, however, the pleasures of walking are largely absent for these older inner-city residents because of the environmental, social, and traffic impediments that they encounter on their walks. At worst, this results in their avoidance of walking and their effective exclusion from the public spaces of their neighborhood. At best, this leads to precautions and behavioral adaptations that not only act as defensive strategies but also reduce the quality of their lives. Finding ways to improve these inner-city public spaces and making sidewalks more inclusive and pedestrian-friendly should be an imperative of just urban design.

MAKING SIDEWALKS MORE INCLUSIVE FOR INNER-CITY OLDER ADULTS

Despite the small sample, the research provided significant insights into the challenges that older adults face while walking around their inner-city neighborhood. Urban designers and planners should act upon this information; sidewalks, as ubiquitous public spaces, should attract their attention and care. A series of simple physical improvements can make sidewalks more inclusive and hospitable to older adults and more enjoyable to a broader public. Systematic development of the urban forest, especially in inner-city neighborhoods, which lack greenery, can offer street trees for needed shade. Additionally, in hot-climate cities, requiring ground-floor building awnings can help create more shade on the sidewalk and protection from the sun. In cold-climate environments, street crossings and curb ramps should take into account the winter conditions and aim to decrease the accumulation of water, snow, or ice at the bottoms of curbs and curb ramps. The strategic location of benches on sidewalks or even parklets in areas where sidewalks are wide or can be widened can offer older adults and other pedestrians some respite and a chance to rest on their way to a destination (figure 15.5). Fixing cracked and uneven sidewalks, picking up sidewalk trash, filling up the potholes, removing obstructions (such as broken phones and abandoned newsstands), installing low-height sidewalk curbs and ramps at intersections,

15.5 Older adults resting on sidewalk benches under the shade of a tree in Portland, Maine. *Source*: https://www.pedbikeimages.org/DanBurden.

as well as pedestrian lighting, would help reduce the chances of tripping and falling.

Traffic calming interventions can help reduce the traffic impediments mentioned by study participants and slow down traffic (Burden 2007). These may include street medians that give refuge to pedestrians crossing a wide street; mid-block curb extensions (chicanes) that narrow the roadway and force motorists to reduce speed; and curb extensions (bulb-outs) that extend the sidewalk and reduce the length of an intersection. At the same time, increasing the length of traffic signal walk cycles in neighborhoods with high concentrations of older adults and implementing scramble crosswalks at high-traffic intersections would also help alleviate the stress that many elders feel when crossing the street.

The COVID-19 pandemic has made outdoor public spaces even more important because the spread of disease is significantly lower outdoors. But as the most vulnerable age group, older adults need more assurances of contagion control so that they can start walking and using public spaces again. The narrow sidewalks of inner-city streets and high densities of inner-city neighborhoods counteract the desire for physical distancing. It is here where the Open Streets movement can do the most good, opening up spaces devoted to cars, giving more ample space for walking, and expanding sidewalk uses. Modest, tactical design interventions—street benches, trees, bus shelters, solar-reflecting materials and cool pavements, and graphic demarcations creating "islands" on the pavement and offering sitting and use priorities to older adults—are some elements of a just sidewalk design, postpandemic (Russell 2020).

Of course, the aforementioned modest design interventions cannot address all the impediments faced by older adults in inner cities. Social problems such as homelessness, drunkenness, crime, and drug dealing represent larger structural issues that hamper the lives and well-being of many inner-city residents. These require larger and much-needed political and financial commitments and interventions that go beyond the scope of this study. Still, age-friendly design interventions can add comfort and reduce fear. Designing sidewalks that are inclusive of older adults would bolster their right to the city.

NOTE

1. The other domains include housing, outdoor spaces and buildings, community support and health services, communication and information, civic participation and employment, respect and social inclusion, and social participation (World Health Organization 2007).

REFERENCES

Banerjee, T., and Baer, W. C. (1984). *Beyond the Neighborhood Unit: Residential Environments and Public Policy*. New York: Plenum.

Banerjee, T., and Southworth, M. (1990). *City Sense and City Design: Writings and Projects of Kevin Lynch*. Cambridge, MA: MIT Press.

Boschmann, E. E., and Brady, S. A. (2013). "Travel Behaviors, Sustainable Mobility, and Transit-Oriented Developments: A Travel Counts Analysis of Older Adults in the Denver, Colorado Metropolitan Area." *Journal of Transport Geography* 33: 1–11.

Burden, D. (2007). *Streets and Sidewalks, People and Cars: The Citizens' Guide to Traffic Calming*. Sacramento, CA: Local Government Commission Center for Livable Communities. https://www.lgc.org/wordpress/wp-content/uploads/2013/08/traffic-calming-guidebook.pdf.

Cao, X., Handy, S., and Mokhtarian, P. (2007). *Residential and Travel Choices of Elderly Residents of Northern California*. Paper presented at the proceedings of the 48th Annual Transportation Research Forum, Boston.

Clark, C. R., Kawachi, I., Ryan, L., Ertel, K., Fay, M. E., and Berkman, L. F. (2009). "Perceived Neighborhood Safety and Incident Mobility Disability among Elders: The Hazards of Poverty." *BMC Public Health* 9 (162). doi:10.1186/1471-2458-9-162.

Clark, F., Carlson, M., Zemke, R., Frank, G., Patterson, K., Ennevor, B. L., and Lipson, L. (1996). "Life Domains and Adaptive Strategies of a Group of Low-Income, Well Older Adults." *American Journal of Occupational Therapy* 50 (2): 99–108.

Horner, M. W., Duncan, M. D., Wood, B. S., Valdez-Torres, Y., and Stansbury, C. (2015). "Do Aging Populations Have Differential Accessibility to Activities? Analyzing the Spatial Structure of Social, Professional, and Business Opportunities." *Travel Behaviour and Society* 2 (3): 182–191.

Jacobs, J. (1961). *The Death and Life of Great American Cities*. New York: Random House.

Kim, S. (2011). "Assessing Mobility in an Aging Society: Personal and Built Environment Factors Associated with Older People's Subjective Transportation Deficiency in the US." *Transportation Research: Part F* 14 (5): 422–429.

Kofman, E., and Lebas, E. (eds.). (1996). *Writings on Cities: Henri Lefebvre*. Cambridge, MA: Wiley Blackwell.

Levy-Storms, L., Chen, L., and Loukaitou-Sideris, A. (2018). "Older Adults' Needs and Preferences for Open Space and Physical Activity in and near Parks: A Systematic Review." *Journal of Aging and Physical Activity* 26 (4): 682–696.

Loukaitou-Sideris, A., and Ehrenfeucht, R. (2009). *Sidewalks: Conflict and Negotiation over Public Space*. Cambridge, MA: MIT Press.

Loukaitou-Sideris, A., Wachs, M, and Pinski, M (2019). "Towards a Richer Picture of the Mobility Needs of Older Americans." *Journal of the American Planning Association* 85 (4): 482–500.

Low, S., and Loukaitou-Sideris, A, (2021). "America under Covid-19: The Plight of the Old." In van Melik, R., Filion, P., and Doucet, B. (eds.). *Global Reflections on Covid-19 Urban Inequalities: Public Space and Mobility*. Vol. 3. Bristol, UK: Bristol University Press, 97–108.

Lynch, K. (1960). *The Image of the City*. Cambridge, MA: MIT Press.

Lynch, K. (1985) "Reconsidering the Image of the City." In Banerjee, T., and Southworth, M. (1990). *City Sense and City Design: Writings and Projects of Kevin Lynch*. Cambridge, MA: MIT Press.

Lynch, K., and Rivkin, M. (1959). "A Walk around the Block." *Landscape* 8 (3): 24–34.

Maratolli, R. (2009). "Safe Mobility for Older Persons." *The Bridge* 39 (1): 27–33.

Mattson, J. W. (2011). "Aging and Mobility in Rural and Small Urban Areas: A Survey of North Dakota." *Journal of Applied Gerontology* 30 (6): 700–718.

Musselwhite, C. (2015). "Further Examinations of Mobility in Later Life and Improving Health and Well-Being." *Journal of Transport & Health* 2 (2): 99–100.

Naumann, R. B., Dellinger, A. M., Haileyesus, T., and Ryan, G. W. (2011). "Older Adult Pedestrian Injuries in the United States: Causes and Contributing Circumstances." *International Journal of Injury Control and Safety Promotion* 18 (1): 65–73.

Rosenbloom, S., and Herbel, S. (2009). "The Safety and Mobility Patterns of Older Women: Do Current Patterns Foretell the Future?" *Public Works Management & Policy* 13 (4): 338–353.

Russell, J. (2020). "Building Public Places for a Covid World." *New York Times*, September 12, 2020.

Satariano, W. A., Guralnik, J. M., Jackson, R. J., Marottoli, R. A., Phelan, E. A., and Prohaska, T. R. (2012). "Mobility and Aging: New Directions for Public Health Action." *American Journal of Public Health* 102 (8): 1508–1515.

Stollof, E. R., and Barlow, J. M. (2008). *Pedestrian Mobility and Safety Audit Guide*. Washington, DC: AARP. https://www.aarp.org/content/dam/aarp/livable-communities/old-plan/assessments/pedesterian-mobility-and-safety-audit-guide-2008-aarp.pdf.

Taylor, B. D., and Tripodes, S. (2001). "The Effects of Driving Cessation on the Elderly with Dementia and their Caregivers." *Accident Analysis & Prevention* 33 (4): 519–528.

World Health Organization (WHO). (2007). *Global Age—Healthy Cities: A Guide*. Geneva, Switzerland: WHO Press.

Yen, I. H., Michael, Y. L., and Perdue, L. (2009). "Neighborhood Environment in Studies of Health of Older Adults: A Systematic Review." *American Journal of Preventive Medicine* 37 (5): 455–463.

CONCLUSION

THE STRUGGLE FOR A PUBLIC CITY

Kian Goh, Anastasia Loukaitou-Sideris, and Vinit Mukhija

Having worked in the field of urban design for years as both scholars
and practitioners, our motivation for conceptualizing and compiling this
book has been twofold. First, we think that the field of urban design has
long been complicit in neglecting issues of justice and compounding
practices of injustice. Arguably, this has become more pronounced and
visible in recent decades. Being trapped within the unjust and exclusive
contours of market-driven urbanism, urban design has been overwhelmingly constrained by profit motives and dictated by dominant narratives
and urban imaginaries, often those of white, political-economic elites.
Second, we believe that urban design pedagogy and urban design practice, if transformed into just urban design, have the potential to contribute to a more spatially just city, which we call the public city.

We began this book by asking three questions: What makes a public
city? Who is it for? How is just urban design made? Through the collective
efforts of this book's contributors, we now can answer these questions, and
we turn to them next. To conclude the chapter and the book, we reflect on
the scope and agency of urban design and its potential for justice.

WHAT MAKES A PUBLIC CITY?

Throughout this volume, we and our colleagues have argued that just
urban design must strive for the public city. We build on progressive

ideals of collective amenities, infrastructure, and resources typically connected with the public commons and public spaces, extend them to the
metropolitan scale of city-regions, and draw from ideas about public culture and credo in a shared destiny. In our conception, the public city is
both the object and subject of urban design justice. Rather than a sharp
analytical distinction between object and subject in urban design, we
consider them intrinsically linked and reciprocal.

The material reality of cities, their built environment, as well as urban
design proposals and ideas that define them, as Kian Goh illustrates in
chapter 11 while discussing the highly influential Rebuild by Design
competition for urban resilience in New York City, are the objects and
conventional focus of urban design practice and pedagogy. They help
determine the spatial, economic, and political opportunities and outcomes associated with cities. Political participation in built environment
and land use decision making, the capacity to play an active role in conceiving and realizing urban form propositions, constitute the subjects and
processes of urban design. Both the objects and subjects of urban design
are mutually reinforcing—they establish the contours of one another and
help determine the limits and expanse of the public city. They play a key
role in determining how underrepresented and disadvantaged groups are
comfortable and successful in advancing their cultural, economic, and
political claims and rights in the city.

Urban designers, we argue, have an important and meaningful role in
addressing the constrained public sphere of cities. Our chapters discuss
how to broaden the boundaries of urban design objects and subjects to
make a public city, or as Chelina Odbert suggests in chapter 9, how to
make a "truly" public city. We summarize below three key lessons from
the book's chapters on advancing such publicness.

First, inclusivity is the touchstone of a public city. Urban design needs
to accommodate and address the diverse needs of residents with differences in abilities, resources, and power. For example, Anastasia Loukaitou-
Sideris, in chapter 15, focuses on walking—a simple everyday activity that
is often taken for granted. She identifies numerous challenges facing Los
Angeles' older adults in underserved neighborhoods and proposes several
urban design tactics for expanding their mobility. As she and Francesca
Piazzoni, in chapter 13, discuss in the case of Bangladeshi street vendors

in Rome, and Teddy Cruz and Fonna Forman argue in chapter 12, while explaining the challenges of Central American migrants and their families at the US-Mexico border region, accepting, learning from, and proactively supporting informal practices and bottom-up initiatives provide a pathway to including disadvantaged groups in the promise of cities.

Along similar lines, in chapter 14, Matthew Jordan-Miller Kenyatta discusses how Black artists and entrepreneurs in Leimert Park, South Los Angeles, have developed economic and cultural strategies for establishing unapologetically Black urbanism. He argues that just urban design cannot be race-neutral—it has to be unapologetically race-aware and focused on privileging the claims and rights of historically marginalized people. Like Kian Goh in chapter 11, Rebecca Choi focuses on ideas and proposals as urban design objects in chapter 7. In her account, she centers on racial discrimination, criticizing the celebrated "Housing Without Relocation" proposal, prepared by a Columbia University team in the 1960s as a response to a competition issued by the Museum of Modern Art, for its disregard for Harlem's Black residents. Like Matthew Jordan-Miller Kenyatta, Choi argues for racial inclusivity and justice as a key benchmark of a public city.

Second, it is necessary to broaden public participation in decision making to make a public city. Iris Marion Young (1990) reminded readers that local control in decision making on its own does not always lead to inclusion. She argued that parochial and elite interests often capture local control. However, the lesson to draw from Young is not to disregard local control but to ensure that decision making takes place within the context of a democratic framework structured across scales, embodiments, and positionalities and that opportunities for participation are inclusive. The chapters in this volume discuss several relevant examples. For instance, Jeffrey Hou in chapter 8 and Rachel Berney in chapter 10 examine participatory processes and community-based efforts by which Seattle's racial minorities, long discriminated against and excluded from decision making, have been able to envision their built environment and actively participate in urban development and design decisions. Similarly, women are also routinely excluded from urban design's institutional processes. In chapter 9, Chelina Odbert shows how gender differences should be taken into account in urban design and how women's participation is crucial in determining the nature and success of urban design interventions.

Finally, differences and disagreements are central to the making of a public city, which should acknowledge and affirm differences among its diverse constituents and work to productively address them. In particular, the chapters in part II—"What Is the Public City and Inclusive Urbanism"—illustrate this argument. Diane E. Davis, focusing on conflict cities in chapter 4, recognizes that contestation and disagreements are expected, but she argues that a democratic process that engages with difference can produce a shared political commitment and a shared identity. Vinit Mukhija, in chapter 5, shows that opinions on housing density, form, and location routinely differ among city residents. Deliberations can be contentious, but the benefits for civic life through all residents participating in the decision-making process can outweigh the disadvantages. Similarly, Alison B. Hirsch, in chapter 6, argues that to be able to move beyond conflict, it is important and productive for urban design to make past conflicts visible—even if they are likely to be painful. Relatedly, Rebecca Choi, in chapter 7, criticizes the idea that a top-down urban design process or a master urban designer can successfully make conflicts vanish. In contrast, a public city needs to engage with conflict and differences.

WHO IS IT FOR?

It goes without saying that we view the public city as belonging to all its residents. However, historically, and even at present, urban design has looked at its focus—the spatial public realm and its users—through very narrow and exclusive lenses. As discussed in chapter 1, its pedagogy and canon draw from theories and ideas promoted almost exclusively by white male designers and design scholars. Urban design praxis has also been mostly exclusive, with spatial interests and attention typically focusing on prime city areas and select groups of users. In cities around the world, urban design has become a spatial tool for neoliberal policies that ultimately benefit the wealthy by ignoring, at best, or excluding and displacing, at worst, marginalized and vulnerable groups. The "rejuvenation" of corporate downtowns, the beautification and eventual gentrification of working-class neighborhoods, the design and branding of cultural districts for "creative" citizens do not serve, and often disparage,

the needs of vulnerable and marginalized groups in the city by perpetu-
ating social inequalities and deepening divisions between wealthy/poor,
private/public, and formal/informal spaces.

Some may argue that the primary role of urban design is to beautify
and not politicize. But, as Michael Rios notes in chapter 3, "aesthetics
is more than the appearance of space. It determines who is included or
excluded, and ultimately what is just." The authors in this book collectively contend that the contours of the public city are currently very narrow, as many social groups do not feel welcome or recognized. We have
argued elsewhere that urban design should expand its *scope* to encompass the ordinary landscapes of everyday life, its *context* to focus on marginalized neighborhoods, and its *process* to include the participation of
vulnerable groups (Loukaitou-Sideris and Mukhija 2015). Rachel Berney,
in chapter 10, says it more eloquently by pinpointing the urban designers' unique role of shaping the "invitations" to use city space and the
"imaginary"—who they are designing for.

To correct historical injustices, however, urban design should not simply add to its repertoire of settings and people. Instead, it should adopt
and advocate for what Kian Goh in chapter 11 calls a "marginalized-first"
response—"one that systematically prioritizes historically vulnerable
people." In other words, a public city cannot be deemed public unless its
most vulnerable social groups—its different racial-ethnic, religious, and
sexual minorities, its women, children, older adults, and residents with
disabilities, its immigrant groups, and its unsheltered denizens feel welcome and designed for. Additionally, as Vinit Mukhija argues in chapter
5, public and inclusive cities are those that provide disadvantaged communities with opportunities to participate and make decisions in design
and planning processes.

Thus, a primary purpose of this book has been to interrogate how
design can proffer justice to the city's most neglected subjects because,
as Diane E. Davis argues in chapter 4, it is at the city level where the
foundations of the public sphere are laid out. Setha Low in chapter 2
and Anastasia Loukaitou-Sideris in chapter 15 suggest design and policy
ways to meet older adults' vital but largely unmet needs to access public
space during ordinary and even extraordinary (like during a pandemic)
times. Diane E. Davis in chapter 4 and Alison B. Hirsch in chapter 6

discuss revisiting and making spatially visible the often-pained histories of nonwhite groups in the city while at the same time rejecting visual symbols and monuments that perpetuate divisiveness. Francesca Piazzoni and Anastasia Loukaitou-Sideris in chapter 13 and Matthew Jordan-Miller Kenyatta in chapter 14 talk about the role of urban design in supporting and making visible in neighborhoods and cities the belonging of groups (Muslim immigrants in Rome and Black Americans in Los Angeles) that are usually "othered" and excluded because of racist prejudices, practices, and policies. Jeffrey Hou in chapter 8, Chelina Odbert in chapter 9, and Rachel Berney in chapter 10 detail how participatory design processes can empower and enable these "other" groups to determine and redefine their neighborhood spaces according to their needs. The work on the ground and the writings of Teddy Cruz and Fonna Forman in chapter 12 give stellar examples of how urban designers can join forces with eager municipalities, universities, and citizens to achieve "social urbanism" and expand "urban rights" for the most unprivileged. Collectively, the contributions of the different authors in this book offer guidance on how urban design praxis can achieve the lofty goal of inclusiveness.

HOW IS JUST DESIGN MADE?

So, we need a just urban design to achieve inclusiveness. And, as we have noted, just urban design begins with a more critical recognition of the public city and an understanding of who it is for. How, then, is just urban design *made*? That is, how is it conceived, formed, and developed? This requires, we believe, nothing less than a thorough remaking of the theories and practices of urban design.

Foundational theories of urban design, as we concluded in chapter 1, have too rarely taken on concerns about justice. To do so effectively requires more than simply an addition to or a minor revision of these theories. Fundamentally, just urban design is made through the repositioning of ideas of justice and publicness in urban design thought and action. This is at once an ontological and epistemological problem. As Setha Low in chapter 2 explains, just urban space demands a deeper interrogation of what constitutes justice in the city. It is a probing and multifaceted view that extends well beyond the generally accepted notions of distribution or procedure. Michael Rios, in chapter 3, also insists on new ways of being and knowing for urban design that resituate city design and city-making beyond currently oppressive structures, such as systemic racism and the associated hegemony of white spatial imaginaries. Just urban design situates itself, both in scholarship and practice, within and in challenge to the often unjust systems and processes of urban change. As should be quite clear by now, design of the city can no longer be seen as something "outside" of the cultural and political-economic forces that determine socioeconomic conditions.

Extending this argument, just urban design is wrought through concepts and practices that both affirm and challenge foundational ideas in urban planning and design. This volume's contributors have found and, in many cases, validated a number of key precepts of more just design. Many of these revolve around processes that hold up what we have already discussed as the constitutive factors of a public city—inclusivity, participation, and difference. These precepts include the following guiding ideals that have also been central in many of the debates on justice and the city. First, just urban design is made through engagement with and for communities on the ground (see chapters by Hou, Odbert, Berney, Goh, Cruz and Forman, and Loukaitou-Sideris). Second, it demands knowledge of and productive interfaces with histories of people and places (see chapters by Hirsch, Choi, Hou, Berney, Goh, and Kenyatta). And third, it insists on the importance of difference and counteracts universalist ideals and efforts to erase difference and othering in cities (see chapters by Davis, Mukhija, Hou, Odbert, Berney, Piazzoni and Loukaitou-Sideris, and Loukaitou-Sideris).

We also find further key factors of transforming urban design and making just cities. These extend and augment the guiding ideals. Four stand out as particularly critical. First, justice in the city requires searching out processes and spaces that may be outside those most commonly understood to be part of the public city. Justice in the public city is also dependent on conditions in the more private city, as Vinit Mukhija in chapter 5 indicates. It also hinges on the mobility and access of those on the margins of legality and belonging, as shown by Francesca Piazzoni and Anastasia Loukaitou-Sideris in chapter 13. We cannot expect idealized urban life in the much-vaunted public spaces of the city without attending to issues of inclusion and equity throughout the multiple and often more hidden spaces of social interactions in the city. Second, if community engagement is to be meaningful, it needs to be developed through processes that are collaborative, sustained over time, and attuned to the power differentials among and within groups. As shown by Jeffrey Hou in chapter 8 and Teddy Cruz and Fonna Forman in chapter 12, this requires long-term, situated partnerships cultivated through the embrace of political realities, cross-disciplinary engagements, and multiple identities and points of view. Third, relatedly, just urban design must allow for and encourage the making of novel organizational structures, whether through new institutional relationships, as Rachel Berney in chapter 10 and Kian Goh in chapter 11 indicate, or new entities of practice, as shown by Chelina Odbert in chapter 9. Newness or innovation in urban design might not always be in the physical form or materiality of a design but in the ways in which design processes are organized and developed. And, fourth, while justice has often been conceptualized in an ideal manner—accessible to and inclusive of all groups across differences of race, ethnicity, gender, class, ability, and so on—the continued systemic injustices of urban development demand that just urban design looks to, centers, and empowers the most marginalized among us, those who suffer first and the most from socioeconomic or environmental threats (see chapters by Goh, Cruz and Forman, Piazzoni and Loukaitou-Sideris, and Loukaitou-Sideris). Such a prioritizing repositions justice not as an abstract liberal ideal but as a clear question of power.

SCOPE AND AGENCY OF URBAN DESIGN

The previous arguments lead us to envision an expansive and ambitious scope for urban design. Similar to Anne Vernez Moudon (1992), we ascribe broad sympathies and interests to urban design, and akin to Kevin Lynch (1981), we aim to broaden the discipline and profession's breadth of concerns. Much like Donald Appleyard (1982), we see little value in confining or narrowly defining urban design's boundaries and find it potentially enriching to identify crucial areas and focus for practice. Correspondingly, we have aimed to foreground the interrelationship between the built environment and justice, providing a new focus and asking and expecting more from urban design.

We have already suggested that the scope and agency of just urban design transcend the conventional dichotomies of object and subject, outcome and process, public and private, and formal and informal. The chapters in this book collectively emphasize a diversity of settings, geographies, and scales for urban design. Many contributors to the volume highlight the importance of small-scale interventions (see chapters by Cruz and Forman, Hirsch, Hou, Loukaitou-Sideris, Kenyatta, Odbert, and Piazzoni and Loukaitou-Sideris). Their case studies acknowledge the role of both professional urban designers and nondesigners. Like David Crane (1960), who saw a "city of a thousand designers," and everyday urbanists (Chase, Crawford, and Kaliski 1999), who associate urban design agency with ordinary people, we see an important role for nonprofessionals in urban design.

Nonetheless, we also see an essential role and central obligation to justice for professional urban designers. Several of our contributors have focused on neighborhood and district-scale interventions conventionally associated with public and private projects employing practicing urban designers. For example, Setha Low, in chapter 2, spotlights neighborhood-serving parks and public spaces typically associated with urban design practice. Rebecca Choi in chapter 7 and Kian Goh in chapter 11 focus on notable projects in New York City that involved some of the better-known urban designers of their era. Similarly, at the heart of Rachel Berney's discussion in chapter 10 is the development of a formidable portfolio of properties owned by Black churches in Seattle's Central District. Indeed, the various scales and arenas of urban design—from the small and unpretentious spaces of everyday life to large and more ambitious citywide (or regional) interventions—are often mutually constitutive. To illustrate, Vinit Mukhija in chapter 5 discusses household-level informal interventions by homeowners to add unpermitted secondary suites; deliberation, opinion surveys, and new policies about them at the neighborhood level by planners and urban designers; and scaling up of new visions of housing and living at the city level by policymakers.

Although most of the chapters in this volume focus on US examples, injustices in the built environment are not limited to the US. Several of our contributors focus on cases from other parts of the Global North, including Jerusalem and Belfast (Davis in chapter 4), Rome (Piazzoni and Loukaitou-Sideris in chapter 13), and Vancouver (Mukhija in chapter 5).

Two contributors share examples from the Global South, including Teddy Cruz and Fonna Forman (chapter 12), who take us to Bogotá, Medellín, and Tijuana; and Chelina Odbert (chapter 9), who discusses her firm's work in Mendoza, Argentina. As Mike Davis and Daniel Bertrand Monk (2007) emphasize, "evil paradises," or market-based exclusionary utopias, are built worldwide, including in Asia, Africa, and South America. Just urban design is in short supply everywhere. The lacuna highlights the broader relevance of our framework and the global necessity to privilege the needs of the vulnerable and marginalized in design decisions.

NOT "JUST" URBAN DESIGN—BUT NECESSARILY JUST URBAN DESIGN

Concluding this book, we believe more than ever that the academic discipline and profession of urban design need engagement with justice for their reinvigoration, development, and legitimacy. The public city is inclusive, participatory, and embracing of difference. It is characterized by attention to those historically vulnerable and disadvantaged. Just urban design makes this public city by searching out the processes and spaces that underlie and perpetuate exclusion; it creates sustained, collaborative engagements attuned to power disparities; it contributes to the development of new, more inclusive institutional structures and practices; and it centers and empowers the most marginalized among us.

We believe in just urban design and maintain its necessity. We also recognize that "just" urban design—that is, "only" urban design—however just, is not enough for achieving the public city. The project of justice in the city also requires social relationships, institutions, policies, political-economic relationships, and other structural changes that might be beyond what might constitute even an expanded scholarship and practice of urban design. And yet, having taken on the project of finding out the what, who, and how questions of justice and designing cities, we can now affirm and insist that urban design has more to contribute to justice than even we, as its scholars and practitioners, had thought. The key aspects of the celebrated public city—its inclusion, participation, and difference—can only really be wrought through ideas and practices that can intervene, in physical, material terms, in the social and spatial processes of marginalization and exclusion that have characterized unjust city-making to date. Just urban design is, indeed, necessary.

REFERENCES

Appleyard, D. (1982). "Three Kinds of Urban Design Practice." In Ferebee, A. (ed.). *Education for Urban Design*. New York: Institute for Urban Design.

Chase, J., Crawford, M., and Kaliski, J. (1999). *Everyday Urbanism*. New York: Monacelli Press.

Crane, D. (1960). "The City Symbolic." *Journal of American Institute of Planners* 24 (6): 280–292.

Davis, M., and Monk, D. B. (eds.). (2007). *Evil Paradises: Dreamworlds of Neoliberalism*. New York: New Press.

Loukaitou-Sideris, A., and Mukhija, V. (2015). "Responding to Informality through Urban Design Studio Pedagogy." *Journal of Urban Design* 21 (5): 577–595.

Lynch, K. (1981). *A Theory of Good City Form*. Cambridge, MA: MIT Press.

Moudon, A. V. (1992). "A Catholic Approach to Organizing What Urban Designers Should Know." *Journal of Planning Literature* 6 (4): 331–349.

Young, I. M. (1990). *Justice and Politics of Difference*. Princeton, NJ: Princeton University Press.

CONTRIBUTORS

Rachel Berney is associate professor of urban design and planning and adjunct associate professor of landscape architecture in the College of Built Environments at the University of Washington, Seattle. She is the author of *Learning from Bogotá: Pedagogical Urbanism and the Reshaping of Public Space* (2017, University of Texas Press) and the editor of *Bicycle Urbanism: Re-Imagining Bicycle Friendly Cities* (2018, Routledge). Her work also appears in *Planning Theory, Journal of Urban Design, The New Companion to Urban Design*, and other volumes.

Rebecca Choi is a postdoctoral fellow and visiting lecturer at the Institute for the History and Theory of Architecture (gta Institute) at the ETH Zürich. Her research considers how movements for racial justice have had a pivotal role in the making of urban America. She holds a PhD in architecture and a master's degree in urban planning from the University of California, Los Angeles. She has contributed writings to the *Harvard Design Magazine, Avery Review, ARDETH* journal, and *Places* journal.

Teddy Cruz is a professor of public culture and urbanization in the Department of Visual Arts at the University of California, San Diego (UCSD). He is the recipient of the Rome Prize in Architecture in 1991. Other honors include representing the US in the 2008 Venice Architecture Biennale, the Ford Foundation Visionaries Award in 2011, and the 2013 Architecture Award from the US Academy of Arts and Letters. With Fonna Forman, he is a principal in Estudio Teddy Cruz+Fonna Forman, a research-based political and architectural practice.

Diane E. Davis is the Charles Dyer Norton Professor of Regional Development and Urbanism and formerly chair of the Department of Urban Planning and Design at Harvard's Graduate School of Design. Among her recent books are *Cities and Sovereignty: Identity Conflicts in the Urban Realm* (2011, Indiana University Press). She is the recipient of fellowships from the John D. and Catherine T. MacArthur Foundation, the Heinz Foundation, the Ford Foundation, the Social Science Research Council, the United States Institute for Peace, the Andrew W. Mellon Foundation, and the Carnegie Corporation of New York.

Fonna Forman is a professor of political theory at the University of California, San Diego (UCSD) and founding director of the UCSD Center on Global Justice. With Teddy Cruz, she is a principal in Estudio Teddy Cruz + Fonna Forman, a research-based political and architectural practice investigating issues of informal urbanization, civic infrastructure, and public culture with an emphasis on Latin American cities. She has coedited *Informal Markets Worlds—Reader: The Architecture of Economic Pressure* and, with Cruz, she is currently completing two monographs—one on citizenship culture at the US-Mexico border and a cross-section of the work of Estudio Teddy Cruz + Fonna Forman, *Top-Down/Bottom-Up*.

Christopher Giamarino is a PhD student in urban planning at the UCLA Luskin School of Public Affairs. His research interests include theories of urban design, the relationship between public space and neoliberal urbanism, and ethnographies of everyday urbanism that reveal how spatiotemporal tactics of appropriation and contestation attempt to transform exclusive public places into urban commons. His most recent coauthored article, "Creativity, Conviviality, and Civil Society in Neoliberalizing Public Space" was published in the *Journal of Sport and Social Issues*.

Kian Goh is associate professor of urban planning at UCLA and associate faculty director of the UCLA Luskin Institute on Inequality and Democracy. She researches urban ecological design, spatial politics, and social mobilization in the context of climate change and global urbanization. As a professional architect, she cofounded design firm SUPER-INTERESTING! and has practiced with Weiss/Manfredi and MVRDV. She is the author of *Form and Flow: The Spatial Politics of Urban Resilience and Climate Justice* (2021, MIT Press). Her recent articles have been published in *Cambridge Journal of Regions, Economy and Society, Journal of the American Planning Association, International Journal of Urban and Regional Research, Urban Studies*, and *Annals of the American Association of Geographers*.

Alison B. Hirsch is associate professor at the USC School of Architecture and director of the graduate program in landscape architecture + urbanism. She is cofounder of *foreground design agency*, a critical landscape practice. She is the author of *City Choreographer* (2014, University of Minnesota Press) and has another forthcoming book, *The Performative Landscape*. She was the 2017–2018 Prince Charitable Trusts/Rolland Rome Prize Fellow at the American Academy in Rome.

Jeffrey Hou is professor of landscape architecture and adjunct professor of architecture and urban design and planning at the University of Washington, Seattle. His publications include *Insurgent Public Space: Guerrilla Urbanism and the Remaking of Contemporary Cities* (2010), *Transcultural Cities: Border-Crossing and Placemaking* (2013), *Now Urbanism: The Future City is Here* (2015), *Messy Urbanism: Understanding* the 'Other' Cities of Asia (2016), *City Unsilenced: Urban Resistance and Public Space in the Age of Shrinking Democracy* (2017), and *Design as Democracy: Techniques for Collective Creativity* (2017). Hou's work has been recognized with the EDRA Places Book Award in 2010, 2012, and 2018. He is also a recipient of the CELA Excellence in Research and/or Creative Work Award in 2019.

Matthew Jordan-Miller Kenyatta is a Provost's Postdoctoral Fellow at the University of Pennsylvania Stuart Weitzman School of Design in the Department of City and Regional Planning. His scholarly work has been honored by the National Academy of Sciences and the Association for Collegiate Schools in Planning and published in *Planning Theory and Practice*. His artistic and cultural work has been featured in the *New York Times*, the *Boston Globe*, and the *Philadelphia Tribune*. He holds degrees in African/African American and urban studies from Stanford University, city planning from MIT, and urban planning and development from USC.

Anastasia Loukaitou-Sideris is distinguished professor of urban planning at UCLA and the associate dean of the UCLA Luskin School of Public Affairs. Her books include *Urban Design Downtown: Poetics and Politics of Form* (1998); *Jobs and Economic Development in Minority Communities* (2006); *Sidewalks: Conflict and Negotiation over Public Space* (2009); *Companion to Urban Design* (2011); *The Informal American City: Beyond Taco Trucks and Day Labor* (2014); *Transit Oriented Displacement or Community Dividends?* (2019); *The New Companion to Urban Design* (2019); *Urban Humanities: New Practices for Reimagining the City* (2020); and *Transit Crime and Sexual Violence in Cities: International Evidence and Prevention* (2020).

Setha Low is distinguished professor of environmental psychology, geography, anthropology, and women's studies, and director of the Public Space Research Group at the Graduate Center, City University of New York. She has been awarded a Getty Fellowship, a NEH Fellowship, a Fulbright Senior Fellowship, a Future of Places Fellowship, and a Guggenheim for her ethnographic research on public space in Latin America and the United States. She is widely published and internationally recognized and translated for her award-winning books on public space and cultural diversity. Her most recent publications are *Spatializing Culture: The Ethnography of Space and Place* (2017), *Anthropology and the City* (2019), and *Spaces of Security* (with M. Maguire) (2019).

Vinit Mukhija is professor of urban planning at UCLA. He is particularly interested in understanding the nature and necessity of informal housing and strategies for upgrading and improving living conditions in unregulated housing. His work also examines how planners and urban designers in both the Global South and the Global North can learn from the everyday and informal city. He is the author of *Squatters as Developers? Slum Redevelopment in Mumbai* (2003, Ashgate; 2017 Routledge), coeditor of *The Informal American City: Beyond Taco Trucks and Day Labor* (2014, MIT Press, with Anastasia Loukaitou-Sideris), and he has a forthcoming book, *Remaking the American Dream: The Informal and Formal Transformation of Single-Family Housing Cities*, with MIT Press.

Chelina Odbert is cofounder and executive director of KDI, an award-winning design, planning, and community development firm. Her expertise includes leadership, participatory planning, social entrepreneurship, urban development, environmental remediation, and social impact design. She has extensive field experience through her work in Africa, Latin America, and the US. She has been recognized by the Van Alen Institute, American Express, and the Aspen Institute for her work. She holds a bachelor of arts from Claremont McKenna College and a master of urban planning from Harvard University.

Francesca Piazzoni is assistant professor at the University of Liverpool, School of Architecture. Her research focuses on the politics of public space with a focus on immigrant urbanisms and critical heritage. Piazzoni's latest research looks at immigrant street vendors in touristic Rome by combining archival and ethnographic methods. She is the author of *The Real Fake: Authenticity and the Production of Space* (2018, Fordham University Press). She holds a PhD in urban planning from the University of Southern California, a PhD in architecture and urbanism from IUAV University of Venice, and a master of architecture from Sapienza University of Rome.

Michael Rios is professor of urban design and vice provost at the University of California, Davis, where he leads the Office of Public Scholarship and Engagement. With over twenty years of community-based research, teaching, and practice, he has collaborated with numerous public agencies, municipalities, and community groups. His research focuses on institutional capacity-building, community engagement, and cross-cultural planning and design. He has authored dozens of journal articles and book chapters and coedited several books, including *Diálogos: Placemaking in Latino Communities* (2013) and *Community Development and Democratic Practice* (2017).

Lawrence J. Vale is Ford Professor of urban design and planning at MIT, where he is associate dean of the School of Architecture and Planning and director of the Resilient Cities Housing Initiative. He is the author or editor of thirteen books focusing on urban design, low-income housing, and the politics of resilient cities, including several prize-winning volumes on the history, politics, and design of American public housing, two editions of *Architecture, Power, and National Identity*, and a co-edited volume, *The Resilient City: How Modern Cities Recover from Disaster*.

INDEX

Sam Bass Warner and Andrew H. Whittemore, *American Urban Form: A Representative History*

John Pucher and Ralph Buehler, eds., *City Cycling*

Stephanie Foote and Elizabeth Mazzolini, eds., *Histories of the Dustheap: Waste, Material Cultures, Social Justice*

David J. Hess, *Good Green Jobs in a Global Economy: Making and Keeping New Industries in the United States*

Joseph F. C. DiMento and Clifford Ellis, *Changing Lanes: Visions and Histories of Urban Freeways*

Joanna Robinson, *Contested Water: The Struggle Against Water Privatization in the United States and Canada*

William B. Meyer, *The Environmental Advantages of Cities: Countering Commonsense Antiurbanism*

Rebecca L. Henn and Andrew J. Hoffman, eds., *Constructing Green: The Social Structures of Sustainability*

Peggy F. Barlett and Geoffrey W. Chase, eds., *Sustainability in Higher Education: Stories and Strategies for Transformation*

Isabelle Anguelovski, *Neighborhood as Refuge: Community Reconstruction, Place Remaking, and Environmental Justice in the City*

Kelly Sims Gallagher, *The Globalization of Clean Energy Technology: Lessons from China*

Vinit Mukhija and Anastasia Loukaitou-Sideris, eds., *The Informal American City: Beyond Taco Trucks and Day Labor*

Roxanne Warren, *Rail and the City: Shrinking Our Carbon Footprint While Reimagining Urban Space*

Marianne E. Krasny and Keith G. Tidball, *Civic Ecology: Adaptation and Transformation from the Ground Up*

Erik Swyngedouw, *Liquid Power: Contested Hydro-Modernities in Twentieth-Century Spain*

Ken Geiser, *Chemicals without Harm: Policies for a Sustainable World*

Duncan McLaren and Julian Agyeman, *Sharing Cities: A Case for Truly Smart and Sustainable Cities*

Jessica Smartt Gullion, *Fracking the Neighborhood: Reluctant Activists and Natural Gas Drilling*

Nicholas A. Phelps, *Sequel to Suburbia: Glimpses of America's Post-Suburban Future*

Shannon Elizabeth Bell, *Fighting King Coal: The Challenges to Micromobilization in Central Appalachia*

Theresa Enright, *The Making of Grand Paris: Metropolitan Urbanism in the Twenty-first Century*

Robert Gottlieb and Simon Ng, *Global Cities: Urban Environments in Los Angeles, Hong Kong, and China*

Anna Lora-Wainwright, *Resigned Activism: Living with Pollution in Rural China*

Scott L. Cummings, *Blue and Green: The Drive for Justice at America's Port*

David Bissell, *Transit Life: Cities, Commuting, and the Politics of Everyday Mobilities*

Javiera Barandiarán, *From Empire to Umpire: Science and Environmental Conflict in Neoliberal Chile*

Benjamin Pauli, *Flint Fights Back: Environmental Justice and Democracy in the Flint Water Crisis*

Karen Chapple and Anastasia Loukaitou-Sideris, *Transit-Oriented Displacement or Community Dividends? Understanding the Effects of Smarter Growth on Communities*

Henrik Ernstson and Sverker Sörlin, eds., *Grounding Urban Natures: Histories and Futures of Urban Ecologies*

Katrina Smith Korfmacher, *Bridging the Silos: Collaborating for Environment, Health, and Justice in Urban Communities*

Jill Lindsey Harrison, *From the Inside Out: The Fight for Environmental Justice within Government Agencies*

Anastasia Loukaitou-Sideris, Dana Cuff, Todd Presner, Maite Zubiaurre, and Jonathan Jae-an Crisman, *Urban Humanities: New Practices for Reimagining the City*

Govind Gopakumar, *Installing Automobility: Emerging Politics of Mobility and Streets in Indian Cities*

Amelia Thorpe, *Everyday Ownership: PARK(ing) Day and the Practice of Property*

Tridib Banerjee, *In the Images of Development: City Design in the Global South*

Ralph Buehler and John Pucher, eds., *Cycling for Sustainable Cities*

Casey J. Dawkins, *Just Housing: The Moral Foundations of American Housing Policy*

Kian Goh, *Form and Flow: The Spatial Politics of Urban Resilience and Climate Justice*

Kian Goh, Anastasia Loukaitou-Sideris, and Vinit Mukhija, eds., *Just Urban Design: The Struggle for a Public City*